Literary New England

William Corbett lives in Boston's South End and teaches writing at Harvard Extension and M.I.T. *Don't Think: Look*, his most recent book of poems, and his forthcoming memoir on the painter Philip Guston are both published by Zoland Books.

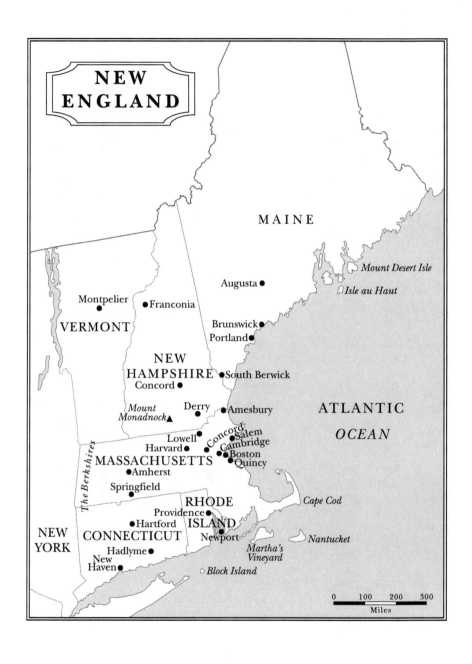

Literary New England

A HISTORY AND GUIDE

BY

William Corbett

Faber and Faber

BOSTON • LONDON

Copyright © 1993 by William Corbett

Library of Congress Cataloging-in-Publication Data
Corbett, William, 1942–
    Literary New England: a history and guide/William Corbett.
        p.   cm.
    Includes index.
    ISBN 0-571-19816-3
    1. American literature—New England—History and criticism.
    2. Literary landmarks—New England—Guidebooks. 3. New
    England—Intellectual life. 4. New England in literature. I. Title.
    PS243.C67 1993
    810.9′974—dc20
93–10887
                                                                CIP

Cover design by Bob Cato
Cover art by Fairfield Porter: "AMHERST PARKING LOT #1, 1969,"
by arrangement with Honolulu Academy of Arts,
Funds from the John Gregg Allerton Bequest, 1989 (5809.1)

Printed in the United States of America

For Trevor Winkfield

CONTENTS

Acknowledgments

———————◆———————

FOR AID, ENCOURAGEMENT, and comfort on the road, my gratitude to Robert Nunnelley and Gerald Coble, Jonathan Williams, Paul Auster and Siri Hustvedt, Russell Banks and Chase Twichell, Jane Gunther, Lee Harwood, Ron Padgett, Joe Brainard, Kenward Elmslie, Robert and Penelope Creeley, Nate Mackey, Helen Power, Jane Hammond, Peter de Lissovoy, Catherina Slautterback of the Boston Athenaeum, Debbie Paddock, Stratis Haviaras of the *Harvard Review*, in which portions of this book appeared in slightly different form, Gay Ellis, Jay Boggis, Linda Simon, Louis and Ellesse Treubner, Doug Bauer and Sue Miller, Joseph Torra, Gerrit Lansing, Bob D'Atillo, Keith Waldrop, Jane Curliano, Jackson Braider, Ben Watkins, and special thanks to Judy Watkins, who made house calls to nurse me through my computer anxiety, tutored me in the use of the machine, and introduced me to the work of her father, the literary historian William Charvat. And my sidekicks —beloved Beverly and Basil, King of Canines— who traveled many a mile.

A book like this is built on other books. I have consulted a great many; a partial bibliography follows the text, but I want to salute a few here. The Works Progress Administration guides, which I found valuable, are now more than fifty years old. They can be found in secondhand bookshops, but it is time to bring them up to date. A good investment by the National Endowment for the Arts or the National Endowment for the Humanities would be to have them redone.

When I began this project, I knew nothing of the work of Edwin M. Bacon. In Brattleboro, Vermont, I chanced upon a copy of his *Literary Pilgrimages in New England,* published in 1902, and have been glad to read and make use of it. Anyone interested in how the map of New England literature was drawn ninety years ago ought to search out Mr. Bacon's book. James D. Hart's fifth edition of *The Oxford Companion to American Literature* and *Benét's Reader's Encyclopedia of American Literature* furnished me with dates and other vital information, but both have holes. There are a number of New England writers and editors of no mean reputation who are absent from both books. Perhaps someone at Oxford and at HarperCollins will take what names they can from this book and add them to the roll.

Introduction:
How to Use This Book

———◆———

I N THESE PAGES Henry James is quoted—"It takes a great deal of history to produce a little literature." There is a great deal more American history in New England than elsewhere in the country, thus New England's abundant, essential literature. Of the thirty-two writers now published in the Library of America series, the edition of American classics that emulates the French Pleiade editions, twenty-one of them—including Ralph Waldo Emerson, W. E. B. Du Bois, Willa Cather, Flannery O'Connor—had close association with New England, and you will find them in these pages.

But classic writers are only part of literary history. This book is for readers who want to know what is underfoot, to know where in literary history they are when visiting the Maine coast, Connecticut suburbs, Vermont's Green Mountains, or walking Boston's streets. This book is for readers seeking instruction and delight.

I have followed, with some exceptions, one rule: the Salinger Rule. Knowing how J. D. Salinger's life has been made miserable by fans and others who refuse to leave him alone, I decided not to include living writers. There are many fine writers who live and work in New England whom you will not find in this book. I realized that there were times this rule had to be broken, but not, I hope, in a way that will spoil any writer's privacy.

This book requires a good map—a road atlas, if you plan to travel extensively with it—and even then, you may want help. I advise you to do what I did and inquire at police stations, town clerk's offices, libraries, post offices (but not at the one in West Dummerston, Vermont, about the Kipling house—the house isn't in that town, and the postmistress has been bothered enough), and general stores. Making use of these will more often than not get you precise directions that would have been tedious, if not at times confusing, to include here.

Other prime sources of information are New England's numerous secondhand bookshops. Often, their proprietors are knowledgeable about writers and writing in their immediate area and beyond. Even if they are not, the pleasure of browsing usually redeems the place. Secondhand shops in every state will have flyers listing all that state's shops and their specialties. I found Maine and Providence, Rhode Island, particularly rich in first-rate shops.

Entries preceded by a pen nib denote places that should not be missed.

"More than a province, less than a nation, New England"—wrote one of this book's tutelary spirits, Van Wyck Brooks—"has always had a certain coherence." You will sense something of the nature and shape of that coherence in this book. But New England is a contrary place, and many of her writers have indulged an independent streak and made it their business, thank God, not to fit.

Every effort has been made to ensure that the information contained in this book is accurate. However, we advise calling ahead to check opening times, as these are subject to change. Please contact the publisher regarding any errors or omissions.

Connecticut

———◆———

ALL NEW ENGLANDERS are Yankees, but the term adheres to Connecticut as to no other state. New York Dutchmen may have been the first to apply it to Connecticut natives. When Yankee peddlers were on the roads, customers were warned not to accept a wooden nutmeg. (Connecticut is the "Nutmeg State.") Mark Twain, a Yankee by adoption, sent one of his Connecticut brethren to King Arthur's court.

Common as the word Yankee is, we still do not exactly know its origins. It descends, we think, from *Janke*, a Dutch nickname for Jan. By 1758 the British were using it to refer to all New Englanders who were, as colonials, younger and less developed in every grace, and, as such, deserving of a derisive nickname. The British soon found that the word fit all colonials, but it was not until 1817 that Southerners applied it in print to Northerners and it stuck.

A Yankee is ingenious—witness Eli Whitney of New Haven, inventor of the cotton gin, or Samuel Colt of Hartford, inventor of the revolver. He is taciturn, shrewd in business, and tightfisted in private life. His sense of humor is dry, and he is pleased to forgo a pleasure. He can hold a poker face that will betray no more expression than a shingle, and he will, if you are not on your toes, put one over on you. "Money," Wallace Stevens of Hartford wrote, "is another kind of poetry." Until recently, Connecticut—by far the wealthiest of the New England states—had no personal income tax. New Hampshire still boasts of having none.

Some find the Yankees uncaring and cold, all dollars and sense, inscrutable and haughty. Others admire them as direct, without a stitch of pretense, respectful of privacy, and true—if undemonstrative—friends. Some are put off by the Yankee who greets them after three days or three years with a "hello" or nod of their head. Others like their lack of fuss and bother.

It is easier by now to find these Yankees in folklore and literature than in the flesh. They are said to have long since disappeared from Connecticut's gold coast, Fairfield County suburbs, and small and large industrial cities. But habits of place, shaped as much by geography and weather as history, persist. Even America's continuous stirring of the melting pot has not entirely blurred this region's distinctive features.

BRIDGEWATER

Born in Plainfield, **Van Wyck Brooks** (1886–1963) spent periods in Cornwall and Westport, and the last fourteen years of his life on Main Street in Bridgewater. He is buried here in the Center Cemetery, and there is a plaque in the Burnham Library dedicating the North Reading Area to his memory.

Perhaps Brooks is too little read today because the best books he wrote are out of fashion, falling into no particular category. He is often referred to as a critic, but this term is meaningless when applied to Brooks. His best books, *The Flowering of New England* (which won the Pulitzer Prize in 1936) and its follow-up volume, *New England: Indian Summer* (1940), are not works of criticism; but are close to literary history. Brooks attempts to give his readers a sense of how the writers of New England's Golden Age imagined what they were doing and how their readers read them as their works appeared. Free of footnotes, rich in detail, and long on quotations these books have been instrumental in the writing of this one.

In 1940, when reviewing *New England: Indian Summer*, Edmund Wilson wrote, "Mr. Brooks's study of New England is, in short, one of the three or four prime light-diffusing works on the history of American society." And so it remains today. You will find volumes of his work on the shelves of most good-sized secondhand bookshops, up and down New England.

BROOKFIELD CENTER

At the director Joshua Logan's house **Thomas Heggen** (1919–1949) and Logan worked to dramatize *Mister Roberts*, Heggen's bestselling novel about naval service in the Pacific during World War II. Their collaboration proved a success, first as a Broadway play and then as a movie. Heggen wrote no other books. Indeed, he is an example of what F. Scott Fitzgerald had in mind when he wrote that in American life there are "no second acts." Eight months short of his thirtieth birthday, Heggen was found drowned in his bathtub, a probable suicide. He is one of the subjects of John Leggett's dual biography *Ross & Tom*. Ross was Ross Lockridge author of *Raintree County*, another postwar bestseller. It was his only book, and he also died young, a suicide and—the biography suggests—the victim of his success. Both Heggen and Lockridge came from the Midwest, and both were published by Boston's Houghton Mifflin Company. Leggett, who shared the same publisher, said it was in "Houghton Mifflin's warren overlooking Boston Common" that he "learned about a dark side of achievement."

CORNWALL

After renting houses in Sandy Hook, Litchfield, Woodbury, and Sharon, **James Thurber** (1896–1961) and his wife Helen bought their "great good place" in 1945. Thurber lived here for the rest of his life. The house still stands adjacent to the cathedral pines of the Mohawk State Forest. In Cornwall, Thurber worked on *The Thurber Carnival, Further Fables for Our Time, Lanterns & Lances,* and others of his late books. His story "The Secret Life of Walter Mitty" is set in nearby Waterbury, where his wife went to have her hair done. As he drives his wife through the rain to her hairdresser, Mitty daydreams a life of heroic adventure, imagining himself captaining a submarine and turning aside a blindfold as he faces a firing squad. The story had its roots in a Thurber family joke. "When I'm on my deathbed," Thurber often snorted, "Helen will be at the hairdresser's." This is exactly where she turned out to be as Thurber began to breathe his last.

Mark Van Doren (1894–1972), brother of the biographer and historian **Carl Van Doren** (1885–1950), summered here for much of his life. He was a professor of English at Columbia University, where the poets Thomas Merton and John Berryman, and the novelist Jack Kerouac, were among his students. Van Doren, while mostly known as a poet—his 1939 *Collected Poems* won a Pulitzer Prize—wrote novels, stories, and critical studies of Thoreau and Hawthorne.

Mark Van Doren's wife, **Dorothy Van Doren** (1896–1993), published four novels and three books of autobiography. *Country Wife* (1950), her first autobiographical book, recounted her experiences as an amateur farmer in Connecticut. Books about cityfolk roughing it in the Connecticut country-side was a popular genre at the time. Their son Charles, himself a teacher of literature at Columbia, became infamous when it was revealed that he had cheated while a contestant on a television quiz show in the 1950s. At first Charles seemed a parent's dream come true, an egghead celebrated for being smart. He was held up as a model of American youth. This made the revelation that he had been fed answers by the show's producers all the more devastating.

CORNWALL BRIDGE

Make Way for Ducklings, which has been one of Boston's most popular books since its publication in 1941, was written here by **Robert McCloskey** (b. 1914). This children's story tells of a family of mallards who live in Boston's Public Garden. Today, near the corner of Beacon and Charles Streets in Boston, bronze ducks walk beside the Garden's path in the footsteps of the originals. Many children get their first taste of Boston from McCloskey's book.

DANBURY

Rex Stout (1886–1975), creator of Nero Wolfe, gourmet, orchidologist, and detective, lived here for more than fifty years in High Meadow, a house he designed. In 1927 Stout bought 18 acres of hilly land through which runs the Connecticut/New York State line. His mailing address was Brewster, New York, but High Meadow actually stands 1,600 feet inside Connecticut. The house, called "the monkey house" by neighbors, is U-shaped, with its fourteen rooms curving around a concrete court. Stout not only designed High Meadow and supervised its construction, he also laid teak floors and built the kitchen cabinets. When he finished in 1930, the house received considerable write-ups in *The New York Times* and various architectural magazines.

Robert Lowell (1917–1977) served six months, from October 1943 to March 1944, in Danbury's federal penitentiary for refusing, in the words of his letter to President Franklin Roosevelt, "the opportunity you offer me . . . for service in the Armed forces." Lowell described the prison as "functional as a tackle box." While Lowell served his time, his wife Jean Stafford commuted to see him from an apartment in New York. Lowell's days as "a fire-breathing Catholic CO" recur throughout his poems.

The novelist **Donald Braider** (1923–1976), who wrote *The Palace Guard* and *Color from a Light Within*, taught from the mid-fifties through the early 1970s at the Wooster School, just past the old fairgrounds on the outskirts of Danbury.

EASTON

From 1938 to 1949, **Edna Ferber** (1881–1968) lived here at her house, called Treasure Hill. Best known for *Show Boat*, which Jerome Kern and Oscar Hammerstein made into a musical, Ferber wrote many successful novels and (with George S. Kaufman) plays. While in Easton, she wrote *Saratoga Trunk* (1941) and *Great Son* (1945).

FAIRFIELD

As precocious as his grandfather **Jonathan Edwards** (1703–1758), **Timothy Dwight** (1752–1817) entered Yale University at the age of thirteen. He attacked his studies with such zeal that he suffered a physical breakdown, which he cured by equally zealous hiking and horseback riding. These experiences later led to his four-volume *Travels in New England and New York*, published posthumously.

Upon finishing at Yale, Dwight became a tutor at the university and began his epic poem on the heroes of the Revolutionary War, *The Conquest of Canaan*. This work and his attempts to add contemporary English literature to the Yale curriculum confirm him as one of the founders of the "Hartford Wits," also referred to as the "Connecticut Wits."

In 1783, Dwight became pastor of the Congregational Church in Fairfield's Greenfield Hill section. He served there for twelve years and wrote the poem "Greenfield Hill" about the community. In 1795, Dwight became president of Yale, an office he held for twenty years. Today a Yale college bears his name.

His brother **Theodore Dwight** (1764–1846) was the most outspoken Federalist of the Wits, and his animus toward democracy drives his speeches and verse.

GREENWICH

As the first wealthy bedroom suburb in Connecticut on the New York–New Haven and Hartford line out of New York City, Greenwich—and its neighbor, Old Greenwich—have been home, if usually for brief periods, to a number of writers.

Ring Lardner (1885–1933) lived here for a year before moving with his family to Long Island. **Willa Cather** (1873–1947) and the muckraking journalist and editor **Lincoln Steffens** (1866–1936) both spent time at the Bush-Holley House, now headquarters of the Greenwich Historical Society. Both Cather and Steffens were working for *McClure's Magazine* at the time. The naturalist **Ernest Thompson Seton** (1860–1946), whose *Wild Animals I Have Known* (1898) and other books on wildlife introduced a generation to grizzly bears, wolves, and the arctic fox, also visited the Bush-Holley House before buying a house in Cos Cob, the next town over toward New York. In the early 1900s Steffens too bought a home here, Little Point, in Riverside. Later, having sold Little Point, Steffens stayed in the area working for a time as a researcher for the journalist Walter Lippmann.

Truman Capote (1924–1984) lived three of his teenage years, 1939 to 1942, in Greenwich and attended Greenwich High School, but he did not stay long enough to graduate. His classmate Thomas Flanagan, novelist and author of *The Year of the French*, remembered the young Capote as "vividly unconventional. He was full of energy and self-confidence, and quite flamboyant, a show-off. He had a sense of himself as a special person, a fact he was under no impulse to conceal from other people." When most Greenwich students were finishing high school and planning for college, Capote was a copyboy at *The New Yorker* and had begun his conquest of New York City.

The journalist **Hendrik Van Loon** (1882–1944) died at his home in Old Greenwich. It is said that he had more than a half-dozen writing projects going at the time. Van Loon's books, *The Story of Mankind* (1921) and *The Story of the Bible* (1923), could be found on the bookshelves of most middle-class homes. In effect, they were popular encyclopedias—sort of James Michener without the fiction. Today they can be found at church book sales and on the dollar table at secondhand shops.

Clare Boothe Luce (1903–1987) married **Henry Luce** (1898–1967) in 1935 in Old Greenwich's First Congregational Church. It was to be a stormy marriage. The Luces kept a house, called The House, in Greenwich. Clare wrote the bitchy, sophisticated, and successful play *The Women* (1936), which also had success as a movie. Henry co-founded *Time* and *Life*. Both magazines promoted themselves as having a significant impact on American life. It is difficult to know if they actually did or, in the case of the still-going *Time*, do today in an age of television's instant journalism. Clare Boothe Luce served two terms, 1943–1947, as a congresswoman from Connecticut. She and her husband were intimates of American presidents from Franklin Delano Roosevelt to Lyndon Johnson and broke bread with most of the world's leaders for three decades.

GREENWICH/THE SUBURBS

The Connecticut suburbs, those towns from which commuters catch the train to work in New York City, begin at Greenwich and end at Fairfield. Stamford, Norwalk, and Westport, the setting for *The Man in the Gray Flannel Suit* by **Sloan Wilson** (b. 1920), are in this chain of towns served by the New York, New Haven, and Hartford railroad. These suburbs had a literary life from the late 1940s to the late '60s, with novels, stories, and occasional sociological works concentrating on the generation that came of age in World War II and moved to the suburbs en masse. This generation is white, middle-class, college-educated, and—in a phrase their appetites gave birth to—upwardly mobile.

John Cheever (1912–1982) is their poet. Although many of his stories are set in Westchester County, New York, they could as easily take place in Connecticut or the suburbs of New Jersey. In stories such as "The Country Husband," "The Housebreaker of Shady Hill," "The Swimmer," and in his novel *Bullet Park* (1969) (with its opening line, "Paint me a small railroad station then, ten minutes before dark"), Cheever registers the mythic rhythm, the ebb and flow of work in the city and home by train at night. He had a well-developed sense of life's absurdities and a gift for creating a physical, touchable world. His stories are tender, funny, melancholy, and quirky enough to have broken *The New Yorker*.

Sloan Wilson's man in gray flannel is middle-brow and takes up the "issues" of the day: conformity and the reality of a workaday routine, after the fear and exhilaration of war. Its title became the tag for all the commuters boarding their trains in their sober get-ups with attaché cases in hand.

Richard Yates (1926–1992) wrote what I believe is the best novel to be set in this time and place—*Revolutionary Road* (1961). In the book, Frank and April Wheeler live "in one of those new little houses on Revolutionary Road not far from Stamford, Conn.," and they want very much, or so they say, to leave it all and go to Europe. Nothing comes of their dreams but grief. Yates is merciless in disclosing their self-deception and the phony values that express the desires of those now living at what must be the end of America's revolutionary road.

GUILFORD

Fitz-Greene Halleck (1790–1867) was born here and late in life he returned to die and be buried in his hometown. His literary career flourished in New York, where he was one of the foremost members of the Knickerbocker Group (the name salutes Washington Irving's *Knickerbocker's History of New York*, 1809) and collaborated with Joseph Rodman Drake on the popular "Croaker Papers," a series of humorous verses published in the New York *Evening Post* in 1819. He was drawn to the work of both Sir Walter

Scott and Lord Byron, and combined their influences in poems that mix schmaltz with sting. In a century of prolific writers, Halleck's output was comparatively thin.

HADLYME

The plays of **William Gillette** (1855–1937)—he wrote thirteen in all, including the farce *Too Much Johnson*—are now forgotten, as is his adaptation of the Sherlock Holmes stories, in which he played the title role and toured for years. Gillette is remembered for having grown up at Hartford's Nook Farm, where he was Mark Twain's neighbor, and for his home, Seventh Sister, overlooking the Connecticut River in Hadlyme. Seventh Sister is now known as the Gillette Castle—a word Gillette himself never used—and is the center-piece of a state park open to the public.

As a boy at Nook Farm, Gillette had passions for the theater and engines. By the time he was sixteen, he had built a steam engine in his house. At Seventh Sister, he built a miniature railroad on which he took guests for rides. Gillette began what has been described as a Rhenish castle in 1915 and it was finished four years later. He designed the place himself and it features furni-ture that runs like railway cars on metal tracks, an ingenious system of mirrors that allowed Gillette to monitor the front door from his bedroom, and other oddments. At his death in 1937 (Gillette is buried in Farmington beside his wife Helen), his will gave the Castle and its surrounding land to the state for use as a park. It is open daily from Memorial Day to Columbus Day, 11 a.m. to 5 p.m. and after that on weekends, 10 a.m. to 4 p.m. until Christmas. There is an admission charge for adults and children over the age of six.

HARTFORD

Founded by pioneers from Cambridge, Massachusetts, in 1635 and incor-porated as Hartford in 1637, the city became Connecticut's capital and for a time in the late 19th century it rivaled Boston and New York as an American literary center.

The Connecticut Wits, also known as the Hartford Wits, gathered at the Black Horse Tavern here for a few years after the Revolutionary War. **John**

Trumbull (1750–1831), generally acknowledged as their leader, was—as were all the others—a Yale graduate. Indeed, he passed the entrance exam at age seven and entered the college at twelve. In 1782 Trumbull published his satire of the British, *M'Fingal.* Perhaps no other group of American writers has been so active in other professions. Several of the Wits, **Joel Barlow** (1754–1812) and Trumbull most prominently, were lawyers. **Timothy Dwight** (1752–1817) was a pastor and president of Yale for more than twenty years, **Elihu Smith** (1771–1798) was a physician, and **David Humphreys** (1752–1818) served George Washington as an aide-de-camp. These men shared a passion for poetry (especially long poems), politics, and patriotism. Humphreys wrote poems titled "The Glory of America: or, Peace Triumphant over War" and "Poem on the Industry of the United States of America." These verses, and much of the Wits' work, is flushed with pride at the nation's birth. In their patriotism the Wits were precursors of those 19th century poets—Emerson, Longfellow, and Walt Whitman—who regarded patriotism as a sentiment worthy of poetry. Modernism broke this connection. Men who found themselves in Ezra Pound's image of trench warfare—"eye-deep in hell"—could not indulge the patriotic impulses of their ancestors. Today, American poets leave the devalued currency of patriotism to television evangelists and other scoundrels.

Nook Farm began in 1853 when John Hooker, descendant of Hartford founder Reverend Thomas Hooker, and his brother-in-law Francis Gillette bought 140 acres along the Park River. Their land fit in a nook formed by the river, which gave the farm its name. The ensuing twenty years saw a community of relatives and friends with an intense interest in politics and literature form around Nook Farm.

Harriet Beecher Stowe (1811–1896) came to the farm in 1871. Her best years as a writer were behind her and her family was disintegrating. Her son Fred, wounded in the Civil War, disappeared in San Francisco and her husband Calvin, losing his mind, was troubled by ghosts. She continued to produce short stories and became involved in controversy when her book, *Lord Byron Vindicated*, alleged an incestuous affair between Byron and his sister. In 1886 her husband died, and she lived for another twelve years, slipping deeper and deeper into senility. Her neighbor Mark Twain remembered she "would slip up behind a person who was deep in dreams and musings and fetch a war whoop that would jump that person out of his clothes." She died on July 1, 1896, and was celebrated as the foremost American woman writer of the century.

Mark Twain (1835–1910; his real name was Samuel Clemens) first came to Hartford in 1868 to do business with Elisha Bliss Jr.'s American Publishing Company. At the time, Hartford had twelve publishers and was one of America's publishing centers. Bliss, like several of the others, published books on subscription. Twain came to work out a contract with him for *The Innocents Abroad* (1869). The subscription publishing system worked backwards. First, the publisher had agents sell subscriptions to a book. If the agents sold enough subscriptions so the publisher would at least break even, the publisher went to press. The books he printed had to be some 600 pages in length, to justify the high price of around $3.50 a volume. Bulk made the books seem like a bargain. Because there were a great many Americans who were far from bookstores, and because these books were sold in the same manner used by encyclopedia salesmen, the system worked. In its first sixteen months, *The Innocents Abroad* sold 85,000 copies for which Twain received nineteen cents a copy—and that was only the beginning. Twain was to be the only writer of literary merit to use and benefit from the system. It made him a very wealthy man, and after establishing his career he used the system as a publisher, most notably with his successful edition of President Ulysses S. Grant's memoirs.

The Innocents Abroad began Twain's fortune. Having recently married Olivia Langdon and wanting to be near his publisher, he came with his wife to Nook Farm in 1871 and rented a house there. Their son Langdon died there in 1872, the first of the tragedies marking their years, Twain's literary success notwithstanding. In 1873, Twain and Nook Farm neighbor **Charles Dudley Warner** (1829–1900) hatched the collaboration resulting in their novel about post-Civil War political and business corruption, *The Gilded Age* (1873).

The Innocents Abroad was followed by *Roughing It*, and Twain's fortune grew. He bought land at Nook Farm, and built in 1874 the house—"The stately mansion," his friend William Dean Howells called it—"in which he satisfied his love of magnificence." The house, still standing, cost Twain $31,000 for the land, $70,000 to build, and $22,000 for furnishings, every penny of which he enjoyed spending. He and his wife loved their house. Even today the care with which they designed and furnished the place and the joy they took in living there are evident. Indeed, it is the only house museum I have visited in New England that doesn't feel the least bit empty and mausoleum-like. It is a short way off Route 84, and well marked.

Twain did little writing in the house. He preferred to work during the summers he spent in his wife Livy's hometown of Elmira, New York, where he is buried. But while he lived at Nook Farm he produced—and the subscription system sold—his great books: *The Adventures of Tom Sawyer* (1876), *Life on the Mississippi* (1883), and *The Adventures of Huckleberry Finn* (1864).

At Nook Farm, Twain was more or less at his leisure. He loved to come and go with his neighbors, to have guests like William Dean Howells visit, and to play. As his literary production attests, Twain could turn out page after page of top-flight prose. Successful as he was as a writer, however, he could not stop himself from becoming involved in get-rich-quick schemes. He had some luck with a scrapbook that had self-adhesive pages, but he was nearly done in by James W. Paige's typesetting machine, which now sits in the basement of his home, the home that its failure caused him to give up.

Believing it to be the best investment he had ever made, Twain, visions of sugarplums blinding him, poured money into Paige's machine. But the linotype developed by Whitlaw Reid, of *The New York Herald Tribune,* did what Paige's typesetter could never do. Twain, who stayed the course, bankrupted himself, and in 1891 he and his family left Nook Farm for Europe—at the time a cheaper place to live—and never returned. Over the next years, Twain paid his debts and recouped his fortune by lecturing worldwide. For a man in his mid-fifties it was a demanding life, and Twain's determination was nothing less than heroic. In August 1895, having finished his world tour in England, Twain had a last tragic bit of news from Nook Farm. His beloved daughter Susy had died of meningitis while staying alone in the house. "It is one of the mysteries of our nature," he wrote a decade later, "that a man, all unprepared, can receive a thunder-stroke like that and live."

Today, Twain's Nook Farm mansion and Harriet Beecher Stowe's "cottage" across from it are open year-round. On my last visit, I had an excellent guide whose dry sense of humor was a wonderful foil for Twain's boisterous sense of amusement.

Not far from Nook Farm is the only Hartford home owned by **Wallace Stevens** (1879–1955). Stevens and his wife Elsie came to Hartford in 1916 when he, a lawyer, took a position with the home office of Hartford Accident and Indemnity Company. After renting in the area, they bought, in 1932, 118 Westerly Terrace—now privately owned—and lived there until Stevens's death. Today there is a holly tree in front of the house. It was planted there by the Stevenses, whose sole child was named Holly. Westerly Terrace is near Elizabeth Park, through which Stevens liked to walk on his way downtown to work. He wrote many of his poems in his head as he walked the three or so miles to his office. In 1934, Stevens became a vice-president of Hartford Accident, his highest position in the firm. He was in charge of bond claims, a highly technical area of the insurance business at which he was expert.

Before the appearance of Peter Brazeau's masterful *Parts of a World*, an oral biography of Stevens, it was the common wisdom that Stevens's life fell into two discrete compartments—insurance work and poetry—and that these did not overlap. But through his interviews, Brazeau demonstrates that Stevens's Hartford Accident colleagues knew of his poetry from the day he started work. His play *Three Characters Watch a Sunrise* had won a prize in Chicago, so Stevens began his Hartford working life as something of a celebrity. He was, Brazeau's witnesses report, all business in the office; but he did not hide his career as a poet, nor was he surrounded by Babbit-types who had no interest in the literary side of him. Stevens's remarkable first book, *Harmonium* (1923), and every subsequent Stevens book was published by Alfred A. Knopf in New York, but he seemed to enjoy being outside New York literary life. He had some literary friendships through the mail with contemporaries such as William Carlos Williams and Marianne Moore, but Stevens's imagination found release in an orderly, middle-class life. He traveled on business and vacationed often, usually by himself, in Florida. For a poet often said to have written French poetry in English, Stevens never visited France, but he kept contact with the language and Paris through letters to a Paris art gallery owner from whom he bought paintings. He had several other letter friendships with people in exotic places. A Dutchman in Ceylon sent Stevens the sort of trinkets he seemed to love, and he wrote long letters to a Cuban friend, explaining his poems in detail.

While the effect of Pound and Williams on American poetry has been much written about, Stevens, while less publicized, has had as decisive an impact. His poems proclaim the primacy of human imagination in a way that is eloquent, mysterious, and often unforgettable. In "The Emperor of Ice-Cream" he writes, "Let be be finale of seem."

Among Hartford's other literary distinctions are America's first cookbook, its forty-six pages written by Amelia Simmons and published by Hartford's Hudson and Goodwin, and the world premiere of the Virgil Thomson–Gertrude Stein opera *Four Saints in Three Acts*. This was the work of A. Everett "Chick" Austin, the adventurous director of the Hartford Athenaeum. The opera, one of two by Thomson and Stein, is based on St. Teresa of Avila. On February 8, 1934, an all-black cast gave the first performance, with St. Ignatius singing "Pigeons on the grass alas . . . " Thomson was present, but Stein stayed home in Paris.

KENT

James Gould Cozzens (1903–1978) entered Kent School in 1916 and graduated in 1922. During those years Kent's headmaster was the legendary Doctor Sills (Dr. Holt in Cozzens's Durham School stories). Cozzens's novel *The Last Adam* (1933) is set—as Cozzens wrote to a friend—in "Kent, Connecticut, with a green like New Milford's along US 7 as it passes through Kent." The novel's hero, a doctor, is one of the professional men who sparked the author's imagination. Cozzens's bestseller, *By Love Possessed* (1957), focuses on a lawyer and his adventures in love.

LAKEVILLE

Georges Simenon (1903–1989), inventor of Inspector Maigret and author of at least 250 novels, came to Shadow Rock Farm here in 1950 and stayed until 1955. During his stay he sat for a *Paris Review* interview. Carvel Collins, the interviewer, described Simenon's study: "On its walls are books of law and medicine, two fields in which he had made himself an expert; the telephone directories from many parts of the world to which he turns in naming his characters; the map of a town where he has just set his forty-ninth Maigret novel; and the calendar on which he has X-ed out in heavy crayon the days (9) spent writing the Maigret—one day to a chapter—and the three days spent revising it . . . " That novel is not identified, but while in Lakeville Simenon wrote *The Brother Rico, Maigret's Memoirs, Maigret and the Headless Body*, and many more. He routinely published six novels a year.

Simenon came to America in 1945 and later wrote that his major adjustment to the country had to do with American attitudes toward alcohol. A heavy drinker since his late teens, Simenon was now an alcoholic who wrote while drinking. Interviewed by Donald Goodwin, M.D., for his book *Alcohol and the Writer*, Simenon claimed, "I did not become truly alcoholic with an alcoholic consciousness except in America." In America Simenon switched from wine to Manhattans and martinis and began to suffer from hangovers and imagined attacks of angina. "In the United States," he said, "I learned shame." And he learned the American style of drinking, which is to keep drinking a dirty secret. He found that "from one end of the country to the other there exists a freemasonry of alcoholics . . . " By the time he left the country he had, in fear for his health, practically given up the sauce.

A footnote: Early in his chapter on Simenon, Goodwin quotes the critic Leslie Fiedler, who contends that writers who excite our admiration have a "charismatic flaw." "Drunkenness appears," in Goodwin's mind at least, "to be the flaw most admired by Americans." The novelist Donald Braider, himself an alcoholic, called alcoholism the "writer's disease." If both Goodwin and Braider have a point, they must be talking about the twentieth-century American writer. Writing and booze do not mix in the 19th century or earlier. Edgar Allan Poe is the significant exception. "Can you name," the alcoholic Sinclair Lewis asked, "five American writers since Poe who did not die of alcoholism?" Dickinson, Melville, Twain, Howells, Stowe . . . and the list goes on, until the generation born with the twentieth century.

LITCHFIELD

Harriet Beecher Stowe was born here a year after her father Lyman Beecher took the pulpit as pastor of the Congregational Church. A Calvinist, Beecher was a throwback to the grimmest strain of Puritanism, and he thundered hellfire and damnation in his sermons. Her father's doctrines of predestination and the elect were to preoccupy Stowe in her novels. At age twelve, Stowe wrote the essay "Can the Immortality of the Soul Be Proved by the Light of Nature?" It won a prize and was read aloud at her graduation from grade school.

During her growing-up years, affluent Litchfield had the nation's first law school. Tapping Reeve was its founder. Stowe's brother, the celebrated Abolitionist preacher Henry Ward Beecher, was also born here. Today, a plaque marks their birthplace.

MERRYALL VALLEY

Josephine Herbst (1892–1969) described the year she and her lover, the novelist **John Herrmann,** spent here during the 1920s as "an interlude of time as clear and uncertain as a drop of water." Though Merryall surely exists, you will not find it in a WPA guide or atlas. Herbst's description of the place in her memoir "A Year of Disgrace," collected in her book of memoirs, *The Starched Blue Sky of Spain,* is so idyllic that even if you could find the valley, it will not be the one she knew. "Two of us," she wrote "could still get by in the country for $600 a year if you took it easy and asked for no more than the essentials." The essentials were a large coal stove, ham, side of bacon and a quarter of a cow hanging in an unheated spare room, a fifty gallon keg of hard cider in the basement, drifted snow up to the windowsills, and an Aladdin lamp to read to each other by. That's the way they spent the winter. In spring the novelists Katherine Anne Porter and Nathan Asch rented houses nearby, and a New York showgirl who was "being put in a book by 'Bunny' Wilson" appeared for a visit.

After a summer spent in the garden, Herbst and Herrmann returned to New York "with the manuscripts of two novels, a basket of currant jelly and summer tans," and the eventual breakup of their relationship.

MIDDLETOWN

Charles Olson (1910–1970) did graduate work at Wesleyan University here. In the biographical note he wrote for his book of poems *The Distances*, Olson claimed to have been "uneducated at Wesleyan, Harvard and Yale." It was here that he began the research into the life and work of Herman Melville that led to his discovery of ninety-five volumes from Melville's personal library including Melville's seven-volume edition of Shakespeare. Melville's heavy annotations in the latter, especially in *King Lear*, became the foundation upon which Olson built his pioneering study of Melville, *Call Me Ishmael*. One of Olson's Wesleyan teachers, the Maine poet **Wilbert Snow** (1884–1977), urged that Olson consider a political career which, during World War II, Olson did when he worked in the Roosevelt administration.

For more than thirty years, the Wesleyan University Press has published a poetry series. On its list are James Wright, Hyman Plutzik, Louis Simpson, Robert Bly, James Tate, Jonathan Aaron, Calvin Forbes, Marge Piercy, Brenda Hillman, and a host of other poets.

NEW CANAAN

Bliss Carman (1861–1929), the Canadian-born poet whose poems have the lyric simplicity of a Eugene Field ("Make me over mother April/Now that spring is here") collaborated with Richard Hovey on the "Vagabondia" series of poems. Although Canada took him as its unofficial poet laureate, Carman lived twenty-one years of his life here.

Scribner's editor **Maxwell Perkins** (1884–1947) made his home here, and for two years, 1925–1927, the poet **Elinor Wylie** (1885–1928) and her husband, the poet **William Rose Benét** (1886–1950), the brother of **Stephen Vincent Benét** (1898–1943), resided here.

NEW HAVEN

Yale University is a series of quadrangles similar in layout to Cambridge University in England. As you enter these, you stroll in the serenity implicit in the phrase "ivory tower." Since Yale's architecture marks the university's many stages of development, there is much to look at, from plain 18th-century brick to 20th-century ribbed concrete. No other Ivy League college has Yale's air of mystery, of the solitariness of scholarly pursuits. Not to be missed is Louis Kahn's Yale Center for British Art. It is a sleek and sensuous marriage of wood and concrete that never overwhelms the art.

The Connecticut Wits could just as easily have been dubbed the Yale Wits as all of their number—Joel Barlow, Timothy Dwight, and John Trumbull being the most renowned—graduated from Yale. Dwight went on to serve the college as president. **Jonathan Edwards** (1703–1758), preacher and leader of the "Great Awakening," graduated from Yale in 1720 at the age of seventeen. Royall Tyler, who made his literary mark in Vermont, graduated from Yale, as did Noah Webster. The novelist James Fenimore Cooper (1789–1851), another Yale prodigy, entered the college at thirteen, but he failed to graduate. No other writer of national reputation attended Yale through the 19th century, but the painter and spinner of Western yarns, Frederic Remington, studied at the Yale School of Fine Arts.

The most famous literary character associated with Yale is undoubtedly Frank Merriwell, the epitome of the all-American college athlete and straight arrow. Merriwell, the creation of **Burt L. Standish** (pen name of **William Gilbert Patten** [1866–1945]), galloped the gridiron, raced around the track, and clouted home runs through more than 200 novels that sold 25,000,000 copies. In 1941 Standish introduced a grown-up Merriwell who faced a man's problems.

The novelist and critic Waldo Frank, playwright Philip Barry, who wrote *The Philadelphia Story*, and the brothers Benét, William and Stephen Vincent, both Pulitzer Prize–winning poets, graduated from Yale. **Thornton Wilder** (1897–1975) finished Yale in 1920 and later bought a house in nearby Hamden where he lived for many years with his sister Isabel. Wilder was the first writer to be awarded a National Medal for Literature. His career in the theater—*Our Town, The Skin of Our Teeth,* and *The Merchant of Yonkers,* on which the musical *Hello Dolly!* was based—has somewhat eclipsed his considerable achievements as a novelist. **Sinclair Lewis** (1885–1951) got through Yale in five years after dropping out briefly, and Donald Ogden Stewart (1894–1980), humorist and screenwriter, graduated in 1916.

Such is the snobbery of major literary reference works that you will not find Yale's greatest poet, **Cole Porter** (1893–1964), included in their pages. Porter wrote several college shows and was a cheerleader before he graduated in 1913. His classmate Gerald Murphy—friend of Hemingway, Picasso, and Fitzgerald, and grand animator in 1920s Paris and the south of France— became, with his wife Sara, the models for Dick and Nicole Diver in Fitzgerald's *Tender is the Night*. Poet, playwright, lawyer, and state department official Archibald MacLeish (1892–1982) was at Yale with Porter and Murphy, graduating in 1915. He later became Murphy's friend in France.

George Pierce Baker (1866–1935) brought his successful 47 Workshop for playwriting from Harvard to Yale in 1925, where it became the seed for Yale's School of Drama. In the 1970s Yale lost its drama school head to Harvard and its American Repertory Theater company.

Clarence Day (1874–1935), author of *Life with Father*—a dramatization of which, written by Howard Lindsay and Russel Crouse, was once the longest-running play (3,224 performances) in Broadway history—attended Yale for a time. In 1919 he helped establish the Yale Series of Younger Poets, which each year publishes the first book of a poet under forty. Judges have been W. H. Auden, Archibald MacLeish, James Merrill, and, currently, James Dickey. Winners: James Agee, Muriel Rukeyser, James Wright, Adrienne Rich, John Ashbery, Robert Haas, James Tate, and, in 1993, Jody Gladding.

John Hersey (1914–1993), who won the Pulitzer Prize in 1945 for his novel *A Bell for Adano*, graduated from Yale in 1936. He returned to the university in 1965, taking up the position of master of Pierson College, a post he held for five years. Hersey's best known work is *Hiroshima*, his nonfiction account tracing the lives of six people who survived the atomic bomb dropped on that Japanese city in 1945. It took up nearly all *The New Yorker* issue of August 31, 1946, and gave America its first sustained look at what the bomb had wrought. In his campaign against the bomb, Albert Einstein passed out countless copies of Hersey's work. Throughout his more than fifty-year career, Hersey alternated between writing novels and nonfiction.

Robert Penn Warren (1905–1989) did graduate work at Yale, and in 1950 he returned as a professor, a post he held until 1973. By Warren's second stint at Yale he had made a reputation as a popularizer of the New Criticism—*Understanding Poetry*, written with Cleanth Brooks, appeared in 1938—and as a novelist—*All the King's Men* won him a Pulitzer Prize in 1946. While he wrote a half-dozen more novels during his years teaching at Yale, he began to give more and more attention to poetry. In 1957 he won a second Pulitzer for *Promises*, and from then until his death he published more than a dozen books of poems that were met, despite some strong demurs, by increasing acclaim. Warren was born in rural Kentucky and as a young writer was associated with the Fugitives. Perhaps the only other writer from the South to spend so much time in the North, so productively, was Mark Twain.

Yale's Beinecke Rare Book and Manuscript Library, a cube with marble windows designed by Gordon Bunshaft, houses Yale's great collection of rare books and manuscripts. Among the American writers represented there are: Barlow, Cooper, MacLeish, Pound, Twain, Melville, Wilder, and Alice B. Toklas. The Beinecke has substantial holdings in William Carlos Williams and prides itself on collecting Nobel Prize winners. It has the papers of Sinclair Lewis, Eugene O'Neill, and recent Nobel laureate Czeslaw Milosz. Step inside the library on a sunny day and enjoy the beauty of sunlight as it shines through the marble walls. Sunken in the courtyard that surrounds the library is a cold yet compelling garden, a product of sculpture and not nature, designed by the sculptor Isamu Noguchi.

For some decades Yale's graduate school in English has ranked among the most influential in the country. In the last fifteen years or so it has been the center of the fashionable school of literary criticism, deconstruction. **Paul de Man** (1919–1983), who taught at Yale for some years, stands as the chief American explicator of this theory. Stood is perhaps the better word, as since his death and the publication of articles he wrote during World War II for a Nazi newspaper in his native Belgium, de Man and his work have been decried, condemned, and as staunchly defended. So hot has been the furor that readers who might normally be only dimly aware of what goes on at Yale, or any other graduate program, can now keep up with the debate in national magazines and books that have become popular, despite the difficulties inherent in the deconstruction theory.

Much to its credit, Yale conferred honorary degrees on two great American writers, Mark Twain in 1888 and Edith Wharton in 1923. Twain was not then the Twain we revere today, but the self-described "funny man" whose slow drawl was magic on stage and who, as he said in accepting Yale's Master of Arts degree, "was the natural enemy of royalties, nobilities, privileges and all kindred swindles, and the natural friend of human rights and human liberties."

Wharton's Doctor of Letters degree made her the first woman so honored by Yale. At first Wharton refused Yale's offer. She was in Europe and did not want to make the crossing, and she feared the demands of "publishers, relations, friends, invitations" when she landed in New York. Yale persisted, and she gave in. It was her only honorary degree.

NEW LONDON

As a child and young adult, **Eugene O'Neill** (1888–1953) spent summers here at Monte Cristo, the only permanent home his parents ever had. The house, which is open to visitors, is named after the play *The Count of Monte Cristo,* in which O'Neill's actor father James toured for years. It looks over New London's harbor and is actually a house with a schoolhouse added on. The schoolhouse addition served as the O'Neills' living room, and it is in this room that O'Neill's greatest play, *Long Day's Journey into Night,* is set. Indeed, the present room has been reconstructed from the play's stage directions. O'Neill wrote *Long Day's Journey* in 1940, but it was not performed in his lifetime. Even in death he did not want the attention its autobiographical character might attract, and so he ruled out a performance for twenty-five years. In 1956 his wife Carlotta overruled her husband's edict, and the tragedy of the Tyrone family opened in New York, winning that year's Pulitzer Prize. Very little happens in the play. In fact, it is all talk—but that talk is maddening, harrowing, and sublime. The Tyrones let their hair down as only Americans do. Two great performances of the play are on film: Frederic March, Katharine Hepburn, and the nonpareil O'Neill actor for our time, Jason Robards, star in an American version, and Sir Laurence Olivier plays the father, James Tyrone, in a version made for British television. *A Moon for the Misbegotten* and O'Neill's comedy *Ah, Wilderness,* in which George M.

Cohan starred, are also set at Monte Cristo, and here in 1916 he wrote *Bound East for Cardiff.* O'Neill was awarded the Nobel Prize in 1936.

There are signs for Monte Cristo on I-95, the major highway running through New London, and these direct you to the city's downtown, where you are on your own. The house is at 325 Pequot Road. Once in New London, it is best to ask for directions. It is open April through December, and there is an admission charge. On my recent visit the guide introduced herself as the fourth Mrs. O'Neill (he had been married three times) and roared through the tour. As might be expected, there is a great deal of theatrical memorabilia, posters and the like, but it is difficult to get a sense of how the O'Neills actually lived.

NORFOLK

In 1938, the poet **Kenneth Patchen** (1911–1972) and his wife Miriam came to this tiny town in northwestern Connecticut to run the office of James Laughlin's New Directions press. Laughlin was, by his own admission, a demanding and difficult boss. Patchen and his wife did all the New Directions drudge work—from packing and sending out books to proofreading—while, Lauglin wrote, "I have the fun of reading manuscripts and corresponding with authors." Patchen remembered that Laughlin cracked the whip if he took so much as a postage stamp for his own use. During these years, the Patchens lived in a cottage connected to the office. Patchen suffered until his death, from undiagnosed back pain that required several operations and eventually disabled him completely.

Through it all he wrote poetry, a great deal of it, and made what he called "picture poems." These may have derived from William Blake's *Songs of Innocence and Experience*, but Patchen's images are cruder, his poems funnier, and they resemble nothing but themselves. By 1940 the Patchens had returned to New York, but they soon wearied of the city and moved in the early 1940s to Old Lyme. Patchens's back continued to degenerate, and so impoverished were he and Miriam, his muse and soulmate, that in 1950 a fund was set up for him by T. S. Eliot. "Yes," Laughlin writes, "T. S. Eliot, who did not like his poetry at all." Thornton Wilder, Archibald MacLeish,

Marianne Moore, e.e. cummings, and other poets gave benefit readings, and there were concerts to raise more money. In 1951 the Patchens left for San Francisco. New Directions continues to keep Patchen's work in print. In his essay "Remembering Kenneth Patchen," Laughlin claims, "the power of Patchen's imagination is evident in his poem titles," and he cites the following: "A Letter to a Policeman in Kansas City," "Do the Dead Know What Time It Is?," "Boxers Hit Harder When Women Are Around," and "The Reason for Skylarks."

OLD SAYBROOK

John Clellon Holmes (1926–1988) met Jack Kerouac and Allen Ginsberg at a New York party in August 1948. That November, during one of their marathon conversations, Kerouac coined the term "the Beat Generation." When Kerouac went on the road shortly afterward, Holmes stayed in New York working on a novel that became *Go* (1952). In light of the Beats' appetite for publicity, the book was to have a curious history. Holmes's paperback publisher paid him a $20,000 advance, which put Kerouac's nose out of joint. Ginsberg disliked Holmes's portrait of him as the fledgling poet David Stofsky. Rumors of lawsuits caused the publisher Bantam Books to withhold the book. This did not seriously disrupt Holmes's friendship with Kerouac or Ginsberg, and did not intimidate Holmes from writing his article "This is the Beat Generation" for *The New York Times* in November 1952. Thus the Beats were launched, but fame came slower in those days. It was not until the publication in 1957 of Kerouac's *On the Road*, the Luce publications, *Time* and *Life*, jumping on the bandwagon with extensive picture stories of Greenwich Village beatniks in beards, berets, and black, that the work of these serious writers was distorted by America's celebrity-making machines. Not that these writers were unwilling victims, but the machines proved to be bigger and more powerful than anyone had imagined. Among the casualties were the words *underground* and *avant-garde*, as they applied to new and innovative writing. No one appearing in *Life* magazine could be underground, and the thirst for the new became so intense the term *avant-garde* became a commercial endorsement. While Holmes was not so celebrated as his colleagues, he continued to publish novels and essays, and for years he taught at the University of Arkansas. From the mid-1950s he kept a home in Old Saybrook, where he died of cancer in March 1988.

REDDING

One of the Connecticut Wits, **Joel Barlow** (1754–1812) was born here, and he wrote at least some of his attempt at *the* epic poem of America, "The Columbiad," at his brother David's farm, which stood into the 1930s on Route 107 but has since been torn down. As did many of the Wits, Barlow graduated from Yale. Barlow became a lawyer and began, with Benjamin Franklin, the 19th-century tradition of American writers serving as diplomats. William Dean Howells, Hawthorne, and James Russell Lowell were to follow. While living abroad Barlow wrote "Hasty Pudding," the poem by which he remains known today. In 1811 he was appointed minister to France, and he died the next year in Cracow, Poland, where he is buried.

Albert Bigelow Paine (1861–1937), a fan, knew Mark Twain only slightly when, at the urging of a friend, he proposed to work with Twain on his autobiography. Twain considered his proposition and responded, "When would you like to begin?" A week later Paine moved into Twain's house on Fifth Avenue in New York, and so began the collaboration, most of which took place in Twain's Redding home, Stormfield. Twain's biographer, Justin Kaplan, describes Paine's relationship to Twain as one of "biographer, constant companion, steward and finally editor and literary executor." Twain commissioned the building of the Italianate villa Stormfield in 1906, the same year he began work with Paine. With his daughter Jean, who was to die there, Twain moved in to the house in 1908. He and Paine did most of their work at the billiard table, a game Twain loved. As he talked, Paine could not help but realize that Twain told the same story in different ways, and he described how Twain's reminiscences "bore only an atmospheric relation to history." This may have intimidated Paine, but it did not dissuade him. Twain kept talking and Paine continued to listen until Christmas 1909, the day after Jean's death by epileptic seizure, when Twain finished his autobiography and announced "I shall never write any more." His health began to fade, and in the spring he sought rest and recuperation in Bermuda, where he declined with such speed that Paine came to take him back to Stormfield. He died there on April 23, 1910, and was buried out of New York's Brick Presbyterian Church wearing his signature white suit. Twain's grave is in Elmira, New York, near his wife Livy's family home. Stormfield burned to the ground in 1923. The Mark Twain Library, which Twain founded in memory of his daughter Jean, stands today at the junction of Routes 53 and 107 and exhibits a collection of Twain memorabilia. Paine's biography appeared in 1912.

RIDGEFIELD

Flannery O'Connor (1925–1964) lived as a boarder at 70 Acre Road (now a private home) with her friends, the Fitzgerald family, from September 1, 1949, until just before Christmas 1950. **Robert Fitzgerald** (1919–1985) has written about this time in his introduction to O'Connor's collection of posthumously published stories, *Everything That Rises Must Converge* (1965). During this year and a half, she worked on her first novel, *Wise Blood* (1952). Just before she returned to her Milledgeville, Georgia, home for the holidays in 1950, she suffered from pains that a doctor diagnosed as arthritis. On the train home, she became seriously ill with a high fever. Blood tests soon confirmed that she had lupus, the disease that eventually caused her death in 1964. All the Fitzgeralds have had a hand in O'Connor's work. At the time of her stay, Fitzgerald was translating *Oedipus Rex* and *Oedipus at Colonnus*. Reading these inspired O'Connor to end *Wise Blood* as she did. Sally Fitzgerald, Robert's wife, has edited a book of O'Connor's letters, *The Habit of Being* (1979), and of occasional prose, *Mystery and Manners* (1969). She is at work on a biography of the novelist, and has edited O'Connor's volume in the Library of America series.

O'Connor is the first contemporary writer, and at this point the only one, to be included in what is the closest thing in America to the French Pleiade. The Fitzgerald's children, Michael and Kathy, produced the John Huston film of *Wise Blood* for which son Benedict wrote the screenplay. Few first-rate novels have been so well served on the screen. After the onset of her illness

O'Connor twice returned to the Fitzgeralds for brief periods, before the family moved to Italy where Robert produced his translation of *The Odyssey*. He followed this with a translation of *The Iliad*. Both are generally considered the translations of their time. From 1965 until his death he was Harvard's Boylston Professor of Rhetoric.

ROXBURY

In 1961, **James Baldwin** (1924–1987) stayed at the home of his fellow novelist and friend William Styron while working on his novel *Another Country* (1962). It was a novel Baldwin would write in parts at New Hampshire's MacDowell Colony, in New York City, and—desiring distance from his frantic life in America—in Turkey. The novel was both acclaimed and roughed up by critics before it reached the desk of FBI Chief J. Edgar Hoover. Undoubtedly, Baldwin's color and his politics caused Hoover to act in his critical capacity. He is said to have found the book similar to Henry Miller's *Tropic* novels. Then he passed it on to the FBI laboratory for "examination," and what happened as a result of this examination is unknown today.

SEYMOUR

A Union captain in the Civil War, **John William De Forest** (1826–1906) was born here when Seymour was Humphreyville, named after Colonel Daivd Humphreys, who established the nation's first large-scale wool mill here in 1806. De Forest called upon his wartime service in writing his novel *Miss Ravenal's Conversion from Secession to Loyalty* (1867). Literary critic and man of letters **Edmund Wilson** (1895–1972) makes much of this realistic novel in his book on Civil War literature, *Patriotic Gore* (1962).

SHERMAN

Malcolm Cowley (1898–1989) rented a house in this small farming town on the New York line in 1926. Eventually he bought an old farmhouse, and this became his base until his death. For years, he spent winters in New York, where he was literary editor of *The New Republic* and an editor at Viking.

While at *The New Republic* he encouraged a great many writers, among them John Cheever, who had recently been thrown out of Thayer Academy. Cheever's story about his dismissal, "Expelled," came in over the transom and Cowley published it, launching Cheever's career at eighteen.

While at Viking, Cowley edited *The Viking Portable Faulkner*, which is worth looking up because it organizes Faulkner's Yoknapatawpha County saga chronologically. Cowley was among the first to champion **Jack Kerouac** (1922–1969) and he edited—alas, with a heavy hand—Kerouac's *On the Road* (1957). When Kerouac saw printed copies and saw Cowley's cuts and changes in punctuation and spelling (Cowley did not let him see galleys) he called his editor "Crafty Cowley" and felt that one had been put over on him. There is some irony in this connection, since Cowley was the spokesman for an earlier rebel generation, "the lost generation." Indeed, his best book is *Exile's Return*, which proclaims itself "a literary saga of the Nineteen-Twenties."

Like Hemingway, Dos Passos, cummings, Harry Crosby, Dashiell Hammett, and Julian Green, Cowley drove an ambulance in World War I. He later paid his Paris dues and returned home, as was true of so many other writers of his generation, to seek his fortune in New York. Hart Crane and Harry Crosby, both suicides, are emblematic figures in Cowley's story. They represent the end of the twenties adventure and Crane especially stands for the wild, hellbent twenties spirit. Cowley's description of the drunk Crane pounding out a poem on his typewriter, in time to a Cuban rumba or Ravel's *Bolero*, is as famous as Kerouac's Sal Paradise and Dean Moriarty driving nonstop to Wardell Gray and Dexter Gordon's blowing "The Chase." It says something about the generations that Kerouac made a novel—several novels—of the sort of experiences that Cowley cast as literary history. Today, writers have classmates in writing programs, and the idea of literary generations seems to have died in the sixties when writing itself began to be overshadowed—for the young at least—by rock and roll, television, and the movies.

Matthew Josephson (1898–1978), who figures in *Exile's Return*, also lived in Sherman. He too was an expatriate, and while in Paris he was one of the few Americans to get close to French intellectual life. His memoir *Life Among the Surrealists* (1962) gives an account of what Breton and his cohort was up to. In addition, Josephson wrote books about an airline, the hotel and restaurant and bartenders' union, 19th-century American industrialists, and several biographies.

SOUTHINGTON

Joseph Hopkins Twichell (1838–1918), who was born here, wrote a biography of John Winthrop, the first Governor of the Massachusetts Bay Colony. But he is best known as Mark Twain's close friend and as the father-in-law of the composer Charles Ives. Twichell and Twain met while Twichell was the pastor of Hartford's Asylum Hill Congregational Church. They hit it off from the start. In 1878 Twain, desiring his company as stimulus, paid for Twichell to join him in Europe, and the month and a half they spent together takes up most of Twain's *A Tramp Abroad* (1879). In the book, Twichell is "Mr. Harris." Ives married Twichell's daughter Harmony in June 1908, with Twichell officiating.

SOUTH WINDSOR

At the old cemetery, a memorial gateway remembers **Jonathan Edwards** (1703–1758), who was born here; his mother; and his father the **Rev. Timothy Edwards** (1669–1758), who preached for sixty-three years in South Windsor's Congregational Church. Jonathan Edwards was another of the Connecticut intellectual prodigies. He began Yale before he turned thirteen, and there he discovered the work of John Locke—who he read like a "greedy miser"—and Bishop Berkeley, both of whom were to have significant impact on his thinking. He already had a keen interest in science, insects in particular. Edwards's youthful observations of spiders inspired Robert Lowell's poem "Mr. Edwards and the Spider." Lowell returned to Edwards again in "Jonathan Edwards in Western Massachusetts" where, in Northampton, Edwards lead the religious revival, the "Great Awakening" of 1734–1735. In 1741, as the Awakening continued, Edwards preached his famous sermon, "Sinners in the hands of an Angry God," at a church in Enfield, Connecticut. Today, a stone on the town green commemorates Edwards's vision of God holding sinners over the flames of hell's fire, testing their resolve. According to the historian Perry Miller, Edwards was not a Puritan. "Edwards led New England," Miller writes, "to a reassertion of the primitive passion, but not within the framework of the ancestral covenant: instead he employed new and revolutionary conceptions of science and psychology." Edwards's stark prose can raise the hair on the back of your neck. "I made a solemn dedication," he begins "A Confession," "of myself to God and wrote it down, giving up myself and all that I had to God, to be for the future in no respect my own, to act as one that had no right to himself in any respect."

STAMFORD

Woodsier and not so posh as Greenwich, Stamford was until recently one of Connecticut's choice suburbs. Now it is becoming a business center, and its woods have been cut down for tract houses. Writers who lived in Stamford have stayed only briefly. **Eugene O'Neill** (1888–1953) boarded at the long-gone Betts Academy for four years; **Maxwell Perkins** (1884–1947) died at the Stamford Hospital, as did the playwright **Maxwell Anderson** (1888–1959; *What Price Glory?, Winterset, Knickerbocker Holiday*), who spent the last four years of his life here. The journalist **Heywood Broun** (1888–1939) had a house here in the 1930s as did the playwright **Elmer Rice** (1892–1967; *The Adding Machine*) in the 1960s. In April 1938, **Edmund Wilson** (1895–1972) married the novelist **Mary McCarthy** (1912–1989) in Stamford, where they lived until 1941.

One night the year before, Wilson, in McCarthy's words, "firmly took me into his arms, misunderstanding my intention." She was spending the night at Wilson's rented house, Trees, when—McCarthy wrote years later in her posthumously published *Intellectual Memoirs*—they "drunkenly made love," thus beginning the love affair that resulted in what was to be an unhappy marriage. As was her habit, McCarthy writes with such candor that it is hard to accept so forceful a woman as a victim. She had, she admits, flirted with Wilson in the past and, perhaps, she was interested in him as a mentor, his career being well established and hers only beginning. In any event, she continued into marriage with Wilson even though she claims to have hoped their affair would end in their parting. She was, after all, a Catholic, and a sense of guilt seems to have complicated her feelings. During her marriage to Bowden Broadwater, her third husband, they referred to Wilson as "the minotaur." As Wilson's biography has yet to appear we do not have his side of the story.

WATERBURY

On December 11, 1860, **Henry David Thoreau** (1817–1862) lectured at Hotchkiss Hall here on "Autumnal Hints." He had a bad cold, passed on to him by Bronson Alcott, and might have stayed home in Concord, but he insisted on giving the lecture. His cold soon became bronchitis, and he was to be housebound all winter.

WEST HARTFORD

Noah Webster (1758–1843) was born at the family farm at 227 South Main Street, which is now open as a museum. Shortly after his graduation from Yale he began his work as a lexicographer, the first fruit of which was his *Spelling Book*. This had such wide use that by 1890 it sold more than 60,000,000 copies. Since the 1806 publication of his *Compendius Dictionary of the English Language* his name has become a synonym for dictionary, but this was not immediately the case. As Webster worked to refine and expand his dictionary, he was engaged in what have been called the "dictionary wars." Webster stood on the side of an American language, and his 1828 dictionary listed some 5,000 American words not included in current English dictionaries. Webster's rival, fellow Yaleman Dr. **Joseph Worcester** (1784–1865) believed Webster had sacrificed tradition and elegance for utility. While Worcester's dictionary was the less popular, it found favor with writers. In *The Poet at the Breakfast Table*, Oliver Wendell Holmes wrote that Worcester's dictionary was one "on which, as is well known, the literary men of this metropolis are by special statute allowed to be sworn in place of the Bible." This held for a generation before Webster's prevailed. As Van Wyck Brook's description of Webster makes clear, Webster was interested in more than words:

> A tall, lean, black-coated man, with black small-clothes and black silk
> stockings and with an odd, quaint, old-fashioned air,—if you had met

him in China, you would have known that he hailed from Connecticut,—always a farmer's son in his heart of hearts, a busy-body, self-important, vain, but upright, and honest, aggressive, enterprising, pertinacious, a schoolmaster, lawyer, journalist who had written on banking and medicine . . .

The Webster House is open year-round every day but Wednesday. Webster memorabilia is on display and is worth a look, but exhibitions do include period furnishings not of the house, and they are changed from time to time. Admission is charged.

Wallace Stevens (1879–1955) lived with his family at 735 Farmington Avenue from 1924 to 1932. His daughter Holly, a young girl during these years, remembered her mother would "brush and comb her long blonde hair in the sunshine: it resembled strands of pure gold." As a teenager Holly's mother Elsie had been the model for the girl on the Roosevelt dime. Holly took enough interest in her father's poetry to make her own selection of his poems, which she published as *The Palm at the End of the Mind.*

WESTON

Franklin Pierce Adams (1881–1960) is one of the few American writers to be known by his initials alone, F. P. A. He lived in Weston from 1932 to 1950. His column, "The Conning Tower," appeared in various New York papers. In it he published his own satirical verse and the work of others. Young writers, especially, were eager to appear there. Once a week, F. P. A. added a diary—modeled on Samuel Pepys's diary—to his column. His initials and name mean little today, and there is no newspaper column in New York or New England that remotely resembles the one he made so widely read and oft quoted.

WESTPORT

This seaside commuter town a few towns up the coast from Stamford once had the reputation of being artsy. In the early 1950s it had one of the first movie theaters showing foreign films and featured cups of espresso to go with your popcorn. Mostly, writers have rented in Westport and moved on, but **Van Wyck Brooks** (1886–1963) spent two-and-a-half productive decades, the 1920s to the mid-1940s, here. He wrote six books including *The Flowering of New England* (1936) and *The World of Washington Irving* (1944) during that time. F. Scott and Zelda Fitzgerald partied through their honeymoon at a rented Westport cottage in the summer of 1920. Sinclair Lewis and Dorothy Thompson also rented a house in 1930, and it was here that Lewis got the call from Sweden telling him he had been awarded the Nobel Prize. The critic Paul Rosenfeld (1890–1946; *Port of New York*, 1924) summered here during the 1920s, entertaining such guests as Sherwood Anderson, Waldo Frank, and the painter Arthur Dove, who farmed in the area.

During one of his American reading tours, Dylan Thomas spent a night or two at the home of the novelist **Peter De Vries**, once an editor of *Poetry* magazine. The Random House editor **Albert Erskine** (1912–1983) lived here for many years. A Southerner, Erskine edited William Faulkner, Robert Penn Warren, James Michener, and Eudora Welty. He is credited with being among the first to champion Ralph Ellison, whose *Invisible Man* he edited; Malcolm Lowry; and Cormac McCarthy. "Erskine didn't try," Ralph Ellison said at his death, "to make the editor's role greater than the writer's." Consequently, he was unknown outside the field as he was respected in it. The novelist Katherine Anne Porter was his first wife.

WEST REDDING

Charles Ives (1874–1954) is one of America's foremost composers and also one of the inventors of life insurance as we know it. Born in Danbury where his father George was the bandmaster, Ives summered in West Redding and retired there. He made a fortune in the life insurance business while writing the music that—despite earning him some passionate partisans—met with much indifference during his lifetime. He wrote about his music, the life insurance business, and politics in two books: *Essays before a Sonata, The Majority and Other Writings*, edited by Howard Boatwright, and *Memos*, edited by the pianist and notable interpreter of Ives's music John Kirkpatrick. Both books were published posthumously in the 1970s. Ives's papers are at

Yale, where he pitched for the baseball team as an undergraduate. His *Concord Sonata,* recorded by Kirkpatrick, among many others, is one of the great evocations of the transcendentalist spirit.

WOLCOTT

The birthplace of **Amos Bronson Alcott** (1799–1888) has long since gone, but in this small town outside Waterbury there is a plaque where two country roads meet acknowledging Alcott's birth and the fact that Louisa May Alcott was his daughter. It does not say that they shared the same birthday and died within days of each other.

Following grade school in a one-room schoolhouse, Bronson Alcott went on to Cheshire, where he attended Cheshire Academy. He was confirmed in Waterbury at seventeen, taught school in Bristol in his late twenties, and met his wife, Abigail May, in 1827 at her father's house in Brooklyn.

The visionary and impractical Alcott, the most un-Yankee-like–of the transcendentalists, was to make his mark as a teacher. The Connecticut Works Progress Administration guide tells us he discovered his vocation in this way: "[Alcott] went to Virginia as a 'Yankee Pedlar' with a tin trunk upon his back, but . . . because of his dislike for trade, sold his pack at Norfolk for five dollars and established a school." In 1830 he and Abigail May married in Boston, in the vicinity of which Alcott spent most of the rest of his long life. He returned but twice to Wolcott, one time to give one of his "conversations" and another time to promote his book *Concord Days* (1872).

Maine

MAINE IS THE largest and most topographically various state in New England. On a map, civilization seems to cling to the coast while the interior is roadless and "empty." These vast acreages over which Thoreau once hiked are now mostly owned and managed by timber and paper companies. Magnificent rivers—the Allagash and St. John—run through these forests, feeding interconnected lakes whose private retreats and fishing camps are accessible only by small plane. In the 200,000-acre Baxter State Park, Mount Katahdin—described by Thoreau as a "vast aggregation of rocks, as if at some time it rained rocks . . . "—rises above it all.

In the north at its crown, where Maine meets Canada, potatoes grow in the fields of Aroostock County. Near the ocean, below the Canadian border, are blueberry barrens, a sort of flat Scotland of blueberry bushes. To the south and west is more lake country, marshy and heavily wooded. Moose, one of nature's most improbably carpentered creatures, thrive here. Then there is the Maine coast, unique in New England and the United States.

Rugged is the word most often used to describe the coast's rocky, sandless shores, and it is accurate as to texture. The coast is a dump of Precambrian bedrock, scored, grooved, and roughened by wind and water. It is as if giant fingers drawing back from the ocean gouged out inlets, estuaries, bays, and coves, and dredged up large and small islands as they worked. Topped by wind-shaped, bristly pine and spruce trees, half lost in the fog that can come and stay for days trapping brine in the air, this coast is shaggy, stern, and fortress-like, and invites endless exploration.

The water off the coast is chill enough, even in summer, to discourage any but the most intrepid or foolhardy swimmer. It is water for the sailor, for the fisherman and lobsterman. (The lobster, as bizarre looking a creature as the moose, is another of Maine's signatures.)

Maine has more homegrown writers of note than any other New England state save Massachusetts, and it likes to boast about them. *Maine: Poets' Corner of America*, an undated booklet apparently printed in the 1950s by the state's Department of Economic Development, begins with a series of questions. "Did you know that America's three greatest sonneteers are all natives of Maine?" You did, if you answered Henry Wadsworth Longfellow, Edwin Arlington Robinson, and Edna St. Vincent Millay. Did you know also that Longfellow's *Hiawatha* is the greatest American Indian epic, and that the first woman to win the Pulitzer Prize was Millay, a Maine girl? The nickname on Maine's license plate is "Vacationland," which partly explains this most un-Yankeelike boasting as a come-on for tourists, but the pride is no less for that.

BLUE HILLS

The Mississippi-born novelist **Ben Ames Williams** (1889–1953) lived here for many years. *Leave Her to Heaven* is his best known novel. He edited Mary Boykin Chesnut's *A Diary From Dixie* in 1949 and wrote the introduction to *The Kenneth Roberts Reader* (1945).

Amos Niven Wilder (1896–1993), poet, Harvard Divinity School professor, and brother of Thornton Wilder, also resided here for many years. He was one of those young Americans who served as a volunteer ambulance driver with the American Field Service in World War I. He wrote about his wartime experiences in poetry, *Battle Retrospect* (1923), and in prose, *Armageddon Revisited: A World War I Journal*, which he completed shortly before his death.

BROOKLIN

E. B. White (1899–1985) knew Maine from childhood summers spent in Belgrade. In 1938, he and his wife **Katherine White** (1892–1977) bought the Brooklin house they had first seen while cruising around Deer Isle five years before. They determined to retire to Maine and do their own work while keeping their hand in at *The New Yorker,* where he was a staff writer and she was a fiction editor. This plan worked until 1943, when the Whites returned to New York. They would not reside permanently again in Maine until 1957.

Both of White's classic children's novels, *Stuart Little* (1945) and *Charlotte's Web* (1952), drew on his experience in Maine. In the winter of 1957–1958, now living in Maine for good, White began his series of essays *Letters from the East* and datelined them Allen Cove—"a small arm of the sea," he explained, "that cradles my pasture." These essays and other "Letters" are collected in *The Points of My Compass* (1962). White is revered for his plain and utilitarian style, and his best selling book is probably *The Elements of Style,* the manual originated by his Cornell University teacher William F. Strunk, Jr., which White revised in 1959. This is one of the few books White wrote after buying his Maine farm in which he does not declare his joy for rural Maine life.

Katherine White, nonpareil *New Yorker* fiction editor, had a garden at their Maine home that became the focal point for her *Onward and Upward in the Garden* essays. Unaccountably, Katherine White has no entry in the current edition of *The Oxford Companion to American Literature.*

BRUNSWICK

Nathaniel Hawthorne (1804–1864) entered Bowdoin College in 1821 with a remarkable class of thirty-eight men, twelve of whom achieved national recognition by middle age. **Horatio Bridge** (1806–1893), whose *Journal of an African Cruiser* Hawthorne edited and who offered the Boston publisher of Hawthorne's *Twice-Told Tales* the $250 required to insure it against loss, was in the class, and so was Hawthorne's close friend Congressman Jonathan Cilley. Franklin Pierce, the fourteenth president of the United States and Hawthorne's friend and patron, was a class ahead, and the prodigy **Henry Wadsworth Longfellow** (1807–1882) joined Hawthorne's class at age fifteen in 1822. Hawthorne began Bowdoin as Hathorne, the family spelling, and experimented with the added *w* as he wrote his name in many of his school-books, now in the possession of the college library.

In 1828, three years after graduating from Bowdoin, Hawthorne published, anonymously and at his own expense, *Fanshawe*, his first novel and the first American novel set at a college. In it, Bowdoin goes under the name of Harley. Hawthorne came to regret the book and burned every copy he could get his hands on, asking his friends to do the same. He did not publish his second novel, *The Scarlet Letter*, until 1850. Hawthorne's wife Sophia did not learn of *Fanshawe's* existence until after his death.

Longfellow had published his first poem at the age of thirteen in a newspaper in Portland, Maine, which was his birthplace. When he graduated, he left for three years in Europe and there studied the Romance languages in order to return and assume the professorship in modern languages Bowdoin had promised him. He taught at Bowdoin from 1829 until 1835, when he again left to study languages in Europe. In addition to his professorship, he was college librarian, responsible for the library's being open one hour a day.

Today Bowdoin's library has a wealth of Longfellow and Hawthorne material. There has not been a biography of Longfellow in more than twenty-five years and demand for his work is slight, but interest in Hawthorne is booming, especially in Japan, and many Japanese scholars journey to Bowdoin to consult the Hawthorne collection.

The library also has major holdings of Sarah Orne Jewett (1849–1909) and Hollis-born **Kate Douglas Wiggin** (1856–1923), author of *Rebecca of Sunnybrook Farm*; a **Marguerite Yourcenar** (1903–1987) collection; and "everything" by Bowdoin alumni and 1935 Pulitzer Prize-winning poet Robert P. Tristram Coffin (1892–1955). Portraits of Hawthorne and Long-fellow hang in the library entrance hall, and a map available there identifies four college buildings still standing from their Bowdoin years.

The poet **Louis O. Coxe** (1918–1993) taught at Bowdoin from 1955 until he retired in 1983. He is best known for his dramatization, with Robert Chapman, of Herman Melville's *Billy Budd*. It played on Broadway to good reviews in 1951.

The Bowdoin College Art Museum displays two portraits of Longfellow, one of Hawthorne, and a Saint-Gaudens bronze relief of Robert Louis Stevenson (1850–1894) reading in bed. In the larger of the Longfellows—painted in 1862 by George Peter Alexander Healy—Longfellow, at fifty-five, is gray and sorrow-eyed. It had been a year since his wife Frances was burned to death in a household accident. The museum also has Assyrian bas-reliefs, a Winslow Homer collection, and a superb John Frederick Peto painting, *Mug, Pipe and Biscuits*.

Harriet Beecher Stowe (1811–1896) set up house at 63 Federal Street—now the Stowe House Motel—in 1850, upon her husband Calvin's appointment as Bowdoin Professor of Natural and Revealed Religion. She was thirty- nine, pregnant with her last child, and she had already begun *Uncle Tom's Cabin*—"something," she swore, "that would make the whole nation feel what an accursed thing slavery is." Family cares kept her from returning to the book until, in February 1851 at the communion service in the college church, she experienced a vision of Uncle Tom's death and, returning home, wrote it down at once. She quickly finished the novel, and it was published in 1852, selling 300,000 copies in that year. It eventually became the first American novel to sell more than a million copies, and it sold more than two-and-a-half million in Europe. Meeting Stowe in Washington during the Civil War, President Abraham Lincoln greeted her by saying, "So this is the little lady who made this big war." Stowe went on to write *The Pearl of Orr's Island*, a novel set in Maine, which had a significant impact on the young Sarah Orne Jewett.

In the lobby of the nondescript motel that today occupies Stowe's house, there is a glass case displaying copies of some of her books.

The Maine Writers and Publishers Alliance, which promotes Maine writers and publishers, has a small bookstore devoted to their work, at 12 Pleasant Street. The Alliance sells a map, "Maine Writers," that identifies places associated with Maine's novelists, poets, humorists, and dramatists, including **John Gould** (b. 1908), who has written many books of down east humor, and playwright **Owen Davis** (1874–1956), who won the Pulitzer Prize in 1923 for his play *Icebound*.

CAMDEN

Edna St. Vincent Millay (1892–1950), born in nearby Rockland, grew up in Camden, where she graduated from high school and wrote her first poetry. Today she is commemorated by a statue that looks out to sea from the harbor side of the public library on Route 1. She was one of three daughters raised by a divorced mother who earned just enough to get by as a practical nurse.

There is a Cinderella story told about Millay's "discovery" and her subsequent education at Vassar. In 1912, Millay's older sister worked at the Whitehall Inn, which still stands, also on Route 1. To entertain the Inn guests, she sang a song one night and then introduced her sister Edna, who read her poem "Renascence":

> All I could see from where I stood
> Was three long mountains and a wood;
> I turned and looked the other way,
> And saw three islands in a bay.

Afterward, so the story goes, a guest in the audience sought Edna out and became her guardian angel, sending her to Vassar, where her career as a poet began. Other sources say that this patron was a family friend. In 1953, the Whitehall Inn dedicated the room in which she read as a memorial to her. After Vassar Millay rarely returned to Camden, but she and her husband did spend many summers on Ragged Island in Casco Bay.

Robert Willis's bronze statue of Millay (the library is on Route 1 and the statue is just behind it) has the poet turned away from Camden. She holds a book behind her back and she is clearly dreaming of other worlds. The spirit of the pose seems right, but Willis's grasp of anatomy is uncertain and he has given Millay an impossibly long waist. A handsome postcard of the statue's yearning head is for sale in Camden's excellent secondhand bookstore, ABCDEF.

Abbie Huston Evans (1881–1983) was known primarily as a nature poet, with Maine's coast and sea her subject. Raised in Camden and "stamped by this rocky corner like a die,/Shaped by these five hills and this edge of sea,"

Evans taught Edna St. Vincent Millay in Sunday school. Later, Millay wrote the forward for *Outcrop*, the first of three books Evans published in her long life.

CASTINE

Robert Lowell (1917–1977) first came here for a length of time when his cousin Harriet Winslow, having suffered a stroke, offered him her Green Street house for half the summer. Lowell once wrote of Winslow that she "was more to me than my mother." Upon her death, he inherited the house and spent summers there through the 1950s and 1960s. When he divorced his second wife, the novelist and critic Elizabeth Hardwick, she received the house in their settlement and later sold it. Now privately owned, it is just up from the public library, catercorner to the Adams School, and fronts on the village green. A Union soldier is on guard there, one of those immortalized in Lowell's poem "For the Union Dead," the statues who "grow slimmer and younger each year."

While Lowell lived on Green Street he worked in a barn—since renovated as a vacation house—looking over the tidal Bagaduce River. In a letter to William Carlos Williams, he described the view from his workroom: "It's right on the bay, which on one side looks like a print of Japan and on the other side like a lake in Michigan as the rocky islands with pine trees ease off into birches and meadows." From his desk, Lowell watched the seals that disport themselves in many of the poems he wrote here. As was his habit and curse, he worked his poems hard, producing a seemingly endless flow of drafts. In "North Haven," her elegy to Lowell, his friend Elizabeth Bishop wrote "You can't derange, or re-arrange,/your poems again."

"Skunk Hour," one of Lowell's most famous poems, is set near Castine. He wrote "Soft Wood," dedicated to Harriet Winslow, here, and many of the poems in *Near the Ocean* are set in this pine-wooded land and rock-islanded seascape Lowell last visited in late August 1977, two weeks before his death. In a photograph taken on a bright, cold day at the beach, Lowell, square-jawed, gaunt, his white hair blowing, looks as formidable as King Lear.

Affluent, well-groomed, and Republican (in the 1980s Mary McCarthy complained that the town was loaded with Reaganites), the staid Castine is a reminder of how patrician Lowell's New England is, a world apart from Robert Frost's hardscrabble farms and Charles Olson's Gloucester fishing port. Finishing his day's work, Lowell liked to play tennis at the country club overlooking the village. When a *Time* cover story made him famous, he drew a crowd there.

Mary McCarthy (1912–1989) bought her Federal-style house here in 1967 and soon afterward painted it yellow, to the alarm of her neighbors. She lived in it for some part of each year, entertaining what her friend and neighbor Robert Lowell referred to as "the beautiful big guests" and running a tight ship (breakfast at eight, lunch at one, and cocktails at seven). She died in 1989. The philosopher Hannah Arendt, perhaps her closest friend, spent six weeks in McCarthy's garage apartment writing her essay "Lying in Politics: Reflections on the *Pentagon Papers*." While in Castine, McCarthy worked on the journalism that distinguished her last years as a writer: her essay on Captain Ernest Medina's trial for the My Lai massacre, and her coverage of the Senate Watergate hearings. McCarthy voted in Castine and took an active interest in local politics, especially what she called a "vacationland" dispute over property taxes and the debate over the Navy's proposed installation of an early-warning radio tower. In Carol Brightman's biography *Writing Dangerously*, the chapter on McCarthy in Castine is titled "The Duchess of Castine." Brightman takes this from Lowell's lines in his sonnet to McCarthy, "Dark Age luminary and Irish hothead/the weathered loveliness of a duchess. . . . " McCarthy is buried in Castine.

COREA

Marsden Hartley (1877–1943), a great American painter who wrote poetry throughout his life and whose volume of collected poems is in print today, was born in Lewiston, Maine, and lived all over the state—Portland, Georgetown, Vinalhaven, and West Brooksville—before coming to Corea in his last years. In Corea, he had his studio in a church, but he had previously worked in a chicken coop, and while painting Mount Katahdin he lived in a lakeside camp. Up and down the Maine coast, there are landscapes that seem to have been copied from Hartley's paintings. Away from the state, he was involved with the avant-garde in both Europe and America. Gertrude Stein wrote a portrait of him in her play *I*; in *Strange Interlude* Eugene O'Neill based the character Charles Marsden partly on him; he showed his work at Alfred Steiglitz's New York gallery 291; and William Carlos Williams called him "a sort of grandpa to us all."

Hartley's poems are straightforward and American in their diction. For all his travel and contacts, he lived an isolated life and his poems reflect a deep engagement with a self closed off from the world. When he died, his friend Paul Rosenberg eulogized him as that "gaunt eagle from the hills of Maine." He must have had in mind these Hartley lines:

> The eagle wants no friends,
> employs his thoughts to other ends—
> he has his circles to inscribe
> twelve thousand feet from where
> the fishes comb the sea,
> he finds his solace in unscathed
> immensity,
> where eagles think, there is no need
> of being lonesome—
> In isolation
> is a deep revealing sense
> of home.

CRANBERRY ISLAND

Cranberry Island was the home of **Rachel Field** (1894–1942), who wrote a bestseller with a perfect bestseller title, *All This, and Heaven Too*. Charles Boyer starred in the movie. Field followed this with the novel *And Now Tomorrow*, whose title seems destined for a soap opera.

CUSHING

Patriarch of the painting Wyeth clan, **N. C. Wyeth** (1882–1945) summered here. His illustrations of *Treasure Island, Kidnapped, The Last of the*

Mohicans, and other novels will forever be the mental images of those stories for readers who read the squarish, oversized editions they appeared in when young. Coming back from watching a local farmer harvest his corn by hand, Wyeth and a grandson were killed in an automobile accident in 1942.

DAMARISCOTTA MILLS

Jean Stafford (1915–1979) and her husband **Robert Lowell** (1917–1977)—it was the first marriage for both—spent nearly a year here in 1945–1946. Stafford bought their house, which stands close to the oldest Catholic church in New England and is in private hands today, with the profits from her bestselling novel *Boston Adventure*. Theirs was an unhappy, at times violent, marriage, and the house was soon up for sale. In her memoir *Poets in their Youth*, Eileen Simpson, the poet John Berryman's first wife, gives a picture of life at the Lowells' during their last summer in Damariscotta.

DARK HARBOR

During the last years of his life, **James Weldon Johnson** (1871–1938) summered here. Educator, editor, novelist, and activist on behalf of civil rights, Johnson wrote the lyrics for "Under the Bamboo Tree" and "The Congo Love Song." His *God's Trombones—Seven Negro Sermons in Verse* (1927) was much read in its time and is in print today. He was killed in an automobile accident in nearby Wiscasset.

DEER ISLE

Helen Nearing (b. 1904) and **Scott Nearing** (1883–1983) spent the last ten years of Scott Nearing's life at their house, Harborside, where Helen Nearing still resides. It is a place of pilgrimage for those who went back to nature in the 1960s, influenced by the Nearings' *Living the Good Life*. A sign at the entrance to their home greets visitors:

> Our mornings are our own
> we'll see visitors 3–5
> Help us live the Good Life.

44

In a recent interview Helen Nearing said, "There are usually about 1,300 visitors a year, but lately I think there have been more, and they're older and more serious now, they really want to change their lives."

Their Good Life began when Nearing, an economist and member of the American Communist Party, was given the boot by the party for questioning the wisdom of Lenin, and he dropped out, sixties-style, to a homestead in Vermont, where he and his wife fed themselves from their garden and lived without electricity. This experience produced their book—something of a how-to *Walden*—which was written in the 1950s and became a sacred book for the 1960s. Thoreau did not expect others to move to a cabin in the woods, but the Nearings wrote a prescription for the modern rural homestead. They expected others to be fed up with the city and to seek self-sufficient country living as they had, and they were right. More than 250,000 copies of *Living the Good Life* are in print today. As a member of the Communist party, Nearing appears in Allen Ginsberg's poem "America."

FARMINGTON

Jacob Abbott (1803–1879), a Congregational clergyman, wrote more than 200 books. He began his Little Rollo books in 1835 and produced twenty-eight in the series. These instructive stories for children, with a Christian bent, were extremely popular.

GARDINER

Edwin Arlington Robinson (1869–1935) was born in the village of Head Tide and reared in Gardiner, which became the model for his Tilbury Town. He began studies at Harvard but did not finish because his father's lumber business (the family also traded in river ice) went broke. His early work impressed President Theodore Roosevelt, who arranged jobs for him in New York City. There he worked, as had Herman Melville, in the Customs House. Leaving New York in 1910, Robinson was able to devote the rest of his life to writing poetry. He spent his summers in residence at New Hampshire's MacDowell Colony.

Robinson's poems are dry, knotty, and heavily ironic. His most widely anthologized works are his portrait poems. "Richard Cory," who kills himself because he can come up with no positive reason for being, the ironist "Cliff Klingenhaven," and the deluded "Miniver Cheevy," who "wept that he was ever born,/And he had reason," are among Robinson's most famous characters. His verse is rhymed and the irony often crushing, as in this final stanza from "Richard Cory":

> So on we worked, and waited for the light
> And went without the meat, and cursed the bread;
> And Richard Cory, one calm summer night,
> Went home and put a bullet through his head.

Gardiner's celebration of this native son might be construed as having a little irony of its own, but the admiration seems genuine. His house, just off the green, is marked by a plaque; the library has a glass case containing various first editions; and on the green there is a monument that proclaims Robinson "Thinker/Seer/Poet." An early reviewer wrote of his work that "The world is not beautiful to him, but a prison house," to which Robinson replied, "The world is not a 'prison house,' but a kind of spiritual kindergarten where bewildered infants are trying to spell God with the wrong blocks."

Laura Richards (1850–1943), author of *Captain January*, wrote biographies of both her father, the Boston doctor and advocate for the blind **Samuel Gridley Howe** (1801–1876), and—in collaboration with her sisters, Maud Howe Elliott and Florence Howe Hall—of her mother Julia Ward Howe, which book was awarded the Pulitzer Prize. Richards also wrote a short life of Edwin Arlington Robinson. She came to Gardiner in 1876 and lived here until her death. Most of the eighty or so books she wrote were for children.

GREAT SPRUCE HEAD ISLAND

The father of **Fairfield Porter** (1907–1975) bought this Penobscot Bay island—the size of New York's Central Park—in 1912, and built a farmhouse, large cottage, and barn. From 1913 until his death, Porter spent nearly every summer of his life on Great Spruce Head, and its meadows, trees, rocks, the bay around it, and the house he and his family lived in are principal subjects of his paintings. Today, after a major retrospective, Porter has taken his place with Marsden Hartley, John Marin, and Winslow Homer as one of Maine's great painters. His friendship with the New York School poets—he painted portraits of Frank O'Hara, Kenneth Koch, and John Ashbery and his close friend **James Schuyler** (1923–1991) is in numerous paintings—led him to write poetry, a book of which appeared after his death. His other book, *Art in Its Own Terms*, also appeared posthumously. It is art criticism of a high order. Indeed, it is the best art criticism written by an American painter in this century.

Porter lived in Southampton on Long Island during the winter and at times kept a studio in New York City. He was in the thick of the 1950s New York art world. When he began to write for *Art News*, he quickly showed his mastery of the short (100 to 250 words) review. His longer essays and speeches are equally adept. Porter's passionate, unorthodox convictions are matched by a lively and lucid prose style. Perhaps the best summary of his aesthetics occurs in one of his letters: "Order seems to come from searching for disorder, and awkwardness from searching for harmony or likeness, or the following of a system. The truest order is what you already find there, or that will be given if you don't try for it. When you arrange, you fail."

After a medical crisis in the summer of 1961, James Schuyler came to recuperate at the Porters, and he ended up staying with them for over a decade. He was a willing model and often read aloud to Porter while he painted. Schuyler's Maine poems (he also wrote beautiful poems on his visits to northern Vermont) display his gift for sharp, original description, his wit, and his intimate, modest, and clear sound. He had a wonderfully amusing way of seeing nature in terms of ordinary life. In "Closed Gentian Distances" he writes:

> A nothing day full of
> wild beauty and the
> timer pings. Roll up
> the silver off the bay
> take down the clouds
> sort the spruce and

send to laundry marked,
more starch.

He ends his poem "Penobscot" that inventories the islands in Penobscot Bay:

From here we see them all, and more,
and the Camden Hills, Mount Desert, Blue Hill, Deer Isle
and ocean facing Isle au Haut
where the breakers roll stones to cannon balls.

The photographer Eliot Porter, Fairfield Porter's older brother, made many photographs on Great Spruce Head, where he summered through the years. These are collected in *Summer Island: Penobscot Bay* and reveal magical paths through pine forests and over wildflower-strewn meadows leading to ocean views.

KENNEBUNK

If Maine had a state writer it would be **Kenneth Roberts** (1885–1957). His historical novels—*Arundel, Northwest Passage, Oliver Wiswell,* and *Lydia Bailey*—have their roots in Maine, and he was a tireless defender of the state whenever he felt it to be maligned.

Roberts was a staunch Republican who, along with his friend John Marquand and other writers, took out advertisements urging Franklin Delano Roosevelt not to seek a third term. Actually, he loathed the president, and he exacted revenge by gluing Roosevelt dimes to the clamshells he used for ashtrays. Thus he could grind his cigarettes out in the president's face. Born in Kennebunk's Storer Mansion on Storer Street, Roberts built his home, Rocky Pastures (now in private hands), in Kennebunkport in 1938 and lived there until his death.

Booth Tarkington (1869–1946) summered near Roberts's Rocky Pastures home. He was a mentor who became a friend. His "Penrod" books, very popular in their time, were behind him, and while he wrote nothing significant set in Maine, he and Roberts surely found pleasure in each other's company and in their mutual dislike for Roosevelt.

Today only some of Roberts's books remain in print, but copies of nearly all of them can be found on the shelves of any secondhand bookshop in the state. His historical novels are well researched, readable, and occasionally stirring. The consensus is that *Arundel* is the best of these. (Late in his career he became obsessed enough by his belief in dowsing to write three books on the subject.)

LIVERMORE FALLS

Poet and critic **Louise Bogan** (1897–1970), who spent most of her career in New York, was born here, but her family moved in 1901 to Milton, New Hampshire, and then to Ballardvale, Massachusetts. They were all small mill towns where her father could get work. Bogan's output was small, but her traditional lyrics are well and sparely made. There is a distinctly New England tone to her voice perhaps best heard in "Question in a Field":

> Pasture, stone wall, and steeple,
> What most perturbs the mind:
> The heart-rending homely people,
> Or the horrible beautiful kind?

Bogan went on to become *The New Yorker*'s poetry editor for thirty-eight years, and she is the subject of an excellent biography by Elizabeth Frank.

THE MAINE WOODS

"I have travelled a good deal in Concord," **Henry David Thoreau** (1817–1862) shrewdly said of himself, and he did, but he had to go to Maine to experience wilderness. On his first trip he was a young man looking for a teaching job. He did not find one, but he caught a glimpse of Penobscot Bay, and in Oldtown he met an Indian who told him, "Two or three miles up the river one beautiful country." In August 1846, he took two weeks off from his Walden cabin and went into that country. He entrained to Portland and from there went by steamboat up the coast and inland to Bangor.

In Bangor he met his cousin George Thatcher and traveled north by stagecoach until the road ended, and they continued by boat up the Penobscot

River through a system of lakes and streams that brought them to North Twin Lake, where the real wilderness began. There were neither cabins nor roads, and to this day, as reported by those who have been there, North Twin Lake is much the same. From the lake, Thoreau, Thatcher, and two Bangor men in the timber business went on foot toward their destination, Mount Katahdin. Since it was late in the summer they were not bedeviled by black flies, but the going was rough through the pathless spruce forests. Thoreau climbed the 5,267-foot Mount Katahdin alone. Later, when he worked up his notes from the trip, he began with this description of what he encountered at North Twin Lake: "It is difficult to conceive of a country uninhabited by men—we naturally suppose them on the horizon everywhere—and yet we have not seen nature unless we have once seen her thus vast and grim and drear—whether in the wilderness or in the midst of cities." Thoreau last visited Maine in September 1853. This time, as he traveled north from Bangor, the "wild fir and spruce-tops, and those other primitive evergreens" were "like the sight and odor of cake to a schoolboy." But his pleasure dimmed when, while on a moose hunt, his Indian guide tracked and slew a moose. Thoreau did not lose his sharp powers of observation, but the skinning of the animal gave him pause, and he exclaimed on the "coarse and imperfect use Indians and hunters make of Nature!" As was his practice, Thoreau built his book on Maine, *The Maine Woods*, from many drafts. At his death the book was unpublished, but there was no question that it was complete, and his sister Sophia saw it into print—with the help of Thoreau's friend Ellery Channing —in 1864.

The Maine Reader: The Down East Experience 1614 to the Present (edited by Charles and Samuella Shain and published by Houghton Mifflin, with a beautiful Fairfield Porter work on its cover) prints "A Moose Hunt" as Thoreau's contribution. More than fifty writers are represented, and there is a helpful bibliography of "Additional Reading." It is a solid introduction to the state's writers and to writing about the state. Robert Lowell is a glaring omission, but perhaps the Shains could not obtain permission to reprint his work.

MOUNT DESERT ISLAND

Marguerite Yourcenar (1903–1987), the first woman to be named to the Academie Française (1981) and the only member to own a home in Maine, first came to Mount Desert Island's Northeast Harbor in the mid-1940s. Born in Brussels, her birthname was de Crayencour, of which Yourcenar is a near anagram. She was visiting the United States when the Nazis invaded France, and she stayed on after the war, becoming an American citizen in 1947. The French government later restored her French citizenship. Her most famous book is the historical novel (a phrase that does not do justice to its rigorous intelligence), *Memoirs of Hadrian.* Yourcenar lived at her home, Petite Plaisance, with her translator and friend of forty years, Grace Frick. The bulk of her papers are at Harvard's Houghton Library, but she maintained a relationship with Bowdoin College, which has a collection and a descriptive catalogue.

Northeast Harbor, "a beautiful resort of summer homes and hotels (no motels)" according to *Maine: A Guide 'Downeast,'* is where Willa Cather occasionally spent vacations. A friend who worked there as a waitress in the late 1930s relates that she "walked around respectfully" stealing glances at Cather as she sat in a rocking chair on the porch of the Asticou Inn.

NORTH HAVEN

It was on this island a ferry ride from Rockland that **Elizabeth Bishop** (1911–1979) wrote her memorial poem to her friend Robert Lowell, "North Haven." She finished the poem in 1978, a year after Lowell's sudden death. As is so often the case with a Bishop poem, the poem's opening stanza effortlessly imprints its picture on the reader's mind:

> I can make out the rigging of a schooner
> a mile off; I can count
> the new cones on the spruce. It is so still
> the pale bay wears a milky skin, the sky
> no clouds, except for one long, carded horse's-tail.

The poem moves as clearly from what she sees and hears, "the white-throated Sparrow's five-note song,/pleading and pleading, brings tears to the eyes," to thoughts of her "sad friend" who now "cannot change."

ORONO

A conference to discuss Ezra Pound's life and art convened here in June of 1985, Pound's centennial year. Pound never set foot in Maine, and the site had no association with him. The conference was the work of C. F. Terrell, publisher of *Paiduma*, the journal of Pound studies, and the National Poetry Foundation headquartered at the University of Maine. Poets Robert Creeley, Allen Ginsberg, and Donald Hall read; Hugh Kenner, Pound's publisher James Laughlin, and Pound's daughter Mary de Rachewiltz spoke; there were numerous panels; and Pound's companion of many years, Olga Rudge, attended from the opening lobster dinner until the end. Elsewhere in America, Pound's centennial received scant notice—nothing like the attention that came to T. S. Eliot in 1988. Given the depth of his disgrace, it is remarkable that Pound was remembered at all. "In the gloom," he wrote in *The Cantos*, "the gold gathers the light against it."

PENOBSCOT BAY

George Oppen (1908–1984), Objectivist poet, and his wife **Mary Oppen**, who wrote their autobiography *Meaning a Life*, rented houses on Little Deer Island and around the bay from 1963 until 1977. That first summer, they arrived with the twelve-foot sailboat he had built with his own hands. The Oppens were passionate sailors among the islands in the bay. During a summer that they could not be in Maine, Oppen wrote the poet Philip Booth that "those silver waters of Castine harbors and those crazy linesqualls shine in our heads." In his poem "Ballad," Oppen sails to Swan's Island where:

> The rocks outlived the classicists,
> The rocks and the lobstermen's huts

And the sights of the island
The ledges in the rough sea seen from the road.

PORTLAND

Henry Wadsworth Longfellow (1807–1882) was born here on Fore Street in 1807. He was descended from an old colonial family and raised at the Congress Street home—Portland's first brick house—of his grandfather, General Peleg Wadsworth. It was from here, still in dresses and accompanied by a black servant, that he began his formal education at the age of three in a school on Spring Street. At fifteen he went on to Bowdoin College. Today the Wadsworth–Longfellow House at 487 Congress Street is open to visitors. In the room where Longfellow wrote "The Rainy Day," there is a display of Longfellow memorabilia.

Portland has not always been so attentive to its most famous son. In 1955, despite efforts to preserve it, Longfellow's Fore Street birthplace was torn down. So complete had been its neglect that bums camped out there and made fires from whatever furniture and pictures were still in the house. In an effort to be more conscious of Longfellow, there is a move afoot to raise money for the cleaning of his statue. An aged Longfellow sits (chairs are to writers as horses are to generals) looking down Congress Street, toward the house in which he spent his childhood.

RAYMOND

The three childhood years **Nathaniel Hawthorne** (1804–1864) spent here, at his uncle Robert Manning's Lake Sebago home, were among his happiest. In the summers he roamed the woods, fished for trout, and hunted partridge. His chief outdoor winter pleasure was ice skating. "I lived in Maine," he later wrote, "like a bird of the air, so perfect was the freedom I enjoyed." Free and solitary. His only companions were his sisters, and Hawthorne also remembered Maine as the place where "I got my cursed habits of solitude." During these years, Hawthorne read a good deal. His two favorite books—

great training grounds for a writer of allegories—were Spenser's *Faerie Queen* and John Bunyan's *Pilgrim's Progress*.

ROCKLAND

Wilbert Snow (1884–1977), the poet, was born here and educated at Bowdoin. Snow's poems, as his book titles *Maine Coast, Down East,* and *Maine Tides* imply, focused on his native state. During his long teaching career, he taught at a number of colleges. At Connecticut's Wesleyan University, one of his students was the poet Charles Olson. Snow also served as Maine's lieutenant governor.

The composer Walter Piston, who wrote a book on harmony, was born here, as was **Edna St. Vincent Millay** (1892–1950) at 200 Broadway.

SEARSMONT

Edwin Denby (1903–1983) was a poet, collaborator on "Horse Eats Hat" (with Orson Welles), America's premier dance critic, and significant presence on the New York art, poetry, music, and dance scenes for more than fifty years. He spent many summers in what he called "lucid Maine," referring, perhaps, to the clarity of its air and the pleasures taken in simple tasks after a winter in frantic New York City. "On July 12, 1983, shortly after arriving in Maine," as Ron Padgett, the editor of Denby's *Complete Poems*, has written, "he sat down at a table, took an overdose of sleeping pills and alcohol and left the world." He acted thus because his keen mind had begun to deteriorate, and he could not bear the prospect of senility.

SOUTH BERWICK

Sarah Orne Jewett (1849–1909) was born and spent her entire life at the house in the center of South Berwick, at the corner of Main and Portland streets, which is now open to the public. It has been refurbished, and is well looked after, but Miss Jewett's bedroom has been preserved as she knew it.

Jewett was something of a prodigy. At thirteen, she read Harriet Beecher Stowe's Maine novel, *The Pearl of Orr's Island.* This led her to see, in the words of M. A. De Wolfe Howe, "the life about her on a printed page." *The Atlantic* published her first story when she was nineteen, and *Deephaven*, the novel that brought her recognition, appeared when she was twenty-eight. Today, she is considered a writer of local color, charming but minor, whose best book is *The Country of Pointed Firs*, a collection of stories. Willa Cather, on whom Jewett's work had an influence, rated her much higher than this.

For all her attachment to Maine, Jewett was not a country bumpkin. She often visited Boston and her great friend Annie Fields, the widow of the publisher James T. Fields and the most celebrated literary hostess in the Boston of her day. Twice they traveled to Europe, meeting Tennyson—a hero to Jewett —Christina Rossetti, and Henry James, who held Jewett's work in high regard.

Jewett died of complications following a carriage accident. *The Country of the Pointed Firs* remains in print today.

WATERFORD

Today **Artemus Ward**—the pen name of Charles Farrar Browne (1834– 1867)—comes up, if at all, in connection with Mark Twain, but during his time he was the toast of two continents and until at least 1929 his birthplace was open to the public. Since he was a humorist—*the* humorist of his day— his relative oblivion is not surprising. Humor generally does not travel across centuries; Twain is the exception.

Yet beginning just before the Civil War, Browne's invention of Ward—an itinerant showman whose wares were "nateral curiosities"—brought him great fame and huge crowds to the "lectures" he began delivering in 1861. These followed his bestseller, *Artemus Ward: His Book*. On the page, Ward's letters from the road were made of comic misspellings, such as "Californy Bare" for California Bear; but on the lecture platform he delivered his extended monologues with a poker face. Part of his shtick, to borrow a word from Lenny Bruce, was to title a lecture "The Babes in the Woods," and then speak about neither babes nor woods. He lectured across the country, as far west as San Francisco, and he was a hit in London as Twain would later be. He died of tuberculosis in Southampton. President Lincoln, with whom Ward imagined a close relationship, was an admirer, as was Twain, whom Ward met while lecturing in Nevada when Twain was the newspaperman Samuel L. Clemens. Twain's platform style borrowed something from Ward's, and one of his popular lectures included Ward among "some uncommonplace characters I have chanced to meet."

WELLS

In Lynn, Massachusetts, there is the "Miracle Mile" of automobile showrooms. Wells, a small town straddling Maine's Route 1, has its own miracle mile, and more, of bookstores. There are *seven* in all. Maine is a great state for books, and most of its antiquarian stores have a card listing Wells's stores on one side with a map identifying them on the other. Harding's Book Shop, right on Route 1, has the largest stock and is by far the best all-around store. It is worth a detour, and while you are there you will want to visit as many of the others as your interest in books allows.

WEST SOUTHPORT

Rachel Carson (1907–1964), a zoologist by training, summered on the ocean she wrote about in this Southport Island town. Stimulated by a ten-day trip on a research ship to the Georges Banks—the prime fishing ground off Maine's coast—Carson blended scientific observation with clear prose to help create a new sort of book, true science for the common reader. *The Sea Around Us*, the middle of her three sea books, reached a wide audience.

But Carson reached, and alarmed, a wider audience with the last book she wrote, *Silent Spring*. Outraged by humankind's contempt for the environment, in particular the use of pesticides, she decried the dangers of what she termed "biocides." Her book had an impact similar to that of another Maine conscience, Harriet Beecher Stowe, and Congress paid heed, outlawing some of the more lethal poisons. Before we had bumper stickers proclaiming "Ecology Now," we had Carson's warning.

Massachusetts

———◆———

A S THE MAYFLOWER stood off the coast of Cape Cod, the company aboard her—among them William Bradford, who named this disparate group Pilgrims—drew up and signed the Mayflower Compact. They designed it to unify their diverse interests and commit themselves to a "civil body politic." "New England was founded consciously," as the historian Samuel Eliot Morison wrote, "in no fit of absence of mind."

At the beginning these Pilgrims were not colonials—that came later; nor were they in the new world drawn by tales of its glories, or to establish trade, or by order of exile. Their purpose was to build a state ruled by the word of their God. New England literature begins on the Mayflower in the accord reached by these educated, single-minded white men and women who would prevail.

Eventually, they took the name for their colony from the Indian tribe the Massachusett, who did not survive the 17th century and who lived along the bay that curved from Plymouth north to Salem. The colonists feared the wilderness that howled around them, but they were a disputatious lot. The Mayflower Compact did not hold on land, and groups soon split off from the Massachusetts Bay—south to Rhode Island and west to Hartford, Connecticut, drafting their own compacts where they settled. As these Puritans carried the word through much of what would become New England, Massachusetts remained the region's center, with Boston as its hub, until after the Civil War when the separate states began to pull away.

Massachusetts, oblong with Cape Cod's upraised arm to fend off the ocean, never was an open door to the west as was New York State. Even after the railroad crossed the Berkshires to Albany, the mountains remained a wall sealing in Massachusetts. To Boston's north the rough mountains, rock-filled soil, and brutal winters attracted immigrants only slowly. Geography helped concentrate a population in Massachusetts that would extend and be nourished by a history unique in America. Literary New England is centered in and achieves its fullest flowering, where New England began and put down its roots.

But no theory of geography or history adequately explains why between 1830 and 1880 within a fifty-mile arc of Boston and in pockets like Amherst and the Berkshires, American literature became both American and literature. Perhaps no theory need ever apply, as it will only tend to corral the particulars that follow, keeping us from musing upon them as we will.

AMESBURY

Born in Haverhill, **John Greenleaf Whittier** (1807–1892) spent most of his life in the Merrimack Valley, living in Amesbury, near the New Hampshire border. From 1836 to 1876 his address was 86 Friend Street. His house is now a National Historic Landmark and open to the public. Whittier is best known for his poem "Snow-Bound." In evoking the snowstorms of his youth, Whittier gives a sharp sense of the isolating harshness of a New England winter. The poem has some powerful images of snow falling:

> A night made hoary with the swarm,
> And whirl-dance of the blinding storm,
> As zigzag wavering to and fro
> Crossed and recrossed the winged snow.

Since "Snow-Bound" is all many readers know of Whittier, the vision of him as a New England sage has obscured his career as a Quaker abolitionist. William Lloyd Garrison published Whittier's early poems in *The Liberator*, and so committed was Whittier to the cause that Van Wyck Brooks calls him Garrison's lieutenant. He wrote pamphlets, faced down mobs, and was responsible for getting Charles Sumner to run for the United States Senate. His gifts as a public speaker were such that he has been credited with making enough money speaking out for the Abolitionist cause to expand the Friend Street house from its original four rooms to what stands today.

The true story is more interesting. In 1903, during renovations on the house, a packet of letters dating from 1847—the year of the enlargement— were found in a wall. One of the letters was from Lewis Tappen, a New York angel of antislavery groups. It had accompanied a check for $100 for editorial work performed by Whittier. "I should think," Tappan wrote, "it could be judiciously invested in real estate for your family." Today, the Friend Street house is open from April to November. The Garden Room, which Whittier used as a study, is as it was in his day.

AMHERST

> It sounded as if the Streets were running
> And then—the Streets stood still—
> Eclipse—was all we could see at the Window
> And Awe—was all we could feel.
>
> By and by—the boldest stole out of his Covert
> To see if Time was there—
> Nature was in an Opal Apron,
> Mixing fresher Air.

Emily Dickinson (1830–1886), the most original American poet of the 19th century, was almost unknown during her lifetime. *Poems*, her first book, published in 1890, began a career that has made her one of the great New England poets of this century and placed her alongside her contemporaries Hawthorne, Melville, Whitman, Emerson, and Thoreau in the American pantheon. She was born in the house at 280 Main Street where she would spend most of her life—a life that has come under as much scrutiny as her poems.

Of all New England writers, Dickinson is not only the most mysterious, but the one whose character, nature, and spirit are constantly reinterpreted and rewritten. She has been seen as the ultimate shrinking violet, a pale and eccentric recluse, unable and unwilling to live in the world. She was, undoubtedly, eccentric (she insisted that her doctor examine her by asking questions through a partially opened door), and beginning in about 1865 she kept more and more to herself, but the poems tell us that her brilliant imagination was firmly of this world. She was as alive to small things, to life's dailiness, as any poet; her work exhibits a wonderful sense of humor, a wide range of reference, and a steely eye focused unflinchingly on Puritan New England's defining subject—death. The legend has, as most do, its own fascination; but so does—as you can see in Richard Sewall's great biography of Dickinson—the life. Her story, and the 900 poems that she left us, will be redefined by every generation to come.

The poems themselves were found after Emily's death by her sister Lavinia. The sisters had been living alone in the Dickinson home since their mother's death in 1882. Lavinia found a small box in which were sixty (she called them "volumes" but the word packets is often used) small books bound with twine. Determined to publish them, Lavinia sought the help of **Mabel Loomis Todd** (1856–1932), an Amherst professor's wife. Todd described her first experience of the poems: "Went in the afternoon to Mrs. Dickinson's. She read me some strange poems by Emily Dickinson. They are full of power." She agreed to help, and began transcribing the poems. Lavinia also contacted Thomas Wentworth Higginson, with whom she knew her sister had been in touch. In 1862, Dickinson wrote Higginson after reading an article of his in *The Atlantic*. She asked him to look at her poems and tell her if they "breathed." They were to correspond for the rest of her life, but Higginson counseled her not to publish. In truth, as he later wrote, he found her poetry "remarkable, though odd," and seems not to have been able to quite accept it as poetry. At first, he discouraged Lavinia and Todd, but they persisted, and he eventually gave the recommendation they needed to convince the publisher. Unfortunately, he could not resist disfiguring the work by altering some rhymes, regularizing the meter, making the language conform to conventional standards, and shifting several of her line arrangements. Since publication, Dickinson's original intentions as read by scholars have been an ongoing controversy. Thomas Johnson's edition of the poems is the best, for this reader, as it is faithful to Dickinson's original punctuation and free of Higginson's interference. Justin Kaplan's *Sixteenth Edition of Bartlett's Familiar Quotations* has seven columns of Dickinson, ending with her last letter: "Little Cousins, Called back." She is buried in Amherst's West Cemetery, and "Called Back" is on her stone.

The Dickinson homestead at 280 Main Street, built by her grandfather Samuel, a founder of Amherst College, is now an Amherst faculty residence but a portion of it is open to the public afternoons by appointment. Between March and December 15th, prospective visitors should call 413-542-8161. On display are a chair Dickinson sat in and her writing desk, but the most evocative thing in the house is an amazingly small dress Dickinson wore as an adult.

Noah Webster was another of Amherst College's founders, and among its graduates are the poets Rolfe Humphries, Richard Wilbur, and James Merrill. **Robert Frost** (1874–1963) had a long association with the college. Between 1916 and 1938, he taught there for eighteen years. From 1931 to 1938, his Amherst home was at 15 Sunset Avenue. In 1972, the Amherst poet **Robert Francis** (1901–1987) published *Frost: A Time to Talk*, an account of Frost and Francis's conversations at Francis's home, Fort Juniper. In 1983, **James Baldwin** (1924–1987) came to the University of Massachusetts here as a lecturer. It was a new world for Baldwin and his approach was unconventional—more talks than formal lectures—but he brought his vivid personality to the classroom for several semesters over a few years.

In Dickinson's time, Amherst was a small college town on the edge of a large wilderness that stretched to the east and north. The wilderness survives in the land around what is today the Quabbin Reservoir, and if you approach Amherst from the north on Route 202 you will pass through a portion of it. Today, Amherst is more college than town. It is home to three: Amherst, the University of Massachusetts, and Hampshire, of the five colleges in the area. Smith College in Northampton and Mount Holyoke in South Hadley, where the Nobel Prize-winning poet **Joseph Brodsky** teaches, round out what is one of the greatest concentrations of college students in the United States.

BELMONT

William Dean Howells (1837–1920) lived here at Red Top, a house he built at 90 Somerset Street, from 1878 until 1881—the year in which he resigned as editor of *The Atlantic Monthly*. In 1878 Belmont was the country, and Howells moved his family to Red Top to get out of Cambridge, where they had lived at several addresses since their arrival in 1866. A frieze in Red Top's library quoting Shakespeare—"From Venice as far as Belmont"—expressed the family's faith that they had made a permanent home.

Howells had met his wife Elinor while serving as U.S. consul to Venice. He held this position throughout the Civil War as a reward for writing President Lincoln's campaign biography. Sadly, the family was to go further than Belmont. Here their daughter Winifred's health began to fail, and Howells suffered a nervous breakdown. After three-and-a-half years at Red Top, the family moved to a Cambridge boardinghouse before taking Winifred on a European trip for her health. During his years in Belmont Howells was mostly occupied with his duties at *The Atlantic*, but he did publish several books. When he left Belmont, Howells's best work lay ahead of him.

McLean Hospital, a psychiatric facility, is located in Belmont, and several writers have spent time as patients there. In 1838 the poet and essayist **Jones Very** (1813–1880) committed himself to McLean. He did so because of increasingly erratic behavior while teaching at Harvard. "Flee to the mountains," he is reported to have told his students, "for the end of all things is at hand." While at McLean, he wrote an essay on Shakespeare that had been "told" him by the Holy Ghost. Many of his religious poems came to him in visions. Emerson, always open to new writing, thought Very was "profoundly sane," and helped edit the one book, *Essays and Poems* (1839), to appear in Very's lifetime. Following his McLean stay, he was briefly a pastor in Maine and Massachusetts, but his intense shyness made it difficult for him to preach. He retired to live as a recluse, cared for by his sister Lydia. In 1886 some 600 of his poems appeared in the book *Poems and Essays*.

The first of **Robert Lowell**'s (1917–1977) many confinements in McLean came in January 1958 after he had been, in the words of his wife Elizabeth Hardwick, "active as electricity" for more than a month. Suffering from a manic-depressive illness, Lowell often returned to the hospital. There he wrote one of his great poems, "Waking in the Blue." It ends:

> We are all old timers,
> each of us holds a locked razor.

Lowell's forthrightness about his illness, and his stature as a poet, helped encourage other poets to write about their mental troubles and time spent in institutions. Indeed, for a time mental illness became a sort of credential verifying one's poetic sensibility. Lowell, hounded by his illness, knew the monster he became under its influence. In his poem "Florence," he exclaims, "Pity the monsters!/Pity the monsters!"

Sylvia Plath (1932–1963), who would be Lowell's student at Boston University, spent four months at the hospital following a suicide attempt before her senior year at Smith. In her novel *The Bell Jar*, Plath wrote about both the attempt and the doctor at McLean who treated her. Plath received electroconvulsive therapy, a standard course of treatment at the time, and was pronounced "cured."

In 1968 **Anne Sexton** (1928–1974), herself sorely afflicted with mental problems at various periods in her life, taught a poetry workshop at the hospital.

 # THE BERKSHIRES

Running the length of Western Massachusetts, the Berkshire Mountains (Mount Greylock, at 3,535 feet, is the highest) are as much a part of New York as of New England. Running north to south, these softly-rounded mountains present a wall to the rest of Massachusetts, and their valleys are a north-south groove keeping traffic away from the mass of New England. Berkshire residents get their television news from Albany, New York's capital, and look to New York City—and not Boston—as their Hub. Bostonians visit the Berkshires, but for them the area has never had the same summer draw as Cape Cod and the Maine coast nor the winter attractions of New Hampshire and Vermont.

The area has a long and rich literary tradition. Indeed, the recent *Berkshire*

Reader, edited by Richard Nunley, is thick enough to do honor to a region three times the size of the Berkshires. Given the character of the place, and that it is not so much a matter of cities and villages but is *the* Berkshires, the usual alphabetical organization of this book will be waived so as better to take on the region as a whole.

Let us begin in Pittsfield, which is near the center of the Berkshires, and which is the region's largest city and the site of **Herman Melville's** (1819–1891) home from 1850 to 1863, Arrowhead. The home is off Route 7 south of Pittsfield—signs point the way—and is open to the public from April to late October, for a small admissions fee. Melville, a New Yorker, settled his wife and young son in Pittsfield because he had fond associations with the area. As a boy he had worked on his uncle's Pittsfield farm, and in 1837 he taught the fall term at a school near the town. By 1850, Melville's South Seas narratives *Typee, Omoo,* and *Mardi* had earned him a measure of literary success. He came to Pittsfield looking for a farm he could work to support himself while he wrote. Finding Arrowhead right for his purposes, he borrowed the purchase price from his father-in-law, Lemuel Shaw, chief justice of the Massachusetts Supreme Court.

In his first year at Arrowhead, Melville wrote *Moby Dick.* Considering the book's bulk alone, more than 600 pages, that simple fact is overwhelming. Melville worked in a room on the house's second floor, which is today much as it was when he began work each day by locking himself in (the key is on display in the room). He wrote at a table set in the middle of the room. The corner fireplace could not have provided great warmth during the winter months, and the room as a whole, at least today, has a stripped-down ship-shape plainness. Melville sat so that he could look out on Mount Greylock. He fancied the mountain had the shape of a whale, and he dedicated his novel *Pierre* to "Greylock's Most Excellent Majesty." Today you can look through the same whorled and striated windowpanes Melville looked out. After *Moby Dick* and *Pierre* ("a rural bowl of milk" Melville described the novel to Sophia Hawthorne), Melville wrote *Israel Potter, The Piazza Tales,* and *The Confidence Man* here. From the key he used to lock the world out, to the chair and desk at which he worked, and the window out of which he gazed in thought, no other New England writer's study I have visited carries the impact of this-room.

The rest of the house is not as redolent of Melville or his family. When they left for Manhattan in 1863, Melville traded the house for his brother Allan's on 26th Street, and after Allan, Arrowhead passed through a number of owners until it came into the hands of the Pittsfield Historical Society in 1974. You enter the house through a barn in the rear, where you can watch a video that promotes the area's relationship with the arts. Melville liked to retreat here with his friend Hawthorne to drink a little rum, smoke cigars, and talk "metaphysics." Here you can buy copies of some Melville titles, Melville and Edith Wharton tee-shirts, all manner of whale gifts, and, among other postcards, one of Arrowhead as it looked in 1852. Then, the trees that today tower over the house were small; plowed fields came right up to the lawn; and there was a large, working barn set back from the house. Melville hated the conventional New England white, so Arrowhead's colors are yellow and green. In the barn/gift shop, the Berkshire poet Michael Gizzi ran a series of poetry readings during the late 1980s, at which **James Schuyler** (1923–1990) delivered, on a flinty November day, one of the half-dozen poetry readings he gave in his life.

Two months before Melville moved into Arrowhead in October 1850, the most significant literary friendship of his life began when he met **Nathaniel Hawthorne** (1804–1864) on August 5 during an outing to nearby Monument Mountain. Hawthorne's journal entry lists Melville among the guests that day, and is altogether matter-of-fact about the ascent of the mountain. But there were at least five other writers, Oliver Wendell Holmes and the New York critic Evert Duyckinck among them—and so we have a full description of the boisterous climb up the mountain in the rain, the champagne drunk at the summit, and the recitation by the poet Cornelius Mathews of William Cullen Bryant's poem "The Story of the Indian Girl" who, scorned at love, threw herself from a precipice. For all this, we know nothing of what conversation passed between Hawthorne and Melville that day. We do know—and the witness is Hawthorne's journal—that a few days later Melville stopped by Hawthorne's Red Shanty at Lenox (it still stands on the grounds of Tanglewood), and that Hawthorne gave him champagne and

showed him the lake. Over the next year and a half their friendship intensified, considerably so in Melville's case.

Shortly after they met, Melville's essay/review "Hawthorne and his
Mosses" appeared, passionate in its admiration, but as Melville disguised his
authorship under the pseudonym—"By a Virginian Spending July in Vermont"—Hawthorne could not have known that this "Virginian," whose view
he so much appreciated, was Melville's. The rest of their relationship was
more forthright, at least on Melville's part. We have many of the expansive
letters he wrote Hawthorne, but we have none of Hawthorne's letters to
Melville. Still, Melville's letters make clear just how important his friendship
with Hawthorne was, and we can assume that the usually reticent Hawthorne
returned that friendship, during the year in which he wrote *Moby Dick*.
Melville responded to Hawthorne's work with such intensity that he clearly
has his own struggles and dreams in mind. Writing to Hawthorne upon the
publication of *The House of Seven Gables*, which was written while Hawthorne was at Lenox, Melville gets off what has become a famous roar:

> There is the grand truth about Nathaniel Hawthorne. He says NO! in
> thunder; but the devil himself cannot make him say yes. For all men
> who say yes, lie; and all men who say no—why, they are in the happy
> condition of judicious, unincumbered travellers in Europe; they cross
> the frontiers into Eternity with nothing but a carpet-bag—that is to
> say, the Ego.

James R. Mellow's *Nathaniel Hawthorne in His Times* contains a full and
excellent account of this friendship, which for all its intensity, distance, and
time, was soon to dissipate. In November 1851, the same month *Moby Dick*
was published, the Hawthornes moved from Lenox to West Newton. There
had been a dispute about rent on the Red Shanty that led to an irritated
Hawthorne quitting the place. Although he kept in touch with Melville, he
was to see him on only one more occasion. This was in Liverpool, England, in
1856. Hawthorne, having been appointed consul by his Bowdoin College
friend President Franklin Pierce, met Melville as he came through on his way
to the Holy Land, Greece, and Italy. Hawthorne found his friend—who
hoped the trip might lift his depressed spirits—older and a little paler but in

sound enough shape. On a walk along the seashore, they paused to have what was to be their last heart-to-heart talk. Hawthorne's journals contain this vivid account of that afternoon:

> Melville, as he always does, began to reason of Providence and futurity, and of everything that lies beyond human ken, and informed me that he had "pretty much made up his mind to be annihilated"; but still he does not seem to rest in that anticipation; and I think, will never until he gets hold of a definite belief.

Hawthorne ends the passage, "he has a very high and noble nature, and better worth immortality than most of us."

One reason Hawthorne could abandon the Berkshires in such haste was that his books, thanks in no small part to his Boston publishers Ticknor and Fields, now earned enough money to support his family. From West Newton, the Hawthornes moved to the Wayside, in Concord, which was to be their American home for the rest of Hawthorne's life.

Although Hawthorne had not been attracted to the Berkshires by its literary life, there was an active one before he arrived for his brief sojourn on the scene. **Catherine Maria Sedgwick** (1789–1867) and her sister **Susan Sedgwick** (1789–1867), both born in Stockbridge, lived and wrote—novels in the main—in the Berkshires throughout their lives. Indeed, Richard Nunley says the "Sedgwick family themselves account for a small regiment of Berkshire writers." **Ellery Sedgwick** (1872–1960), owner and publisher of *The Atlantic* from 1908 to 1938, was a Stockbridge Sedgwick, and the Andy Warhol superstar Edie Sedgwick, subject of one of the earliest "oral" biographies, came from the same family.

The English actress and writer **Fanny Kemble** (1809–1893) visited the region in the mid-1830s and, largely because of her friendship with the Sedgwicks, settled there in the 1840s. She lived for more than forty years, many of these at her house The Perch, which no longer stands. She not only wrote "letters" (these appeared in newspapers), poems, and a novel—*Far Away and Long Ago* (1889) about the Berkshires—but she read Shakespeare from stages in Pittsfield and Lenox and was an energetic and charming hostess.

Charles Dickens came through the region in 1842 and wrote about his impressions of the Shaker Colony at Mount Lebanon; Thoreau climbed Greylock; Longfellow spent two summers, one of them his honeymoon with his second wife Fanny, in Pittsfield; the historian Francis Parkman (1823–1893) crossed the Berkshires in 1842 on the newly completed railroad line to Albany—"the longest day's journey I ever made," he noted in his journal—and Emerson visited the area, but he turned down the entreaties of Caroline Sturgis Tappen, from whom the Hawthornes rented, and others, to take up residence. He did send his daughter Ellen to Mrs. Charles Sedgwick's (Catherine's sister-in-law) Stockbridge school, The Hive.

In 1849 **Oliver Wendell Holmes** (1809–1894), whose great-grandfather Jacob Wendell had owned tens of thousands of acres in Pittsfield, built a summer home—a twenty-four room "cottage"—at Canoe Meadows. The house, now in private hands, still stands on Holmes Road just down from Melville's Arrowhead, whose proper address is 780 Holmes Road. Holmes and his family spent seven summers here before the house became too expensive to maintain. During that time he planted 700 trees on his property. In 1861, Holmes published his novel *Elsie Venner*, in which Pittsfield appears as "Rockland."

Edith Wharton (1862–1937) came to Lenox in 1899 because she wanted to escape the "watering-place trivialities" of Newport for "the real country." Before she sold her Newport house, Land's End, she paid "$40,600 for 113 Lenox acres" and, in 1901, began to build The Mount, where she summered for a decade and which is open to the public today. Wharton's interest in architecture, design, and gardening was personal and professional. In 1897 she published *The Decoration of Houses*, and in 1903 she published *Italian Villas and Their Gardens*, which exerted enough influence on American interior design that Edmund Wilson called Wharton "not only one of the great pioneers, but also the poet, of interior decoration." Sadly, The Mount displays little of this imagination today. We really do not know what the interior of the place looked like when Wharton lived there, and after she sold the house in 1911 it went through the hands of several owners, one of them a girl's boarding school, until it became a National Historic Landmark in 1971. Still, the interior proportions suggest Wharton's taste, and the exterior and grounds evoke the European models on which she based her grand and dignified home. The Mount, designed by architect Francis Hoppin after Christopher Wren's Belton House in Lincolnshire, England, stands atop a hill and was originally, as Henry James wrote, "mirrored in a Massachusetts pond." This can no longer be seen from the house, but the view is available on postcard. You enter the grounds on a long drive designed by the landscape architect Beatrix Farrand, who also designed the walled kitchen garden that is at one end of the lime walk running the length of the house's front. At the other end is the "Red Garden." While the interior is mostly bare, and part of it is off limits because it houses the actors of Shakespeare & Company who perform plays in a small amphitheater adjacent to the house, it is still possible to imagine what James described as "an exquisite and marvellous place." He visited in the fall of 1904 and again in the summer of 1905. On his first visit, he and Wharton and her husband motored constantly through the Berkshires and to the Hudson River—country that James found "too terrifically big." It was country Wharton got to know intimately enough to make good use of it in her fiction. "My two New England tales," she wrote in her autobiography, "*Ethan Frome* and *Summer*, were the result of explorations among villages still bedrowsed in a decaying rural existence . . . " An actual sleigh riding incident on Lenox's Courthouse Hill provided Wharton Ethan Frome's climactic scene. The Mount is off Plunkett Street, which is at the junction of Routes 7 and 7A in Lenox. It is open for guided tours from Memorial Day to the end of October. In addition to the tour, Tina Packer's Shakespeare & Company has adapted several of Wharton's fictions into "Matinee Plays," which are put on afternoons in the Drawing Room at tea time from Memorial Day through Labor Day. Call the Shakespeare & Company box office for more information: 413-637-3353.

Great Barrington, on the Housatonic River eighteen miles south of Pittsfield, is the birthplace of **W. E. B. Du Bois** (1868–1963), historian, essayist, novelist, autobiographer, and champion of the black race. In 1909 Du Bois, having rejected Booker T. Washington as too conservative, helped found the National Association for the Advancement of Colored People, an organization that he came to condemn as inadequate to redress America's racism. Du Bois—a child, as he wrote, "of Negro blood, a strain of French, a bit of Dutch, but thank God! no 'Anglo-Saxon'"—spent his childhood in what he later described as a "paradise: there were mountains to climb and rivers to wade and swim; lakes to freeze and hills for coasting." Blacks accounted for at most one percent of Great Barrington's 5,000 inhabitants. The Du Bois family (long ago a Dutchman had married a Bantu woman) was among the oldest in the area. Du Bois's awareness of how much his black skin set him apart from his white neighbors seems to have been gradual, but none the less cruel and permanent for that. He had his heart set on going to college at Harvard (he would get his Ph.D. in history there) but he went South to Fisk University instead where, as he wrote, "They needed trained leadership. I was sent to furnish it." Great Barrington's four Protestant churches contributed to the cost of his Fisk education. Today, Du Bois has a volume in the Library of America series, but like many American black intellectuals and writers who insist on going their own way, he suffered for it. His acceptance of the Lenin International Peace Prize in 1958, membership in the Communist party a few years later, and his becoming a citizen of Ghana before his death, was more than white America could take.

Williamstown, the northernmost Massachusetts town in the Berkshires, is the home of Williams College, whose handsome buildings straddle Route 7. William Cullen Bryant briefly studied here, as did the mid-19th century newspaper poet and precursor of Edgar Guest, **Eugene Field** (1850–1895), who wrote "Wynken, Blynken and Nod" and who is remembered for authoring the line, "He could whip his weight in wildcats." The social critic and founding editor of the radical magazines *The Masses* and *The Liberator*, Max Eastman (1883–1969) graduated from Williams in 1905. It was Eastman who, after questioning Hemingway's masculinity, fought with him in their editor Maxwell Perkins's Scribner's office, and who passed on the Italian anarchist Carlo Tresca's word that Sacco was involved in the crime that cost him his life but not Vanzetti with whom he was convicted. Stephen Sondheim (b. 1930), lyricist and composer whose *Company, Sweeney Todd*, and *Sunday in the Park with George* reinvented the Broadway musical, also graduated from Williams.

The restless **Sinclair Lewis** (1885–1951) stopped twice in Williamstown before buying Thorvale Farm in 1946. Here he wrote *The God-Seeker*, whose hero was a missionary from the Berkshires. It is one of Lewis's many forgotten novels. He died in Italy while Thorvale was up for sale. During his time here Lewis employed the novelist **John Hersey** (1914–1993), then just starting his career, as his secretary. Hersey has left an account of Lewis's sad, decline. Alcoholism is accepted as contributing to Lewis's difficulties, but Hersey claims he never noticed Lewis having a drinking problem.

James Gould Cozzens (1903–1978) lived here, at his house Shadow-brook, from 1958 to 1971. Something of a hermit, he was basically in retirement, and published but one more novel—*Morning, Noon, and Night* (1968). When he moved to Florida he sold his library of 3,000 volumes to a Vermont bookseller, and abandoned a large record collection in the house.

BOSTON

William Blaxton or **Blackstone** (1595–1675), the Shawmut peninsula's first white resident, settled in 1625 on the western slope of what became Beacon Hill. Blackstone had a Master of Arts degree from Cambridge University and was an Anglican clergyman with a library of 186 volumes. He enjoyed his own company, and his books, for five years—until the arrival of **John Winthrop** (1588–1649) and 900 Puritan colonists. Disliking Puritans, Blackstone decamped for Rhode Island.

Winthrop, the first governor of the Massachusetts Bay Colony, had landed in the new world on the *Arbella*. During the crossing, he wrote out his hopes for the colony in *A Model of Christian Charity*, taking as his text Matthew 5:14: "Ye are the light of the world. A city that is set on a hill cannot be hid." Winthrop's "City upon a hill" would be sounded again when Senator John Fitzgerald Kennedy declared his candidacy for president at the Massachusetts State House in 1960, and yet again during President William Jefferson Clinton's inauguration in 1993. As Blackstone brought the first books to Boston, Winthrop laid out the idea for the city in his words. By 1637 Boston had a "bookebynder's" shop and a decade later its first bookstore. By 1646, there were at least 130 graduates of Oxford and Cambridge in New England. These Puritans were a well-educated, bookish lot. **William Bradford** (1590–1657), the first governor of Plymouth Colony, set down that colony's history in *History of Plimmoth Plantation*, which was lost and not discovered until 1850 in England. It was Bradford who called his fellow Puritans Pilgrims, the name we most often use for them today. In the early decades of settlement, these religious dissenters were too busy battling "the howling wilderness," making homes and an economy for themselves, to write much of what today we consider literature. The poet **Anne Bradstreet** (c. 1612–1672) did arrive on the *Arbella* and was writing poems, but these were first published in England. Her fellow colonists had neither the time nor the interest for such frivolities as plays and poetry, but they were constantly attending to the word of God in the Bible and in the long sermons—four hours were not uncommon—delivered on the Sabbath. The forms of Puritan literature, the sermon and the journal or diary, we consider secondary today, and the questions of law and government to which they applied themselves are not ours; but no other group of immigrants to America has been so imbued with the word.

Members of the Mather family are the preeminent writers of the 17th century and America's first literary dynasty. **Richard Mather** (1596–1669), founder of the line, arrived in Boston—Dorchester, to be precise—in 1635. He wrote numerous pamphlets on government and church theory and contributed to the *Bay Psalm Book* (1640). He fathered **Increase Mather** (1639–1723), the first Mather to be educated at Harvard and the author of 130 titles. Increase was the father of **Cotton Mather** (c. 1663–1728), the greatest of the Mather clan, who entered Harvard at twelve, learned seven languages, and had a library of over 2,000 volumes. No other American of his time was as widely read, and none came close to equaling the 444 books he produced, including the 1,300-page *Magnalia Christi Americana,* which took issue with the methods used in the Salem witch trials, and his narrative of several of those trials, *The Wonders of the Invisible World.* Cotton wrote in every form but the novel, and, like his father, was active in politics and interested enough in science to support inoculation against smallpox. His arrogance and intimidating intellectual powers made him many enemies. In his essay on Cotton Mather, the poet Robert Lowell came down hard on him. "The Salem witch hanger, was a professional man of letters employed to moralize and subdue," Lowell wrote. "His truer self was a power-crazed mind bent on destroying darkness with darkness, on applying his cruel, high-minded, obsessed intellect to the extermination of witch and neurotic." Few of Mather's pages are read today. Cotton's son **Samuel Mather** (1706–1785), one of fifteen children, was the last of the line. He avoided the political world that so attracted his forebears and stuck to the ministry, producing a paltry—in terms of his bloodline—twenty books. A contemporary described him as "as weak a man as I ever knew." Samuel is buried with his father Cotton and grandfather Increase in the North End's Copps Hill Burying Ground. A plaque identifies their grave.

Throughout the 18th century, Boston's literary energy flowed into politics and revolution. Through periodic upheavals, it remained a small (population 20,000 by 1797) Puritan city that in 1750 prohibited the performance of plays. Boston's great architect, planner, and builder **Charles Bulfinch** (1763–1844) built the city's first theater in 1794, but in order to mount plays, the theater had to advertise itself as "a school of virtue."

The few writers born in Boston during this century, Benjamin Franklin (b. 1706), at 17 Milk Street, Royall Tyler (b. 1757), and Daniel Pierce Thompson (b. 1795) did their work elsewhere. The "Mother Goose Songs" did appear in Boston, but their history is murky. We know that **Elizabeth Vergoose**, the original Mother Goose, lived on Devonshire Street when it was Wilson's Alley, but we do not know her dates. It was her son-in-law, **Thomas Fleet**, who copied down and published the songs she sang her grandchildren. Fleet is buried in the Granary Burying Ground on Tremont Street. *Boston: The Official Bicentennial Guide* (1976) takes us from there: "Next to Thomas Fleet's stone is a marker for 'Mary Goose.' Unfortunately this is not Mother Goose, but her husband's first wife Mary. If you find a stone around here for Elizabeth Foster Goose (or Vergoose), then you've found the real Mother Goose." I must report that I have yet to find such a stone.

The poet **Phillis Wheatley** (1753–1784) had the century's most unlikely literary career. She came to Boston as a slave from Senegal, West Africa. Seven years old and sickly on her arrival, she was bought for household use by Susannah Wheatley and her merchant husband, John. Exceptionally intelligent and quick, Phillis—named after the ship that carried her to Boston—learned English in sixteen months and began writing poetry, conventional neoclassical verse dedicated to God or great men. Rejected for publication in Boston, her first book, *Poems on Various Subjects Religious and Moral,* was published in England in 1773, the same year the Wheatleys freed her. She married unhappily, or so legend has it, and had three children who died, the last shortly before Wheatley's own death at thirty. Visitors can learn her story on Boston's Women's Heritage Trail and the Freedom Trail. The Old South Meeting House displays a first edition of her book, along with other memorabilia.

It was **Gilbert Stuart** (1755–1828), the painter famous for portraits of George and Martha Washington, who named Boston "the Athens of America." He died a pauper and was buried in an unmarked grave on Boston Common, not to have a proper stone until a decade ago. Today, Stuart's phrase is most often encountered in the sports pages of Boston newspapers when the Red Sox play the New York Yankees (Sparta). But it can still be applied to the intellectual ferment and the outpouring of original writing that set Boston apart in the 19th century.

This "Golden Age" did not begin with the century. **Ralph Waldo Emerson** (1803–1882), born and raised in Boston close enough to the Common so that he pastured the family cow there, said of Bulfinch's city (Bulfinch himself left in 1817), "From 1790 to 1820 there was not a book, a speech, a conversation, or a thought in the state." Despite the city's population doubling to 40,000 by 1817 and the huge influx of Irish immigrants, (more than 200,000 between 1845 and 1855), Boston remained a Puritan city. **Oliver Wendell Holmes, Jr.** (1841–1935) remembered, "The Boston of my youth was the still half-Puritan Boston, with the 'unutterable ennui' of its Sundays . . . it was a Boston with no statues, few pictures, little music outside the churches, and no Christmas." Still observed was the Puritan Sabbath, beginning at Saturday nightfall. And yet a congeries of forces—the Transcendentalist spirit, the abolitionist cause, and the Civil War—turned Boston into the Hub, the "Hub of the Solar System" according to Oliver Wendell Holmes, some 200 years after its birth. "It takes," Henry James noted, "a great deal of history to produce a little literature."

When did Bulfinch's Boston end and the "Golden Age" begin? Perhaps in 1832 when Emerson, believing that we ought not "in an altered age . . . worship in the dead forms of our forefathers," resigned his pastorate of the Second Church, originally the Old North Church of the Mathers, at

Audubon Circle on Commonwealth Avenue. After this Emerson moved to Concord, but his intellectual presence and example were crucial to Boston all his long life. Certainly, his resignation is a faultline representing a separation from the Puritan past. Three years before this, at Park Street Church, **William Lloyd Garrison** (1805–1879), not yet twenty-four, gave on Independence Day his first public speech against slavery. In 1831 Garrison founded *The Liberator*—"Our Country is the World, our countrymen are all Mankind"—which he edited until 1865. The Abolitionist cause galvanized New England's writers. You simply could not avoid it. Hawthorne, for one, tried, as he found the Abolitionists self-righteous, shrill, and humorless, but even he was drawn into the fray. Garrison, who also supported women's suffrage, vegetarianism, and a smorgasbord of causes, was dedicated to the point of sleeping many nights on the desk beside his printing press. He once infuriated his townsmen enough that they dragged him through the streets with a rope around his neck, but he did not back down and today his likeness sits on the Commonwealth mall between Dartmouth and Exeter streets. Under his chair are newspapers and an inkwell. The text carved at the base of his statue proclaims: "I am in earnest. I will not equivocate. I will not excuse. I will not retreat a single inch and I will be heard." You can hear in this what so put off Hawthorne and the fire and brimstone, the absolute righteous belief that stirred so many to action.

The slave narratives of William Wells Brown, James Williams, Thomas H. Jones, and Sojourner Truth were printed in Boston. Many of the Abolitionists were women—Lucretia Mott (1793–1880); the Grimke sisters Angelina (1805–1879) and Sarah (1792–1873), who came from a slave-owning Southern family to Boston; and Lydia Maria Child (1802–1880) were among those who orated and wrote for the cause. Lucy Stone (1818–1893), an Abolitionist who took up the cause of women's suffrage, edited the *Women's Journal* out of 5 Park Street. There were attempts at confrontation as well most famously during the May 1854 trial of Anthony Burns, who was charged under the despised Fugitive Slave Law. In Faneuil Hall the preacher Theodore Parker (1810–1860) and the lawyer Wendell Philips (1811–1884), who were as influential in their day as any writer, spoke to an overflow crowd and were later charged with inciting a riot. A mob led by **Thomas Went-**

worth Higginson (1823–1911), who commanded black troops during the Civil War and was the only literary figure ever contacted by Emily Dickinson, disrupted Burns's trial in a failed attempt to free him. Higginson wielded a battering ram and in the melee got a scar on his chin, of which he was proud for the rest of his life.

Oliver Wendell Holmes (1809–1894) was born in Cambridge, educated at Harvard, and studied medicine while beginning his poetry career in 1830 with "Old Ironsides," which saved the U.S. frigate *Constitution* from being destroyed. He studied in Paris and taught at Dartmouth before returning to Boston, and for thirty-five years he was Harvard's Parkman Professor of Anatomy and Physiology. With the extraordinary stamina of so many Victorians, Holmes had two professional lives. He poured out poems and essays, gave *The Atlantic Monthly* its name, and was famous as "the autocrat of the breakfast table" after his magazine columns and book of that title. At the end of his long life, he lived at 296 Beacon Street. In 1915, Boston placed a memorial seat and a sundial on the Esplanade behind his house where Holmes could have seen it from his library. His son Oliver Wendell Holmes, Jr., associate justice of the United States Supreme Court for thirty years, is today more famous than his father. He wrote extensively on the law and fought for the Union in the Civil War. His *Touched With Fire* (1946) is a collection of his War diaries and letters.

The elder Holmes knew everyone in literary Boston—but then all the writers knew one another. **Edgar Allan Poe** (1809–1849), born in Boston in a trunk—as his parents were itinerant actors—was so irritated by the chumminess of Boston writers that he satirized the city as "Frogpondium." He did have his first book, *Tamerlane and Other Poems* (1827), published anonymously in Boston, but it sank without a trace.

Not all Boston's writers swam together in the pond Poe imagined. Hawthorne, shy by nature, and Thoreau, contrary and antisocial, surely spent less time in Boston than any of the other writers associated with the city during this period. Hawthorne, with the help of his sister-in-law educator **Elizabeth Palmer Peabody** (1804–1894), spent two years working at the Boston Custom House and living in boardinghouses. He liked the outdoor work on the Boston and East Cambridge wharves, but left to join **George Ripley**'s

(1802–1880) commune, Brook Farm, in West Roxbury. It is hard to imagine a more unlikely communard than Hawthorne, yet he lasted for nearly eight months and years later drew on the experience for his novel *The Blithedale Romance* (1852). Today the site of Brook Farm is a National Historic Landmark but it is not open to visitors.

Hawthorne and Thoreau had the same Boston publisher, Ticknor and Fields, who published Holmes, Longfellow, Lowell, and Emerson. Founded by **William Ticknor** (1810–1864) in 1834, the house added **James T. Fields** (1817–1881) in 1854. They published *Walden*, rescued Hawthorne from years of publishing for little or no money, and in *The Atlantic Monthly*—which they bought in 1859, making Fields editor—produced the top literary magazine of its time. Ticknor and Fields occupied for many years what is today the Old Corner Bookstore at the corner of School and Washington streets. Before Ticknor died, in Philadelphia while on a trip with Hawthorne, he and Fields had the sound business sense to publish English writers like Dickens and Thackery, and to pay them royalties. Prior to this, American publishers simply pirated English books. Ticknor and Fields not only developed an excellent list, but helped keep their American writers from being pirated in England. After Ticknor's death, Fields, who edited *The Atlantic* until 1871, prospered. He and his wife **Annie Adams Fields** (1834–1915), who wrote *Memoirs of a Hostess* and was by all accounts a woman of exceptional intelligence and charm, had a salon at their 148 Charles Street House. Mrs. Fields—as she signed her book—lived on until 1915, and penned biographies of Stowe, Hawthorne, and her friend Sarah Orne Jewett, whom Ticknor and Fields also published. The present day publishing firm of Houghton Mifflin on Park Street descends from Ticknor and Fields.

An imaginative, reliable publisher was as crucial to the city's "Golden Age" as the antislavery cause, but the Age's pre-Civil War Transcendentalist soul breathed through the original thought and action of individuals. Hawthorne's sister-in-law Elizabeth Palmer Peabody, one of the original Transcendentalists, was such an individual. Intelligent, honest to the point of insensitivity, and a busybody, Peabody is credited with introducing kindergartens to Boston, but more important was the bookstore she ran at 13–15 West Street. In this shop **Margaret Fuller** (1810–1850), editor of *The Dial* and a feminist long before the term was coined, gave her "conversations." She began on Wednesday evenings in 1839 and continued, intermittently, until April 1844. Her biographer Thomas Wentworth Higginson tells us they covered "the best of French, German, Italian and English literature." Fuller described them as "a point of union to well-educated and thinking women, in a city, which, with great pretensions to mental refinement, boasts, at present, nothing of the kind." It was in the back parlor of the same shop that Peabody's sister Sophia wed Nathaniel Hawthorne, and her other sister, Mary, wed the educator Horace Mann. Elizabeth Peabody remained single and gave her considerable energies to intellectual and social causes through another of the long lives common among Boston writers of this period. Peabody was active enough, thirty years later, that Henry James used her as a model for Miss Birdseye in *The Bostonians*. Fuller's end came too soon, when she drowned off the coast of New York while returning from Italy where, true to her principles, she had taken part in the revolution of 1848.

The Peabody bookshop is today a parking lot next to Boston's Brattle Bookshop. George Gloss, who often spoke on radio encouraging listeners to rummage in their attics for old books that might make them a fortune, ran the shop for years from behind tottering stacks of books; now his son Kenneth is in charge.

George Ripley left the Unitarian church to found Brook Farm, on which he hoped to "prepare a society of liberal, intelligent and cultivated persons, whose relations with each other would permit a more wholesome and simple life than can be led amidst the pressures of our competitive institutions." Brook farm was a 170-acre dairy operation in what was then a rural part of Boston. Margaret Fuller was enthusiastic as for a time as was Hawthorne. Ripley approached Emerson, who gave him his blessing but did not join. Although ultimately a failure, Brook Farm kept going for almost nine years. Ripley then went to New York, where he is credited with introducing the concept of daily book reviews in the *New York Tribune*.

As the Transcendentalists experimented, Boston streets were filling with wretched, mostly illiterate Irish peasants who, unlike many immigrants, did not have the money to move on after their arrival. Poverty forced them to stay where they had been shipped. Literary Boston seems to have paid little attention to them. For their part, they accepted the authority of church and state, and thought Emerson and his followers were unconscionable for questioning such authority. One C. M. Keefe, noted, "we Irishmen are not yet reduced to that moral nakedness which startles and appalls us in Mr. Emerson." These Irish Catholic anti-Abolitionists were soon to fight in the Civil War beside the Yankee Protestants who now looked down on them, and *Uncle Tom's Cabin,* published in Boston by John P. Jewett, Co., in 1852, helped bring this about. In its first year Stowe's novel sold 305,000 copies in America.

Boston literary life made two major contributions to the Union cause during the Civil War, and both were published in *The Atlantic.* **Edward Everett Hale** (1822–1909), whose over-large statue stands today in the Public Garden where the path crosses Charles Street, published there his story of Philip Nolan, "The Man Without a Country." While on trial for conspiracy with Aaron Burr, Nolan cries, "Damn the United States. I wish I may never hear of the United States again." He gets his wish, and is exiled to spend the rest of his life at sea, never to have word of his country. This cautionary tale of patriotism held a place on school curriculums into the 1960s. The other work is **Julia Ward Howe**'s (1819–1910) "Battle Hymn of the Republic," her one stroke of genius as a writer. She wrote the poem at one sitting in Washington, D.C., on a night in 1862 as she heard Union troops marching through the streets. "The grapes of wrath" and several other of the song's phrases have entered the language, and many Americans can still sing every word. Howe married into Boston and became a fixture in the city's intellectual life. When Oscar Wilde visited Boston, Howe entertained him at her 241 Beacon Street home. She had an outsider's perspective on Boston, and she possessed a tart tongue. Passing Boston's Charitable Eye and Ear Infirmary, she is reported to have said, "Oh, I did not know there was a charitable eye or ear in Boston!"

Van Wyck Brooks begins his *New England: Indian Summer* with a chapter titled "Dr. Holmes's Boston." After the war the Transcendentalist spirit dimmed, the Abolitionist cause triumphant, and a postwar boom created by Union victory, the man of letters—which Holmes so surely was—dominated Boston literary life. Edmund Wilson saw Holmes as inventing the "Brahmin," which intellectual cast became synonymous with Boston. "The distinguishing mark of the Brahmin," wrote Wilson, "is that, from generation to generation, he maintains a high tradition of scholarship: the Brahmins are all preachers, lawyers, doctors, professors and men of letters." One of the disciplines Brahmins took up was history. During this century, Boston abounded in historians who produced a body of work unparalleled for its scope and emphasis on story. **William Hickling Prescott** (1796–1859) concentrated on an overlooked Mexico and the Spanish conquest of South America in producing his *History of the Conquest of Mexico* (1843), which places Cortes at the center of dramatic events, and *History of the Conquest of Peru* (1847), which revolves around Pizzaro. Prescott's house at 55 Beacon Street bears a plaque honoring him. **George Bancroft** (1800–1901), adept politician and patron of Hawthorne during the latter's years at the Boston Custom House, published a ten-volume history of the United States that appeared from 1834 to 1876. When Bancroft served as ambassador to Berlin, he was asked by a British diplomat to explain why American ministers appeared at court "all dressed up, like so many undertakers." "Because we represent the burial of monarchy," replied Bancroft. A grade school in Boston's South End named after Bancroft has a bit part in Anthony Lukas's *Common Ground.* The school has since been transformed into condominiums and Bancroft's name has been erased.

John Lothrop Motley's (1814–1877) *The Rise of the Dutch Republic* (1856) endured in Robert Lowell's youth as a Boston classic. The poet recalled poring over it and finding its three volumes in every Beacon Hill and Back Bay house. Bostonians must have found inspiration in the story of a small country whose sea power came to dominate the world.

Of Boston historians, **Francis Parkman**'s (1823–1893) sense of story and his mastery of narrative drive, his evocation of forest, river, and the hard distances traversed by the colonial French, English, and their Indian allies and adversaries place him at the top. His major works, currently in print in the Library of America, are totally engrossing. He makes the past come alive as few contemporary historians, who rely on statistical data, are able to do. Parkman, a graduate of Boston Latin High School (as were Motley, Emerson, and Edward Everett Hale), actually climbed the mountains, walked through the forests, and canoed down the rivers he wrote about. After an adventurous youth, illness made it so difficult for him to see that he could write only for brief periods, and many of the original documents on which he relied had to be read aloud to him. From 1864 until his death, Parkman worked in his townhouse at 50 Chestnut Street on his masterworks on Champlain, La Salle, the Jesuits, and the struggle between France and England in the new world. He also kept a house on Jamaica Pond where he raised roses, a passion enjoyed by Bancroft and Henry Adams, himself a historian of great stature. Historian Simon Schama gives a detailed portrait of Parkman in his recent *Dead Certainties*, a book that means to put the story back in history and is not shy about that ambition. The centerpiece of the book is the murder of Parkman's brother, Dr. George F. Parkman, Harvard professor and one of Boston's leading citizens, by another Harvard professor, John White Webster. The trial caused a sensation. Oliver Wendell Holmes was among those who testified, and Chief Justice Lemuel Shaw, Herman Melville's father-in-law, presided. Boston Common's Parkman Bandstand, from which Martin Luther King, Jr., once spoke, was a gift to the city from the historian.

As Boston literary life continued to thrive, it attracted outsiders—the most significant of whom, **William Dean Howells** (1837–1920), arrived in 1866 to become assistant editor at *The Atlantic*. Howells quickly made friends with William and Henry James, who were, like him, from a Swedenborgian family, and the old and "proper" Cambridge and Boston writers Holmes, Longfellow, and Lowell. In 1871 Howells succeeded James T. Fields as editor of *The Atlantic*, and he proved to be hospitable to a wide range of writers, including his friend Mark Twain, who was to have a thorny relationship with Boston, and the western novelist Bret Harte. Howells introduced both of them to the Saturday Club, which had been active since the 1850s, and to its members Agassiz, Emerson, Longfellow, etc. During the decade he edited *The Atlantic* Howells published a number of books; however, he did his best work, and the most significant in terms of Boston, after he resigned from the magazine in 1881. In July 1883, Howells returned from a European trip and rented 4 Louisburg Square, where he wrote his novel of a romance between New Englanders in Florence, *Indian Summer*. He soon bought the house still standing at 304 Beacon Street and here wrote the best Boston novel of the century, *The Rise of Silas Lapham* (1885). Lapham is *the* post-Civil War captain of industry. His fortune has literally gushed from the ground in the form of a base for the paint he manufactures. He is bent on building himself a house in Boston's Back Bay, itself a post-Civil War creation, and he does so only to lose his fortune in the panic of the early 1870s and see his house accidentally burned to the ground. Lapham is pitted against the Brahmin Bromfield (there is a Bromfield Street in downtown Boston) Corey, although he does not know it and Corey could never admit it. The Laphams' coming to dinner at the Coreys is the best scene in the novel, and many critics feel it is the finest thing Howells ever wrote; the outcome is hilarious and jarring. As new money mixes with old, what was rock solid in Boston has begun to change. "It's a perspective," agonizes Corey, "without a vanishing point."

Twain, who often came to Boston to visit his friend Howells, found the city intimidating. He spoke for many a writer and performer when he wrote: "Tomorrow night I appear before a Boston audience—4,000 critics." On December 17, 1877, at the Hotel Brunswick he addressed a dinner in honor of Whittier's seventieth birthday, and his discomfort got the best of him. He put his foot in his mouth by telling a story about three tramps that looked like Emerson ("a seedy little bit of a chap"), Holmes ("fat as a balloon"), and Longfellow ("built like a prize fighter"). All three were in the audience, and Twain could see that they did not know what to make of his story. When he finished only one person laughed. Ten days later, mortified, he wrote letters of apology. Twain, wearing a sealskin coat and hat and speaking in his slow drawl, caused some Bostonians to think he drank. At least that's what the wife of **Thomas Bailey Aldrich** (1836–1907) thought, when her husband brought Twain to their 84 Pinckney Street home for dinner. Aldrich—who edited *The Atlantic* from 1881 to 1891—and Twain stayed friends, but Boston fell out of Twain's orbit after Howells left for New York City in 1885.

When **Henry James** (1843–1916) began his friendship with Howells, James was living in his family's Cambridge home and just beginning his career. As editor of *The Atlantic*, Howells helped James into print, serializing *Watch and Ward* (1871), his first novel, *Roderick Hudson*, in 1875, and a great deal of other fiction, including the novel *Washington Square*, and journalism. James's biographer Leon Edel thinks Howells gets too much credit for discovering James, but clearly James's *Atlantic* connection was important to his career. James knew Boston well, and he knew the older writers, as his father, Henry Sr., had many friends among them. That James felt a kinship with Hawthorne in particular is evident from the book he wrote about him.

Upon the death of James's mother in the spring of 1882, James's father and sister Alice left the Quincy Street home in Cambridge and took a small house at 131 Mount Vernon Street in Boston. James returned to England after his mother's death, only to sail again for Boston when his father died at the end of the year. This time James stayed on in Boston, writing away through the winter—in particular a story set in Boston, "A New England Winter"—and absorbing the impressions that he would distill into his novel *The Bostonians*. James had set other of his novels in Boston. He conceived *Watch and Ward* as a study of Boston manners, and in 1878 *The Atlantic* published *The Europeans*, which emphasized Boston's parochialism. This got the goat of Thomas Wentworth Higginson, who panned the novel. He delighted in pointing out that James had horse cars in Boston streets before they were there. *The Bostonians* is a finer novel by far than *The Europeans*, and next to Howells's *The Rise of Silas Lapham* there is no better picture of upper-class late 19th century Boston life. James wanted his novel to be "a very *American* tale, a tale very characteristic of our social conditions" and to accomplish this he determined to focus on "the situation of women, the decline of the sentiment of sex, the agitation on their behalf." The novel is a romance in the form of a triangle. Basil Ransom, Southerner and antifeminist, comes between Olive Chancellor and Verena Tarrant, two enthusiastic champions of women's rights. Olive lives on Beacon Hill, and her view toward Cambridge and "the long low bridge that crawled, on its staggering posts, across the Charles" must have been the one that James saw from Mount Vernon Street and that can still be seen today. Charles Street plays a part in the novel, as does Cape Cod, and Miss Birdseye—whom Bostonians saw as modeled on Elizabeth Palmer Peabody—lives in Boston's South End. When the moviemakers James Ivory and Ismail Merchant came to film *The Bostonians*, they set much of the action in this neighborhood, where there are more Victorian brick townhouses than anywhere else in the United States.

The Century, a New York magazine, serialized *The Bostonians* in 1886, as it had *The Rise of Silas Lapham*. James's next novel, *The Princess Casamassima*, did appear in *The Atlantic*, but his connection with the city both as writer and as a man was all but over. The writers who had created Boston's Golden Age were dead, dying, or gone to New York. Bronson Alcott, among the last of the Transcendentalists, died at his daughter Louisa May Alcott's 10 Louisburg Square house in 1888; Louisa May herself died the day after his funeral. Thomas Bailey Aldrich continued to edit *The Atlantic*, but he stepped down in 1890. In that year, the Irish poet and adventurer **John Boyle O'Reilly** (1844–1890), who had been editor of the nation's oldest Catholic newspaper, *The Pilot*, since 1876, died. O'Reilly is remembered by a large Daniel Chester French memorial that stands at the Boylston Street end of the Fenway and by a South Boston grade school that bears his name. State Senator William "Billy" Bulger, the quintessential Irish pol of his generation, went to that school, and he enjoys quoting an O'Reilly stanza now and then.

The Golden Age passed as all ages must, but beginning in 1885 when Howells left Boston to go to New York and write a regular column for *Harpers*, Boston also lost its position as leader in American literary life, a position it has never regained. New York became America's London or Paris, and Boston became a shrine, its past towering over its present. Howells's departure draws a line, but his leaving did not prevent Boston writers from continuing the city's rich literary tradition. What happened to transform the city of Emerson, Parkman, and Longfellow into a city known to generations by the phrase "Banned in Boston"? It is, of course, too much to ask that tradition be unbroken. One extraordinary generation died out, and there was not another to take its place. What did come in had its roots in the preceding generation. Howells's Bromfield Corey, the Brahmin scholar, represents a dried up intellectual life, a life of contemplation and connoisseurship resting as much on social position as on intellectual effort. Brahmins did not help make Modernism, but they gathered in the sort of clubs (e.g., the Saturday Club) that 19th-century Boston writers, beginning with the Transcendentalists, had favored. The clubbiness that so rankled Poe could not create an atmosphere conducive to the production of literature. One could study, yes, and one could write about writing, but Emerson's "one wild line out of a private heart" would never arise from a gathering, no matter how artistic or earnest its individual members. Another factor in Boston's decline must have been the political shift from the Yankee–Brahmin aristocracy to Irish Catholics embodied in the life and career of James Michael Curley. In the 20th century, Boston became as much an Irish city as a Brahmin one, and between the faith of the one and the manners of the other, literature suffered—or at least it was not encouraged. The Modernism scanted by Boston's Brahmins was deemed illegal and immoral by the Catholic church and Boston's Blue Laws. The attitude typified by the banning of such books as Hemingway's *A Farewell to Arms* is one that is inhospitable to whatever is new. (It is a small irony that Hemingway's papers are now in President Kennedy's library in Dorchester, where scholars sift through them and Hemingway symposiums are held. When *Scribner's Monthly* published *A Farewell to Arms*, the offending words were "balls" and "cocksucker". To be acceptable in Boston, they had to be printed "b__ls" and "c__k_____r.")

Ernest Fenollosa (1853–1908), a pioneer in Oriental studies and a curator at the Museum of Fine Arts, made Boston's signal contribution to Modernism, but he was unaware of doing so. At his death Fenollosa left a number of notebooks that his wife happened to pass on in London to just the right man, Ezra Pound. Pound took the notes Fenollosa had made on his visits to Japan and turned them into a book on the No plays and his own translations, *Cathay*, which introduced Chinese poetry into the 20th century and became a foundation for Pound's own poetics. Pound also translated Fenollosa's *The Chinese Written Character as a Medium for Poetry*. Otherwise, Boston at the beginning of the century was, in the words of Harvard student T. S. Eliot, "quite civilized but refined beyond the point of civilization." Eliot mildly satirizes the city in his short poem "The Boston Evening Transcript":

> The readers of the Boston Evening Transcript
> Sway in the wind like a field of ripe corn.

Today the old Boston Evening Transcript building, which once housed the city's largest newspaper, still stands across from the Old South Meeting House, and Eliot is famed for decrying a wasteland on another continent.

In the 20th century, the literary history of Boston does not unroll so much as occur randomly. The unifying forces of the previous century have disappeared, and the writers associated with Boston—with some notable exceptions—might have done their work in any city. Some, like the poet and publisher **Harry Crosby** (1896–1928), who was "of a socially prominent Boston family," as the obituaries said after his New York suicide, did their work in Paris. There, Crosby ran the Black Sun Press and published himself, Hart Crane, and D. H. Lawrence, among others. Rich and bohemian, he flamboyantly rebelled against his strait-laced Beacon Street upbringing. Malcolm Cowley found him representative of their generation's mad despair, and he ends his "literary saga of the Nineteen Twenties," *Exile's Return*, on Crane's death. (It was a double suicide in a New York hotel room. Crane's partner was the twenty-two-year-old wife of a Harvard graduate student.) e.e. cummings, another Boston rebel, wrote this epitaph for the suicides:

<blockquote>
2 boston

Dolls;found

with

Holes in each other

's lullaby.
</blockquote>

Not all Boston's literary rebels abandoned the city. **John Brooks Wheelwright** (1897–1940) never traveled beyond Albany, New York. His Wheelwright ancestors came to Boston with the Puritans in the 1630s, and on his Brooks side he could count the six-term governor John Brooks. There had been money in the family, but Wheelwright, though he did as he pleased, was not wealthy. He spent his time between the Somerset Club and the South End, where he attended Socialist meetings. Indeed, he combined both socialism, as a member of the Socialist Labor Party, and Anglo-Catholicism (he had been raised a Unitarian) in his freewheeling personality. The poetry he wrote (his *Collected Poems* is published by New Directions) is as original as his behavior. Whether he demanded dinner at the Ritz though not garbed as ritual required, or napped on a Commonwealth Avenue bench, "Wheels" vividly recalled the original independence of mind that has distinguished Boston. When he was run down and killed by a drunken driver on Massachusetts Avenue, Wheelwright's poems were little known. They are so unconventional that they will always be out of fashion, but John Ashbery, who is

Phillis Wheatley.

Negro Servant to Mr. John Wheatley
of Boston.

Pendleton's Lithog.? Boston.

Since we have no idea what the Boston poet Phyllis Wheatley looked like, this is an idealized portrait. The engraver has given her the pose we like to imagine writers adopt just before the lightning of inspiration strikes. Today, there is a Wheatley school in Boston, and if you walk Boston's Freedom Trail you will encounter the desk on which she wrote. (Boston Athenaeum)

For several generations the bearded Henry Wadsworth Longfellow was what many imagined a poet to look like. His beard marks a most tragic episode in his life. The fire which took the life of his wife Fanny burned his face so badly that it became intolerably painful for him to shave, and thus he grew the beard. (Boston Athenaeum)

In this photograph Harriet Beecher Stowe holds a copy of her recently published novel *Uncle Tom's Cabin*. Published in 1852, the novel had enormous impact; she was hailed in the North and vilified in the South and in England. (Boston Athenaeum)

In this engraving Cotton Mather looks more benign than he could have possibly been in life. The great historian of American Puritan thought Perry Miller admired Mather's prodigious intellect, but declared him to be "the most nauseous human being." Mather entered Harvard at age twelve and wrote unceasingly throughout his life. Somehow he balanced a keen interest in science with a belief in witchcraft. (Boston Athenaeum)

Frederick Douglass is pictured here beside the frontispiece of the first of his three autobiographical works. Douglass toured the North and East for the book's publisher, William Lloyd Garrison's Anti-Slavery Society, speaking out against slavery. He was one of the most powerful orators of the time. (Boston Athenaeum)

Louisa May Alcott's novels *Little Women* (1868), *Good Wives* (1869), and *Little Men* (1871) have sold millions of copies, and the Marches, whose life they chronicle, are household familiars. Her first claim to literary fame was a fictional account of her brief service as a nurse during the Civil War, *Hospital Sketches.* (Boston Athenaeum)

We know neither the date of this hitherto unpublished photograph of Henry James nor exactly where it was taken. As he
appears to be in early middle age, he must have already been
living in Europe for many years, and is probably in America
visiting his brother William. The dashing vest suggests the lively, witty James that those who read his letters encounter.
(Boston Athenaeum)

Sarah Orne Jewett was born, lived, and died in this colonial-style house in South Berwick, Maine. It was built around 1750, and acquired sometime thereafter by her grandfather, a well-to-do owner and builder of ships. (Photograph by `Ben E. Watkins)

William Lloyd Garrison, abolitionist and editor of *The Liberator*, once so outraged the citizens of Boston that they dragged him through the city with a rope around his neck. Today he sits on Commonwealth Avenue with the air of someone whose ideals have triumphed. (Photograph by Ben E. Watkins)

The Cambridge Cemetery, across from the Mount Auburn Cemetery, holds the James family plot where Henry lies beside his brothers, sister, father, and mother. The O. M. stands for Order of Merit, the highest distinction that the British Crown bestows on civilians. It was awarded to James on January 1, 1916. (Photograph by Ben E. Watkins)

Historian and sailor Samuel Eliot Morison is perched atop a boulder on Boston's Commonwealth Avenue esplanade. He seems to be perpetually contemplating what he has just seen through his binoculars. (Photograph by Ben E. Watkins)

DOCTOR SAX

Yet often now I had a dream that I was sitting on the
sidewalk on Moody Street, Pawtucketville, Lowell, Mass.,
with a pencil and paper in my hand saying to myself "Describe the wrinkly tar of this sidewalk, also the iron pickets
of Textile Institute, or the doorway where Lousy and you
and G.J.'s always sittin and dont stop to think of words
when you do stop, just stop to think of the picture better
—and let your mind off yourself in this work."

Book One

"TI JEAN"
JOHN L. KEROUAC
MAR. 12, 1922 — OCT. 21, 1969
— HE HONORED LIFE —
STELLA HIS WIFE
NOV. 11, 1918 — FEB. 10, 1990

This is one of eight red granite stelae that form a memorial to Jack Kerouac on Lowell, Massachusetts's Bridge Street. Ben Woitena was the sculptor, and all of the stelae bear short texts by Kerouac that were selected by Lowell native Brian Foye. One of Lowell's cotton mills, now holding apartments, stands in the rear. (Photograph by Ben E. Watkins)

This is Jack Kerouac's grave in the Sampas family plot in Lowell's Edsom Cemetery. It is a sacred place for many, and there are usually offerings around it. The pencil to the right in the photograph is one such offering. "Ti Jean" means Little Jean. (Photograph by Ben E. Watkins)

This is the grave of the poet John Boyle O'Reilly. For many years he was editor-in-chief of *The Pilot*, the nation's foremost Irish newspaper. His stone stands in the cemetery behind the Chestnut Hill Mall in Newton, just outside of Boston. (Photograph by Ben E. Watkins)

The granite posts and chains mark the site of Henry David Thoreau's Walden cabin. From his front door between the posts on the left, he could look out on the pond. During his residence few trees obscured his view. The cairn behind the house was begun by his friend Bronson Alcott. (Photograph by Ben E. Watkins)

Robert Frost lived in this Derry, New Hampshire, farmhouse from 1900 until 1912, when he and his family sailed for England. While he lived here Frost struggled to farm the place but had to supplement his income by teaching at Derry's Pinkerton Academy. (Photograph by Ben E. Watkins)

Poet Robert Lowell lies beside his mother and father in the Stark family cemetery in Dunbarton, New Hampshire. Charlotte Winslow descended from John Starks, Revolutionary War hero. All the gravestones in this fenced-in family plot face a statue of Christ, who offers them his blessing. (Photograph by Ben E. Watkins)

This is the view of Mount Monadnock from the Shattuck Inn in Jaffrey Center, New Hampshire, where both William Dean Howells and Willa Cather were guests. Thoreau climbed the mountain, Emerson wrote a poem about it, and Galway Kinnell titled a book *Flower-Herding on Mount Monadnock*. (Photograph by Ben E. Watkins)

Willa Cather's Jaffrey Center, New Hampshire, gravestone looks toward Mount Monadnock. The small footstone to the right of Cather's is that of her friend and companion Edith Lewis. "The Old Burying Ground" has several other stones of interest, especially those of Isaac and Moses Spofford, which are beautifully carved. These can be found by consulting the map, visible in its frame on the shed wall uphill from Cather's grave. (Photograph by Ben E. Watkins)

Opposite: H. P. Lovecraft's grave is in Providence's Swan Point Cemetery. A few days before this photograph was taken, one of the many who visit the grave used a burning candle (its stub was in the grass) to accentuate Lovecraft's last name. (Photograph by Ben E. Watkins)

Incorporated in 1831, the Providence Athenaeum took up residence in this Greek Revival building on Benefit Street in 1838. Its stated purpose is to maintain a library "larger, better arranged, more useful and more attractive than within the means of any individual shareholder." Edgar Allan Poe courted Sarah Helen Whitman in this building. (Photograph by Ben E. Watkins)

This statue of the teenaged poet Constance Witherby stands on the esplanade that runs down Providence's Blackstone Boulevard. It is the only statue of a writer in the city. Witherby died while still in her teens. (Photograph by Ben E. Watkins)

passionate about the work, gave one of his 1989 Harvard Norton lectures on Wheelwright.

Another Bostonian who stayed was the historian **Samuel Eliot Morison** (1887–1976). Morison, a professor of American history at Harvard, wrote a history of the university and of the United States, but his specialty was maritime history. During World War II he served as the Navy's official historian and produced fourteen volumes detailing that war's naval engagements. He won a Pulitzer Prize for his biography of John Paul Jones, and published a short memoir, *One Boy's Boston*, about his youth. Morison wrote and published into his eighties, and today is commemorated by a statue—the only 20th-century writer to be so honored in Boston—on the Commonwealth mall near Exeter Street. He wears sailing gear and is perched on a boulder as if peering out at the sea.

A third Bostonian who stayed was the journalist **William Monroe Trotter** (1873–1934), after whom Boston named a grade school. Trotter's founding of the Boston Equal Rights League in 1901 had an impact on W. E. B. Du Bois, who began the National Association for the Advancement of Colored People nine years later. To provide a forum for civil rights issues Trotter founded, also in 1901, the *Boston Guardian* newspaper. It, and Trotter, were in the forefront of the protest that ultimately lead to D. W. Griffith's film *Birth of a Nation* being banned in Boston. After Trotter's death his sister Maude Trotter Stewart and her husband Dr. Charles Stewart published the *Guardian* until 1957.

The poet and painter **Kahlil Gibran** (1883–1931) was one writer who came to Boston. He emigrated from his native Lebanon, and a monument in Copley Square thanks the Denison Settlement House, Boston Public Schools, and the Boston Public Library for his early care and education. Gibran's most famous work is the poem *The Prophet*, which achieved cult status in the 1960s. Indeed, passages from it were read at thousands of weddings held in fields, uniting barefoot men and women, or in churches as a friend played the guitar. Gibran's monument is across Dartmouth Street from the library's main entrance, and it bears a plaque which is the work of his namesake and relative, the Boston sculptor Kahlil Gibran.

One outcome of the rise of universities in Boston and Cambridge is that many more writers are now educated here and move on as a matter of course. This first began during the 1920s and 1930s, when the news of Modernism came from everywhere but Boston. Lincoln Kirstein, a Filene's department store heir, went to Harvard where he founded the influential magazine *Hound and Horn*, but his writing and lifelong involvement with ballet has taken place in New York. James Laughlin, who also attended Harvard, became interested in literature there but had to go elsewhere to find the sort of writing he wanted to publish at his firm, New Directions. *The Atlantic*, under the editorship of Ellery Sedgwick, had not kept up with the times and did not care to. Gertrude Stein, who admired the magazine, could speak of wanting to be published there, but the force of Modernism—while it passed through some of Boston's schools—did not leave a strong imprint on the city.

The novelist **Helen Howe** (1905–1975), raised in Boston, detailed the mainstream of Boston's 20th-century literary life in her book *The Gentle Americans* (1965). It is subtitled "Biography of a Breed," but the central figure is Howe's father, **Mark De Wolfe Howe** (1864–1960) who as editor, biographer, and antiquary contributed a shelf of books about Boston. He edited Mrs. Fields's memoirs, wrote a history of *The Atlantic*, and compiled more than a dozen volumes of letters by George Bancroft and Charles Eliot Norton, among others. For all his strength of character and liberal attitudes, he was more a curator of tradition than one who could, in Ezra Pound's phrase, "make it new." Browse in any Boston secondhand bookstore today and you will come across some of Mark De Wolfe Howe's many titles and copies of his daughter's indispensable book about a breed whose determined lack of flamboyance has left them on the margin.

The novelist **John P. Marquand** (1893–1960), a Howe family friend, figures in Helen Howe's book. Like William Dean Howells and Henry James, Marquand was not a Boston native, and like them, he wrote one of the novels by which the city is most known. Marquand's *The Late George Appley*, for which he won a Pulitzer Prize in 1937, presents itself as the memoir of a Boston Brahmin. George Appley is the sort of stodgy Bostonian who would have moved away had Silas Lapham attempted to build his house next to his. The novel is satiric, but mild enough so that Bostonians took to it. **Walter Muir Whitehill**, the Brahmin whose *Boston: A Topographical History* (1968) is *the* book on the city's growth and development, quotes with pleasure Appley's description of his father's leaving Boston's South End. Appley, a child of seven, remembers his father's exclamation when he looked across the street to a figure on the steps of a brownstone house:

> "Thunderation," Father said, "there is a man in his shirt sleeves on those steps." The next day he sold his house for what he had paid for it and we moved to Beacon Street. Your grandfather had sensed the approach of change; a man in his shirt sleeves had told him that the days of the South End were numbered.

Marquand also created the Japanese detective Mr. Moto and wrote a number of more or less successful novels of manners that are pretty much forgotten today.

The other famous Boston novel of this century was also the work of an outsider, Rhode Island–born and Notre Dame–educated **Edwin O'Connor** (1918–1968), whose *The Last Hurrah* (1956) was popular as a book and movie. The novel's hero is Boston's mayor scoundrel Frank Skeffington, who is running for office yet again. No one in the city needed the Cliff notes to tell them that Skeffington was based on James Michael Curley. Skeffington, like Curley, is an outsize character with a great gift for blarney and the manner of a rogue but beloved by all. Spencer Tracy played him in the film directed by John Ford, Hollywood's great spinner of Irish yarns. O'Connor's image of Curley stuck until the recent biography, *The Rascal King*, by *Atlantic* editor Jack Beatty, who puts flesh and blood on what has been a cardboard knight. O'Connor's next novel, *The Edge of Sadness*, also set in Boston, won him the Pulitzer Prize in 1961.

Around the time O'Connor created Skeffington, the Irish-American writer **J. P. Donleavy** (b. 1926) worked on his first novel, *The Ginger Man*, whose American hero Sebastian Balfe Dangerfield raises hell in Dublin, on Poplar Street in Boston's West End. Poplar Street was leveled in the urban renewal that destroyed the West End, but in the year Donleavy spent there he found it "a fantastic ghetto where you had the whore coming home at night, and the baker across the street." To escape from work, Donleavy entertained himself reading *The New York Times* on a bench in the Public Garden. Before he left Boston to return to Ireland, Donleavy showed his book to a Boston publisher. "There's libel and obscenity in that book," was the publisher's response, "and we would be tarred and feathered were we to publish it in Boston."

Malcolm X (1925–1965) did not become a part of Boston's literary history until his *Autobiography*, written by the journalist Alex Haley, appeared in 1964; but it was in the 1940s and 1950s that he lived and went to prison in Boston. X—Malcolm Little then—came to Roxbury, the now-derelict house at 72 Dale Street, where he lived with a half-sister, as a teenager. At one point he worked as a busboy at the Parker House, where the Saturday Club had met and where Ho Chi Minh once bussed tables, as a busboy. In the mid-1940s, X headed a gang that got caught after a few successful suburban burglaries. X went on to spend six years in area prisons, where he learned to read and write. At the Norfolk Prison Colony southeast of Boston, he converted to Islam. On Wellington Street in the South End, he preached its gospel in a neighborhood where he had previously hung out in bars and jazz clubs. No plaque identifies any of these places and the Dale Street house is boarded up, but current interest in Malcolm X, fueled by Spike Lee's biographical film, may soon result in some sort of commemoration.

Born in his grandfather Winslow's Beacon Hill house, the poet **Robert Lowell** (1917–1977)—descendant of poets James Russell and Amy, a Harvard president, a Revolutionary War general, and millionaire cotton merchants—became the one Boston writer of this century to rival those of the Golden Age. He was raised at 91 Revere Street, after which he titled the prose memoir that appears in his breakthrough book, *Life Studies* (1959). As had generations of Lowells before him, he went to Harvard but transferred after two years to Kenyon, where he studied under the poet John Crowe Ransom and impressed upon his schoolmates his ambition to be a great poet. Upon graduating, he married the novelist **Jean Stafford** (1915–1979) who is yet another outsider who wrote a good Boston novel, *Boston Adventure* (1944). Lowell had in him a streak of Boston contrariness and reformer's zeal. For a time he converted to Catholicism, and his declaration of conscientious objection to World War II landed him in federal prison. He began to publish dense, gnarled, powerful, but not always coherent poems soon after leaving

Kenyon. In 1946 he won the Pulitzer Prize for *Lord Weary's Castle*. Critics considered his technically accomplished verse to be first-rate if conventional. In the mid-to-late 1950s, while living on Boston's "hardly passionate Marlborough Street," he began to change his work, to open its form and use as subject matter (with the example of Allen Ginsberg in mind) his family and himself. *Life Studies* was the result, and its impact was great in part because an aristocrat—not a beatnik but a bona fide intellectual—had let his hair down in poems that came to be called "confessional." From this vantage point, that label's implications seem wrong. Lowell's frank poems do not so much ask for forgiveness as seek understanding. They sound more like what we say to therapists than to priests. Lowell followed this book with *For the Union Dead* (1964), which takes its title from the best Boston poem he ever wrote. The poem's centerpiece is the St. Gauden's Robert Gould Shaw memorial across from the Boston statehouse. Shaw commanded the Union's first regiment of black troops, the 54th, which was composed of free Massachusetts blacks. Most of the regiment, including Shaw himself, met their deaths at Fort Wagner in South Carolina. Thirty years later, William James spoke at the monument's dedication. Lowell writes at a moment when a garage is being dug under the Boston Common and the Shaw memorial has been propped up by planks. The poem recalls Boston's Abolitionist past, contrasting it to the country's sorry present, in which black schoolchildren have to be escorted to school by federal marshals and everywhere, as the poem ends, "a savage servility/slides by on grease." "For the Union Dead" was something of a valediction for Lowell, as shortly after publishing the book he and his wife, the novelist Elizabeth Hardwick (they had been living at 239 Marlborough Street), left for New York and the intellectual big leagues, where his reputation grew and he appeared on the cover of *Time* magazine. He returned to Boston to teach at Harvard, and the city is everywhere in the late sonnets and other poems he wrote. But like Howells's leaving to write for *Harper's*, Lowell's departing the scene emphasized that Boston is now a backwater.

In the late 1950s Lowell taught at Boston University and had, in his graduate seminar, an unusually talented bunch of students—**George Starbuck** (b. 1931), who would also teach at Boston University; Sylvia Plath; and Anne Sexton, whose career as a poet touched a number of Boston institutions. She began writing poems as a suburban Boston housewife and then enrolled in the poet **John Holmes**'s (1904–1962) writing class at the Boston Center for Adult Education on Commonwealth Avenue. In 1958 she joined Lowell's seminar, where her work took off, becoming much more revealing than her mentor's. Houghton Mifflin published her, and in 1972 she was made a full professor at B.U. Death-haunted and beset by severe emotional turmoil, Sexton killed herself in 1974.

V. R. "Bunny" Lang (1924–1956)—poet, playwright, and one of the animating spirits of Cambridge's Poets' Theater—lived in her family's Bay State Road home until her much-mourned death from Hodgkin's disease. The poet Peter Davison, active in the Poets' Theater at the time, describes her as the Theater's "Lady Gregory." She combined madcap wit, bohemian charm, and a genius for drawing people to her. The poet Frank O'Hara (1926–1966) and she were so close that one of her poems was published in his *Collected* and went unnoticed for years. Her poems and plays were published by Random House in the mid-1970s and are now, for no good reason, out of print. Alison Lurie, the novelist and a friend of Lang's, contributed an excellent memoir which—in often hilarious detail—recalls a brief period when the academy and the arts fertilized one another.

No contemporary city is as cohesive as were those of the 19th century. Writers are born and die, come and go, in Boston not because they have any real connection with the city but because fate places them there. **Edward Dahlberg** (1900–1977) was born here, the illegitimate son of the red-haired lady barber he would later write about in *Because I Was Flesh* (1900). **Elizabeth Bishop** (1911–1979), who came to teach at Harvard, spent her last years on Long Wharf, and died in Boston in 1979. **Robert Frost** (1874–1963) died in Boston's Peter Bent Brigham Hosptial in 1963. Among his last visitors was Ezra Pound's daughter, Mary de Rachewiltz, who thanked him for helping her father get out of St. Elizabeth's Hospital in Washington, D.C., and who said of Frost, "He was a great poet and a great romantic." **Eugene O'Neill** (1888–1953) spent his last years at Boston's Shelton Hotel before dying in Boston. Only his wife, Carlotta, attended his funeral. He is buried under a pink quartz boulder in Jamaica Plain's Forest Hills Cemetery, where e.e. cummings is buried under a stone that spells his name in capitals.

Merrill Moore (1903–1957), one of the Fugitives, practiced psychiatry in Boston (Robert Lowell was one of his patients) and wrote an enormous amount of poetry, all in the sonnet form. **Nat Hentoff**, jazz critic and journalist, grew up in Boston's Roxbury neighborhood (his book *Boston Boy* chronicles those years) and his book *The Jazz Life* gives a picture of the jazz scene in and around Copley Square after World War II. Hentoff also wrote a memoir about his early years on Blue Hill Avenue. The poet **Cid Corman**, born in Boston, had a radio program in the late 1940s called "This Is Poetry." Robert Creeley, farming in northern New Hampshire, picked it up one night "by a fluke of the airwaves" and began a correspondence with Corman, which resulted in Corman's contacting Charles Olson (1910–1970) and beginning the important magazine *Origin*. When Olson heard Corman's plans for a magazine he exclaimed:

> Well, the thing you ought to know, is that, that you have the will to make a MAG is a very fine thing, and is hailed, by this citizen, (especially, I suppose that it is also BOSTON: by god, how long is it, that except for harvard sheets, which is not Boston, there has been SUCH A THING! all the way back to Emerson's DIAL, i do declare, almost, isn't it?

Corman left Boston for Japan, where he continued the magazine before returning to Boston in the 1970s to open a Japanese restaurant on Newbury Street, between Clarendon and Dartmouth. He ran this for a few years, then returned to Japan, where he continues to write the spare poems of which he has produced many thousands. At some point in the mid-1950s the poet **Jack Spicer** (1925–1965) worked at the Boston Public Library in Copley Square. He claimed he was fired because while examining the library's only copy of the *Bay Psalm Book* he cracked the spine. In his brief time in Boston, Spicer had a circle including the poets Robin Blaser, Steve Jonas, and John Wieners, who attended Black Mountain College after hearing Charles Olson read at the Charles Street Meeting House on the night of Hurricane Hazel.

The last gasp of Boston's book banners took place on July 7, 1966, when the Massachusetts Supreme Court declared William Burroughs's *Naked Lunch* not obscene. The novel had been published in New York in 1962, and

Boston-area book stores had already broken the ban, but Norman Mailer, Allen Ginsberg, and the poet John Ciardi testified on the book's behalf and carried the day. But not by much. The court based its ruling on the Supreme Court doctrine that found the novel *Fanny Hill* to be obscene. Two Massachusetts justices dissented, and one of these, a Judge Reardon, declared *Naked Lunch* "a revolting miasma of unrelieved perversion and disease."

Many writers live in Boston and teach literature or writing at the many colleges and universities in the area. The 1992 Nobel Prize winner **Derek Walcott** teaches at B.U., where he is in the process of building a theater company. B.U. advertises its creative writing program by reminding potential students that Lowell's famous class sometimes convened over drinks at the Ritz and pointing to the success of novelist Sue Miller, who got her start there. The university supports William Phillips's *Partisan Review*, and the *Agni Review* under the editorship of fiction writer and essayist Askold Melnyczuk. The poets Robert Pinsky and Stuart Dischell and the novelist Leslie Epstein also teach at Boston University. Poets Martha Collins and Lloyd Schwartz teach at the University of Massachusetts, Boston campus. Emerson College in the Back Bay also has a magazine, *Ploughshares*, under the direction of Dewitt Henry. Poets Bill Knott and Sam Cornish teach there. The novelist George V. Higgins, a Boston College graduate, teaches at B.U., but he was a practicing lawyer when he wrote his novel set in Boston, *The Friends of Eddie Coyle*. Robert Mitchum played Coyle in the movie. Robert Parker, the inventor of the private eye Spenser, taught a course in hardboiled detective fiction at Northeastern before he became famous. Parker's novels are full of references to Boston and environs, and the television series based on his books was filmed locally.

The Atlantic continued to operate out of its Arlington Street office until its move to Boylston Street in 1989. Edward Weeks, who followed Ellery Sedgwick as the magazine's editor and held the post for thirty-three years, published a memoir, *My Green Age*, which takes him up until he took over the magazine. Weeks tells a few tales about *The Atlantic*'s problems with Boston's Watch and Ward Society when that society served as a guardian of the public's moral good health. The magazine's current editor, William Whitworth, came to *The Atlantic* from *The New Yorker*, which has not reversed the effect of Howells's move a century ago.

The Boston Athenaeum, one of the oldest and most distinguished independent libraries in America, has been open since 1807, and has been located at its 10 Beacon Street address since 1849. Emerson, Bronson Alcott, Longfellow, Parkman, Daniel Webster, Lydia Maria Child, and Amy Lowell have been members. Visitors to the Athenaeum are welcome. They must sign in at the entrance and stay below the second floor, where there is gallery space for shows. The Athenaeum's art collection is on display throughout the building and visitors can see works by John Singer Sargent, Gilbert Stuart, Washington Allston, and a Bradley Philips (he was married to the poet V. R. Lang) of a man smoking a joint over breakfast as he looks out on Brighton, England. The serenity and elegance of the place—as if books by themselves bring calm, order, and beauty—offers uncommon pleasure to visitors.

For research into all manner of things having to do with Boston, the Bostonian Society at 206 Washington Street is the place to try. Movie producers use it to determine just what people were wearing in Boston fifty years ago; city planners who might want to take a look at the West End before it was so foolishly demolished in the name of urban renewal will find pertinent photographs; students come to work on papers about the history and composition of the city's neighborhoods; and anyone with a Boston question for which they have been unable to find an answer is welcome.

The John Fitzgerald Kennedy Presidential Library in Dorchester and Fenway Park, home of the Boston Red Sox, on Jersey Street in Boston also have literary interest. Kennedy scholars from all over the world do research at the library, and so do those interested in the work of Ernest Hemingway, whose papers are there. It seems right that the glamorous president and writer are together under one roof.

Fenway Park can be visited, for the price of a ticket, during the baseball season. John Updike wrote "Hub Fans Bid Kid Adieu," one of the best pieces of writing on baseball, after watching Ted Williams play his final game there. Today Peter Gammons, in my opinion the best baseball writer in America, regularly practices his craft from Fenway's pressbox.

BREWSTER

Conrad Aiken (1889–1973)—novelist, poet, critic, and contemporary and friend of T. S. Eliot at Harvard—lived here in a house at 457 Stony Brook Road. He named the house Forty-one Doors, and lived in it from 1940 to 1967, after which he summered there until shortly before his death. Although Aiken produced high quality short stories ("Silent Snow, Secret Snow" has been anthologized), novels (Freud is said to have read his *Blue Voyage*), poems (his selected poems won a Pulitzer Prize in 1929), and criticism, he never seemed to get his due in his lifetime, and now his work is largely out of print and unread. The critic Randall Jarrell once guessed that Aiken's poems were neglected because of his singularly off-putting titles, such as *The Pilgrimage of Festus* and *The Coming Forth by Day of Osiris Jones*. Perhaps a certain self-conscious artiness has kept readers from Aiken. Whatever the reason, his work is less known than it ought to be.

BROOKLINE

Amy Lowell (1874–1925), distant cousin of the poets James Russell and Robert Lowell, was born here in Sevenels, named by her father, Augustus Lowell, for the seven Lowells living in the house. Amy's birth, eighteen years after her brother Abbott Lawrence—a future president of Harvard—caused her to be nicknamed "Postscript" by her family. Her other brother, Percival, gained fame as an astronomer. We know that Amy Lowell wrote her first poem on October 21, 1902. "It loosed," she noted, "a bolt in my brain and I found out where my true function lay." In 1913 she read the issue of *Poetry* in which Ezra Pound launched Imagism, and she discovered that she was an Imagiste. This moved her to go to England and eventually take over the Imagist "movement," and ultimately she declared of Pound: "Poor Ezra, he had a future once, but he has played his cards so badly that I think he has barely a past now." Lowell published numerous books of poetry, a biography of John Keats, and, in collaboration with Florence Ayscough, a book of translations from the Chinese. She is known to have smoked cigars, several of which are in her archive at Harvard's Houghton Library, and to have had a "Boston marriage"—defined by the critic Steven Watson as having "the domestic rhythms, emotions and devotion of a marriage," with the actress Ada Dwyer.

President John Fitzgerald Kennedy's (1917–1963) birthplace is now a National Historic Landmark. It has literary significance only in matters of biography, but Kennedy is included here because he won the Pulitzer Prize in 1956, while a United States senator, for *Profiles in Courage*. Kennedy is the only president to have won the prize. Today there is some question as to just how much of *Profiles* Kennedy actually wrote. We know that his speechwriter and confidante, Theodore Sorenson, helped with the book, but the exact nature of his editorial work is unknown. We accept that recent presidents do not write the words they speak and, Harry Truman aside, hardly write anything while in office, so it will shock few if it is discovered that Kennedy's book is not entirely his own work.

Leonard Bernstein (1918–1990) was born in Brookline. He is mentioned here not because of his many collaborations with writers, the great lyricist Stephen Sondheim (*West Side Story*) and the poet Richard Wilbur (*Candide*) among them, but because he gave the Norton Lectures in Poetry at Harvard. He was not the first musician to do so; Igor Stravinsky preceded Bernstein, and John Cage followed him. Bernstein titled his lectures "The Unanswered Question," taking Charles Ives's orchestral piece of that title as his text. As anyone knows who has seen his television talks on music, Bernstein compelled the same sort of attention as a lecturer that he did as a conductor. Harvard University Press continues to keep Bernstein's lectures in print.

CAMBRIDGE

Most visitors to Cambridge stroll through Harvard Yard and around Harvard Square, and while they may venture as far as Longfellow's house on Brattle Street, they stay within what can be called Greater Harvard. If they arrive at the Square having come from Boston on Massachusetts Avenue, they are usually surprised, as they pass through Central Square, to find that Cambridge is more than Harvard. Literary Cambridge is not Harvard alone, but it is so concentrated there that working-class Cambridge and the grand homes off Fresh Pond Parkway are another world. America's oldest and most prestigious university began in 1636 and took its name in 1638 from John Harvard, who bequeathed the school £780 and his library of 320 books. A mind-boggling number of American writers, far too many to list here, have been educated and/or have taught at the university. Literary Cambridge is not Harvard alone but almost. Increase Mather graduated from Harvard in 1656, and his son Cotton Mather in 1678. Emerson, Thoreau, Oliver Wendell Holmes, Richard Henry Dana, Jr., historian John Lothrop Motley, and Francis Parkman not only graduated from Harvard, but were taught composition by the same man, Edward Tyrell Channing, Boylston Professor of Rhetoric. Oliver Wendell Holmes, Jr., who went on to teach law at the law school; Thomas Bailey Aldrich, editor of *The Atlantic*; William James; Owen Wister, who wrote *The Virginian*; and George Santayana graduated from Harvard, as did Van Wyck Brooks, Samuel Eliot Morison, T. S. Eliot and Conrad Aiken. Wallace Stevens, Robert Benchley, e.e. cummings (who was born in Cambridge), John P. Marquand, John Dos Passos, Thomas Wolfe (whose papers are in Houghton Library), poet Howard Nemerov, the novelist William Burroughs, William Gaddis, Norman Mailer, Harry Mathews, Harold Brodkey, John Updike, and playwright Arthur Kopit.

And the list goes on: Horatio Alger, Jr., Frederick Goddard Tuckerman, Bernard Berenson (whose Florentine villa, I Tatti, now belongs to Harvard), the composer and music critic Virgil Thomson, Edwin Arlington Robinson, poet John Hall Wheelock, poet John Wheelwright (whose architect father designed the Harvard Lampoon building, home of Harvard's humor magazine), James Gould Cozzens, Countee Cullen, George Ripley, John Reed, Charles Olson . . . all received degrees from Harvard. Robert Frost spent two years studying at Harvard, 1897 to 1899, but left before graduating.

W. E. B. Du Bois took a Ph.D. Such was the status of members of his race that he read with Santayana, away from class, in Santayana's attic and William James, whom Du Bois said had an influence on him second only to his mother's, was alone among Harvard teachers in asking him to his home. In 1949, these poets were at Harvard: John Ashbery, Kenneth Koch, Frank O'Hara (roommate of Edward Gorey), Robert Creeley, Donald Hall, L. E. Sissman, Robert Bly, Adrienne Rich (who was at Radcliffe), Gerrit Lansing, and Kenward Elmslie. Why this unprecedented concentration of poets? Perhaps because Harvard's prestige, since dimmed somewhat by the rise of schools across the country like the University of Michigan and Stanford, was such that students who did well in school automatically applied here. And Harvard's wealth of scholarships probably had some effect. Recent graduates include Jonathan Kozol, Robert Grenier, William Ferguson, Richard Tillinghast, Sidney Goldfarb, Michael Palmer, literary agent Andrew Wylie, Katha Pollitt, Mary Jo Salter, and Dana Gioia. And there are the graduates of Radcliffe, Harvard's sister school: Gertrude Stein, whose studies in psychology with William James had lasting importance for her; Helen Keller; the historian Barbara Tuchman, and the novelist Rona Jaffe. This roll of names must not suggest that Harvard had a similar impact on each one of them. There are those—Thoreau is an example—who found the place difficult to take, and those for whom Harvard determined their future. Norman Mailer, who entered as an engineer and left to become a writer, is one.

As much as Harvard is HARVARD, monolithic and enduring, Harvard is also no more nor less than who teaches there. Henry Wadsworth Longfellow taught languages, and during his tenure Jared Sparks, editor of George Washington's writing and Benjamin Franklin's works, was president of the university. Louis Agassiz taught Henry Adams, and Adams, who also taught at Harvard, declared him his favorite teacher. Charles Eliot Norton, for whom the Norton Lectureship is named, taught art history, and was the literary executor of both Ruskin and Carlyle. James Russell Lowell both graduated from and taught at his alma mater. Francis J. Child, the ballad collector, held the Boylston Professorship of Rhetoric, a chair once held by John Quincy Adams. Few teachers had greater impact than William James, who from 1872 to 1907 urged his students to "plunge into the ruddy stream of things." George Pierce Baker conducted his 47 Workshop in playwriting for more than twenty years. Thomas Wolfe was one of his students. George Lyman Kitteridge taught Shakespeare for many years, producing editions of the plays still in use. Irving Babbitt taught T. S. Eliot, and Charles Townsend Copeland, ("Copey") taught generations of students expository writing. Many of them kept their corrected papers for the rest of their lives. F. O. Matthiessen, whose *American Renaissance* (1941) is a pioneering look at 19th-century American literature, and Harry Levin developed their ideas in

Harvard classrooms. Archibald MacLeish taught a writing workshop to Donald Hall's generation, and poets John Berryman, John Ciardi, and Delmore Schwartz taught briefly at Harvard, as did the novelist Wallace Stegner. David Reisman, whose *The Lonely Crowd* had an impact in the 1950s, and B. F. Skinner, whose novel *Walden Two* inspired some sixties communards, taught at Harvard. The novelist Monroe Engel taught several generations of fiction writers. Robert Lowell spent two years at Harvard before transferring to Kenyon College from which he graduated, but he returned to teach at Harvard in 1963. He had great influence on the poet Frank Bidart, among many others. Lowell's friend the playwright and poet William Alfred taught Anglo-Saxon for many years until his recent retirement. Nobel-Prize–winning poet Derek Walcott taught briefly at Harvard, and so did Elizabeth Bishop. The critic Helen Vendler and the poet Seamus Heaney, scientist Stephen Jay Gould, and the historian Bernard Bailyn are among the writers who teach at Harvard today.

The Norton Lectures are Harvard's most significant literary event. They occur in clusters—there were five in the 1980s—and the delivered texts, with some revisions, are published by the Harvard University Press. T. S. Eliot gave *The Use of Poetry and the Use of Criticism* in 1933. Robert Frost lectured in 1936. Frost's relationship with Harvard began in 1926, and over the years held a number of faculty positions, the Ralph Waldo Emerson Fellowship in Poetry among them. During the time he spent at Harvard Frost lived at 35 Brewster Street. Robert Lowell, who visited Frost there, remembered "the barish rooms, the miscellaneous gold-lettered old classics, the Georgian poets, the Catullus by his bedside, the iron stove where he sometimes did his cooking, and the stool drawn up to his visitor's chair so that he could ramble and listen." The artist and photographer Ben Shahn titled his lectures *The Shape of Content*; painter Frank Stella gave *Working Space*; and composers Igor Stravinsky, Leonard Bernstein, and John Cage have also given the lectures. e.e. cummings titled his Nortons "nonlectures," and began, "Let me cordially warn you, at the opening of these so-called lectures, that I haven't the remotest intention of posing as a lecturer. Lecturing is presumably a form of teaching; and presumably a teacher is someone who knows. I never did, and still don't know." Some lecturers—Stella for one—drew large (upwards of a thousand) crowds to each of their six lectures. Others, such as critics Harold Bloom and Dame Helen Gardner speaking on more recondite subjects, drew smaller audiences. Nobel Prize winner Czeslaw Milosz gave his Norton Lectures as Solidarity emerged in Poland. In 1989, John Ashbery lectured on poets important to him: Thomas Lovell Beddoes, John Clare, Raymond Rousell, Laura Riding, David Schubert, and John Wheelwright. That book has yet to be published.

Harvard claims to house 100 libraries, holding more than 13,000,000 volumes. Two have special literary interests. Houghton Library is the rare book library of Harvard College. It opened in 1942 and stands between Lamont Library and Widener, Harvard's main library. Houghton holds a fabulous collection of books, manuscripts, and memorabilia. Its Fiftieth Anniversary Exhibition exhibitions are open to the public) displayed 102 items spanning thirteen centuries, among them a Gutenberg Bible, Beethoven autographed scores, Herman Melville's annotated Shakespeare, Lewis Carroll's own copy of *Alice in Wonderland,* Ticknor and Fields's original contract for *Walden,* one of the 197 volumes of Emerson's complete journals owned by the library, the manuscript of Hawthorne's *The House of the Seven Gables,* and John Updike's corrected copy of his novel *Rabbit, Run* among 102 items spanning thirteen centuries. The Woodbery Poetry Room, under the stewardship of novelist Stratis Haviaras, has, besides its poetry book and magazine catalogue, a number of rare recordings and tapes, including readings by Alfred Lord Tennyson ("The Charge of the Light Brigade") and Vladimir Mayakovsky, as well as all the Norton Lectures and the many readings that have taken place over the years at Harvard. The Poetry Room is in Lamont Library and is open to the public.

A few odds and ends: one book of John Harvard's original bequest survives. *Christian Warfare* exists today because it was overdue when a fire on January 24, 1764 destroyed Harvard Hall and the other 400 volumes of John Harvard's library. Frank Norris (1870–1902) spent one year at Harvard, during which he completed his novel *McTeague* (1899) on assignment for a class. Vladimir Nabokov (1899–1977) lived from 1942 to 1948 at 8 Craigie Circle. The view from his third-floor window is used at the beginning of his novel *Bend Sinister* (1949). During his years in Cambridge, Nabokov worked at

Harvard, part-time at the Museum of Contemporary Zoology. Certainly the most famous recent novel associated with Harvard is Erich Segal's *Love Story*, in which upper-class Harvard student Oliver meets and marries working-class Jenny, and in the end there's not a dry eye in the house. The novel gave America the line, "Love means never having to say you're sorry."

The Poets' Theater and its short-lived reincarnation, the New Poets' Theater, while not formally connected with Harvard, drew most of its actors, playwrights, staff, and audience from people involved with the university. The novelist Mary Manning, one of its founders, contributed her adaptation of James Joyce's *Finnegans Wake*; John Ashbery had a play produced by the theater, as did the poet V. R. Lang and Frank O'Hara acted in its productions; Dylan Thomas read under its auspices, and William Alfred, poets Felicia Lamport, Peter Davison, Lyon Phelps, Richard Wilbur, Richard Eberhart, and playwright Ethan Ayer were in the company. Edward Gorey designed posters and sets, and many productions were staged in a 49-seat theater where the Harvard Coop Annex is today. A history of this group has yet to be written, but Alison Lurie affords a glimpse of its many colorful personalities in her introduction to V. R. Lang's collected poems and plays.

 Henry Wadsworth Longfellow (1807–1882) was Professor of Modern Languages at Harvard, but his presence in Cambridge only begins there. His mansion at 105 Brattle Street, which has been described as better known than any house in America save George Washington's Mount Vernon, is cared for by the National Park Service and is open year-round. In 1837, Longfellow began residence in the house as a lodger. His landlady, the Widow Craigie, had rented rooms since 1819. Among her other boarders were Josiah Quincy, who wrote a two-volume history of Harvard; Harvard president and renowned orator Edward Everett; Jared Sparks; and dictionary-maker Joseph Worcester. It was already a famous house because General George Washington lived in it for ten months beginning in July of 1775 when he took command of the Continental Army. His wife Martha joined him, and they celebrated a wedding anniversary here. Longfellow continued to live in the house after Mrs. Craigie's death, and he wanted to buy it but did not have the money. In 1843, he married Frances Appleton of Boston and her merchant father Nathan bought the house for the Longfellows as a wedding present. All six Longfellow children were born here, but Frances, or Fanny, was to die here in 1861, the victim of a terrible accident. While using hot wax to seal locks of her daughter's hair as keepsakes, the wax ignited her dress. On fire, she ran to her husband, who grabbed a rug and smothered the flames, but Fanny was horribly burned and did not survive. Longfellow's face was so disfigured by the flames that in order to hide the scars he grew the white beard he is commonly remembered as wearing. In this house, as lodger and owner, Longfellow wrote much of the poetry that made him world-famous in his own time. There is a bust commemorating him in Westminster Abbey's Poet's Corner, and he is the only major American poet of the 19th century to be genuinely popular. Today's middle-aged Americans can still recite the Longfellow poems they memorized in school: "The Children's Hour," "The Midnight Ride of Paul Revere," "The Courtship of Miles Standish," "Hiawatha," and "Evangeline." And one of Longfellow's best-known poems, "The Village Blacksmith" (whose "spreading chestnut tree" once stood at the corner of Brattle and Story streets) is kept alive by a poetry reading series presided over for the past twenty years by poet Gail Mazur at Brattle Street's Blacksmith House. Wood from the original tree was made into a chair, on display in Longfellow's study, that was presented to Longfellow on his seventy-second birthday by the children of Cambridge. Throughout Longfellow's years, only Emerson's Concord home commanded as many literary visitors. Hawthorne —who passed on to Longfellow the story that became "Evangeline"—called here as did generations of Harvard literati and visiting English writers such as Charles Dickens and Matthew Arnold. Here the Cambridge Dante Society met and aided Longfellow with his translation of *The Divine Comedy*. Having retired from Harvard in 1854, Longfellow remained Cambridge's chief literary eminence until his death in 1882. His descendants maintained the house as it was during his lifetime, until they passed it on to the Longfellow House Trust in 1913. Today it is in splendid shape, and visitors can get a strong sense of what his achievements meant in terms of everyday life. Behind the house there is an Italian garden built to Longfellow's plan. Its sundial bears a line from Dante that, as translated by Longfellow, reads: "Think that this day will never dawn again."

James Russell Lowell's (1819–1891) house, Elmwood, still stands at 33

Elmwood Avenue, and is used by Harvard for faculty housing (the current president lives there now). Lowell lived here throughout his life. He taught at Harvard, served as *The Atlantic's* first editor and as editor of the *North American Review*, and was an Abolitionist who later in life became a Republican. President Garfield appointed him minister to Spain and then to the Court of Saint James. He published his first book of poems at twenty-one, wrote numerous essays, including the satiric "Biglow Papers," and is best remembered for his "Ode Recited at the Harvard Commemoration," known as the "Commemoration Ode" and written to honor Harvard men who died in the Civil War. His older brother Robert Traill Spence Lowell (1816-1891), grandfather and namesake of the 20th-century poet, was a teacher and writer remembered for his poem "The Relief of Lucknow." The Lowell wealth did not flow through this branch of the family, where poets and preachers predominated.

William Dean Howells (1837–1920), fresh from Europe, bought his first Cambridge house at 41 Sacramento Street in 1866, and became a fixture in Cambridge–Boston literary life until he left for New York in 1881. He later lived at 3 Berkeley Street and built the house at 37 Concord Avenue that today bears a commemorative plaque. The gregarious and likable Howells made friends with all the great Boston writers of his day, but he was especially close to the young Henry James and to Mark Twain, who came in from Hartford, Connecticut, to see him. Howells and James spent many hours talking the candle down at Sacramento Street, and they enjoyed walking the city streets at night and rowing on Fresh Pond. During his Cambridge years, Howells often returned to his native Ohio to visit his parents. His biographer Kenneth S. Lynn gives this account of one such visit:

> Once summer, for instance, in the early 1870s, Howells and his father stopped overnight at Garfield's (James A. Garfield an old friend of the family and soon to be President of the United States) home, and as they were sitting with the Garfield family on the veranda that overlooked their lawn, Howells began to speak of the famous poets he knew. Suddenly, Garfield stopped him, and ran down into the grassy space, calling and waving to his neighbors who were sitting on their

back porches. "Come over here!" he shouted. "He's telling about Holmes, and Longfellow, and Whittier!" Soon dim forms climbed over the fences and followed the Congressman to his veranda. "Now go on!" Garfield called to Howells, and Howells did, while the whip-porwills soared about in the cool of the evening and the hour hand of the town clock drew toward midnight.

Oliver Wendell Holmes (1809–1894), **Richard Henry Dana** (1787–1879), and **Richard Henry Dana, Jr.** (1815–1882), author of *Two Years Before the Mast* (1840), were born in Cambridge, as was **Margaret Fuller** (1810–1850), who was raised on Cherry Street in what is now the Cherry Street Settlement House and spent a year and a half at 42 Brattle Street in what is now the Cambridge Center for Adult Education. **Thomas Wentworth Higginson** (1823–1911) was also born in Cambridge. He entered Harvard at thirteen, and later graduated from the Divinity School. This fiery abolitionist, secret backer of John Brown and correspondent with Emily Dickinson, settled again in Cambridge in 1878 and lived here until his death. Among his many books are biographies of Longfellow and Whittier. Given all the writers born, schooled, passing through, and living in the city, it is no wonder that visiting novelist Bret Harte (1836–1902) said of Cambridge, "You cannot shoot in any direction without bringing down the author of one or two volumes."

But Cambridge's role in the history of literature in the Commonwealth is not limited to writers. New England's first printing press was set up here in 1639, and the following year it was used to print the first book published in the Colonies, *The Bay Psalm Book.* Just more than two centuries later, in 1855, **John Bartlett** (1820–1905) created another sort of book. Bartlett, owner of Cambridge's University Book Store, earned a reputation for identifying the sources of quotations. His answers to customers evolved into his reference work *Familiar Quotations,* now in its sixteenth edition, edited by the biographer and Cambridge resident Justin Kaplan.

The graves of many notable writers are located in Mount Auburn Cemetery on Mount Auburn Street. Chartered in 1835, Mount Auburn was the nation's first garden cemetery, a cemetery landscaped to invite tranquil walking and meditations on the here-and-now as well as on the eternity to come. Edward Everett, the greatest orator of his day, spoke at the cemetery's opening. He later gave the oration—more than two hours long, as custom called for—at the dedication of Gettysburg Cemetery. President Lincoln followed Everett and over the years his address upstaged what earwitnesses judged an exceptional oration. An excellent map of the cemetery is available at the office just inside the North Entrance off Mount Auburn Street. Louis Agassiz, Thomas Bailey Aldrich, John Bartlett, Nathaniel Bowditch, and Concord's William Ellery Channing are buried here. Mary Baker Eddy has a Greek temple above Halcyon Pond. James T. Fields and Oliver Wendell Holmes, whose work Fields published, are both here. Asa Gray (1810–1888), botanist, author, and Darwinian, has a garden and fountain in his memory. The poet Lorine Niedecker composed an elegy for Gray by drawing on a phrase from his letters some seventy years after his death:

> Asa Gray wrote Increase Lapham:
> pay particular attention
> to my pets the grasses.

Julia Ward Howe, known as not only the author of "The Battle Hymn of the Republic" but the founder of Mother's Day, is buried at Mount Auburn, as are Longfellow, the Lowells (James Russell and Amy), the historians Francis Parkman and William H. Prescott, the philosopher Josiah Royce, Jared Sparks, and Joseph Worcester. The abolitionist and close friend of most of the writers of his time, Senator Charles Sumner (1811–1874) is buried here. His impassioned speech against the Fugitive Slave Law provoked a Southern opponent to attack and beat Sumner within an inch of his life on the senate floor. Author Buckminster Fuller, inventor of the geodesic dome and participant in the first Happening ever at Black Mountain College, is buried here, but his grave has yet to make the map. The office staff will tell you where to find it. V. R. Lang is here in the Lang family plot. The cemetery is splendid in fall and spring and is a great walk under full summer leaf or even in bleakest winter.

Across Coolidge Avenue, which runs on the east side of Mount Auburn, is the Cambridge Public Cemetery where William Dean Howells is buried not far from his friends, the James family—America's preeminent intellectual family of the 19th century. **Henry James, Sr.** (1811–1882)—wealthy, restless Swedenborgian and a lecturer and writer, settled down in Cambridge in 1866, after moving back and forth between America and Europe while educating his children. He rented and then bought 20 Quincy Street, where the Harvard Faculty Club stands today. A blue oval sign designates this as the site of the James home. Henry, Sr., knew Emerson and Thomas Carlyle well, and he often lectured on them. He was particularly drawn to the utopian Fourierist ideas of men like George Ripley, Brook Farm's founder. James and his wife Mary lived at 20 Quincy Street until their deaths. Son **Henry James, Jr.** (1843–1916) lived there long enough to begin his lifelong friendship with Howells, but he had already started to make his way in the world, and for some years he moved every bit as restlessly between Europe and America as he had as a child. Six months before his death in England in 1916 he became an English citizen, but his ashes are interred in the family plot. His older brother, **William James** (1842–1910), had by far the greatest impact of any James on Cambridge life. After studying medicine at Harvard, he began his teaching career there, as instructor of physiology, in 1872, and ended it as professor of philosophy thirty-five years later, when he gave his last lecture on January 22, 1907. In 1889, he built the house at 95 Irving Street where he and his family lived until his death. He can be called a philosopher—*Pragmatism* (1907) qualifies him for the title—and he can be called a psychologist, *The Principles of Psychology* (1890) being long used as a college text. But in the end, the breadth and depth of his interests resist categorization. In our era of specialization, it would take several "experts" to cover the ground James did. Today on Kirkland Street, across from a Swedenborgian church stands Harvard's William James Hall. **Alice James** (1848–1892), Henry's and William's sister, also is buried in the family plot. She suffered from psychosomatic illnesses, as did her brother William, as a teenager and from severe depression over the last decade and a half of her life. Today she is remembered by the poets who continue the Alice James Press, a cooperative named in her honor. The Jameses left an enormous number of books, and have had an equally enormous number of books written about them. Harvard's F. O. Matthiessen's "group biography," *The James Family*, which includes large selections from the writings of all the Jameses, is an excellent introduction to the life of their individual and collective minds. Inquire at the office just inside the gates of the cemetery for directions to their grave.

For more than fifty years, Plympton Street—four blocks toward Boston from Harvard Square—has been the home of the Grolier Bookshop, *the* poetry bookshop in New England and one of a handful of such shops in the country. Gordon Cairnie, graduate of Ontario Agricultural College (also the alma mater of Harvard professor, economist, ambassador, and author John Kenneth Galbraith) and erstwhile potato inspector on Prince Edward Island, began the shop with a friend. They put together their rooms full of books, but the friend soon dropped out, and until his death in 1973 Cairnie ran the store in unforgettable style. He made change from a wallet and his pants pocket; priced out-of-print books at $8.75 and $17.50 and refused to sell them if he didn't think they were going to a good home; had a hand-lettered sign on the door warning "No Textbooks, No Science Books . . . Just Literature!"; shouted "Shut the Goddamn Door!" at all who entered, and actually loved poets, famous or forever unknown, for themselves. He arranged books in no discernible order, and the store's center table held a midden of little magazines, broadsides, pamphlets—who knew what all. Allen Ginsberg stood on this table hawking copies of "Big Table," banned in Boston for carrying chapters of William Burroughs's *Naked Lunch*, until the police came and carried him away. Regular customers included Robert Lowell, Charles Olson, Elizabeth Bishop, Richard Eberhart, Donald Hall, Helen Vendler, Robert Creeley, Jim Harrison, Paul Hannigan, Gail Mazur, and the photographer Elsa Dorfman. Also regulars were generations of Harvard undergraduates and legions of poets whom Cairnie let have books on the cuff, loaned money to, and asked to mind the store while he nipped out for a glass of Black Horse Ale. In an apartment above the store, Cairnie's friend Conrad Aiken greeted the novelist Malcolm Lowry, whose father had apprenticed him to Aiken, and in an evening of rough-housing Lowry managed to crack Aiken's skull and fracture an arm. In Cairnie's last years, potential customers often stopped after opening the door, and refused to enter because the room was dense with smoke and ribald talk. It became something of a men's club, forbidding to women, though some did persist. One was Louisa Solano, who became Cairnie's friend and took over the store upon his death. Cairnie was supported by his wife's inheritance, but Solano needed to make a go of the business. She transformed the shop and has kept it open through thick and all too much thin. The shop is at 6 Plympton Street, and on the little wall space not taken up by bookshelves there are photographs, most of them unpublished, of past and present Grolier poet customers.

CHICOPEE

Edward Bellamy (1850–1898), world-famous in his time, is Chicopee's only writer of note, and the city has done him proud. His house is a National Historic Landmark, his papers are at the public library, and a school bears his name. A lawyer who never practiced law, Bellamy became a journalist, and began publishing fiction in 1879 with the novel *The Duke of Stockbridge*. His utopian romance, *Looking Backward* (1888)—intended by Bellamy "as a forecast, in accordance with the principles of evolution, of the next stage in the industrial and social development of humanity, especially in this country"— struck a nerve here and abroad. Through the book, Bellamy became a spokesman for what he called "nationalism." He promoted these theories in a weekly journal, *The New Nation*, and founded the Nationalist party. Bellamy Clubs formed to keep the discussion going here and in Europe. He finished *Looking Backward*'s sequel, *Equality*, just before his death from tuberculosis. In his introduction to Bellamy's book of short stories, *The Blindman's World*, William Dean Howells compares Bellamy favorably with Hawthorne. Van Wyck Brooks seconds this, but felt that Bellamy "was merely reproducing Hawthorne's dreamwork." *Looking Backward* remains in print today long after the interest in Bellamy's utopia has passed.

CONCORD

No other town its size in New England or America has the literary history of Concord. Today, more authors' homes and literary sites are open to the public here than anywhere else in the United States. Since Concord is unique, its entry here will be organized in a unique way in this book. Instead of alphabetically by author, the guide will proceed from site to site, exactly as the visitor who tours Concord will.

For most Americans, as for those throughout the world familiar with American literature, literary New England *is* Concord. They will know it as home to Ralph Waldo Emerson, the Alcotts, and Nathaniel Hawthorne, and as the place where American Minutemen fought British regulars at the "rude bridge that arched the flood." They will know it as the birthplace and home of **Henry David Thoreau** (1817–1862) and the site of Walden Pond.

Walden is first among American sacred literary places. Not that the crowds who throng the pond on hot summer weekends nor the fishermen who fish there do so with reverence—nor is there reverence in those who currently seek to buy the adjacent woods so they can build condominiums. (Imagine what some copywriter will do to sell a porch overlooking the pond on which Thoreau's cabin stood!) Walden is more sacred in the American imagination, where it represents independence, self-reliance, getting-away-from-it-all, and a return to nature, a world the American soul holds to be "truer" and "realer" than that of the city. "When I wrote the following pages, or rather the bulk of them," Thoreau begins his book, "I lived alone, in the woods, a mile from any neighbor, in a house which I had built myself, on the shore of Walden Pond, in Concord, Massachusetts, and earned my living by the labor of my hands only. I lived there two years and two months. At present I am a sojourner in civilized life again."

Thoreau's *Walden* (1854) is key to how Americans imagine themselves. Few graduate from high school without some exposure to the book, but even unread, Thoreau is a folk hero, and the years he spent at Walden are symbolic of the American's right to pursue whatever life he can imagine for himself, no matter how nonconformist, eccentric, or antisocial that life might be. Thoreau began building his cabin on Emerson's Walden Pond woodlot in the spring of 1845, and he moved in on that July Fourth, Independence Day. It was the only house he ever owned. Thoreau did not exile himself to Walden. He often walked into Concord, had dinner at his parents' house and with the Emersons, and even took leave of his cabin for as long as a month at a time. While in residence he worked on his first book, *A Week on the Concord and Merrimack Rivers* (1849), planted a two-and-a-half-acre garden of beans, corn, and potatoes; studied the pond's ice; attended to all manner of natural events; kept his journal; began writing *Walden*; and got jailed for one July night in 1846 for failure to pay several years' poll tax. Thoreau's action was in protest against what he considered the state's role in upholding slavery. He championed the antislavery cause at Walden, where he hosted an Anti-Slavery Society fair, and throughout the rest of his life. His 1854 pamphlet "Slavery in Massachusetts," was well known at the time, and in response to John Brown's attack on Harper's Ferry, Thoreau delivered his tribute, "A Plea for Captain John Brown," to audiences in Concord, Boston, and Worcester.

Today, Walden Pond is a state reservation open to all, every day of the year. The site of Thoreau's cabin is an easy fifteen-minute walk from the parking lot across from the pond. At the lot stands a replica, one of three in Concord, of the original cabin. You will sense from it how close Thoreau's 10' × 15' Walden quarters were. The site itself is well marked. The cabin stood a little farther into the woods than one might think. Near the cabin's original foundation Bronson Alcott left the first stone of what has become a cairn. Take the long way back and walk completely around the pond. The path follows the shoreline, and you will have the woods to your right and the open pond on your left. It will take you but a half-hour to accomplish this beautifully varied walk.

A second replica of Thoreau's cabin is behind the Thoreau Lyceum at 156 Belknap Street. The house that holds the Lyceum has no associations with Thoreau, but he did survey Belknap Street. As headquarters of the Thoreau Society, the Lyceum is open seven days a week from April 1 through December, and intermittently from January to March. No other American writer is served by a place like this. Curator Anne McGrath and her staff are there to answer questions visitors have about Mr. Thoreau, whose name they pronounce "Thorough." Visitors sit in the Lyceum's main room, where a bust of Thoreau rests on a table between two standing lamps and looks funereal. The last time I visited, I heard Dick O'Connor tell a group what Thoreau's attitude toward corporal punishment really was during the two weeks he taught school; how Thoreau got along at Harvard; and the many speculations about Thoreau's affection for Emerson's wife Lydian. Since the 1960s Thoreau has been increasingly idealized as a hermit, environmentalist and peacenik, but the actual man was—as you can learn at the Lyceum—not nearly so simple. "The best you can write," he knew, "will be the best you are. Every sentence is the result of a long probation—the author's character is read from title page to end—of this he never corrects the proof." There is a bookstore at the Lyceum, where a great many books by and about Thoreau are available, as well as walking sticks, a video, denim clothes-patches bearing Thoreau's motto "Beware of all enterprises that require new clothes," cards, notes—heaps of stuff whose proceeds support the place.

The Old Manse on Monument Street, built by Ralph Waldo Emerson's grandfather, the Reverend William Emerson, was the first Concord home of **Nathaniel** (1804–1864) and Sophia **Hawthorne**. Before the Hawthornes' 1842 arrival, the Old Manse already had literary associations. Waldo (he was not known as Ralph) Emerson came here as a boy to visit his grandfather, and returned in 1834, a widower, with his mother, to live for a year. Emerson wrote his first book, *Nature*, here, about which he had written in his journal, "I like my book about Nature" two years before he actually wrote it. Clearly, *Nature* was already formed in Emerson's mind, and all he had to do was put the words down, which he did through the summer of 1835, looking out over a landscape that prompted him to write, "Art cannot rival this pomp of purple and gold." *Nature*, all of ninety-five pages, appeared anonymously—a custom of the time—the following year. By then Emerson had remarried and moved to the Concord house where he would spend the rest of his life.

Hawthorne and his bride came to the Old Manse—he gave the house its name—on July 9, 1842, directly from their wedding in Boston. They rented the place for $100 a year and spent the next three-and-a-half years there, on a sort of long honeymoon, becoming acquainted with the entire Transcendentalist circle. Emerson and Thoreau were particular friends of the Hawthornes. Indeed, as his wedding present to them, Emerson commissioned Thoreau to plant a garden for the newlyweds. One winter day, Sophia Hawthorne looked out a rear window to the Concord River that flows just behind the house, and saw the three men ice skating. She wrote down this charming collective portrait:

[Thoreau] figuring dithyrambic dances and Bacchic leaps on the ice—very remarkable, but very ugly, methought. Next him followed Mr. Hawthorne, who, wrapped in his cloak, moved like a self-impelled Greek statue, stately and grave. Mr. Emerson closed the line, evidently too weary to hold himself erect, pitching headforemost, half lying on the air.

In other seasons, the Hawthornes enjoyed the river in the boat they bought from Thoreau and christened the *Pond Lily*. It was in that boat that Hawthorne, in company with Ellery Channing and others, discovered the body of a young schoolteacher who had drowned herself in the river. Hawthorne wrote that he heard his "voice tremble a little when I spoke, at the first shock of discovery, and at seeing the body come to the surface, dimly in the starlight."

During his years in the Old Manse Hawthorne published some twenty stories and sketches that would go to form his book *Mosses from an Old Manse*, "The Birth-Mark," "Rappaccini's Daughter," and "The Celestial Rail-Road" among them. Hawthorne would not write a first novel (he had disowned, and been successful in suppressing, his youthful novel *Fanshawe*) for another five years. At the Old Manse, he worked in a back upstairs study at a small half-moon foldup desk he had built into the wall so he could keep his back to the view. The desk is there today, and it must have been uncomfortable enough to use that it concentrated Hawthorne's attention on his work. On a pane in the north window of this room, the Hawthornes, during their first year in the house, incised several inscriptions on an April afternoon:

Man's accidents are God's purposes. Sophia A. Hawthorne, 1843
Nathaniel Hawthorne. This is his study, 1843.
The smallest twig leans clear against the sky
Composed by my wife and written with her diamond.
Inscribed by my husband at sunset, April 3 1843. On the gold light. S. A. H.

A second windowpane, in the back parlor on the floor below this, was also inscribed by the Hawthornes. Both inscriptions are visible today, and just before my last visit to the house, a third windowpane had been discovered in the attic. It was broken, but the signature on it is clearly Hawthorne's. When it came time for the Hawthornes to leave the Old Manse, they did so because Hawthorne had been able to use his political influence within the Democratic Party to gain the post of Surveyor in the Salem Custom House. He needed the money as his daughter Una was born in 1844, and son Julian was soon to follow the move to Salem. The Old Manse, now owned and managed by the Trustees of Reservations, is open from mid-April to the end of October. The furnishings are original to the house, and my last guide was knowledgeable and enthusiastic. There is a gift shop complete with postcards —both inscribed windows are on cards—and books, but blessedly little junk.

Just behind the Old Manse is the bridge over the Concord River where the Minutemen, memorialized by Daniel Chester French's famous statue, gathered on April 19, 1775, to repel the British Redcoats and fire what Emerson called "the shot heard round the world." Emerson's grandfather was among that company, and he left an account of the battle. His family watched the action from the window in what became Waldo Emerson's and Hawthorne's study. The bridge came down in 1793 and was not replaced until 1874. On July 4, 1837, a granite obelisk that still stands was unveiled, and on it, irregularly carved, blackened letters remember "the first forcible resistance to British aggression." To commemorate the battle's centennial, a celebration was held in 1876 to coincide with the Declaration of Independence's hundredth birthday. Mark Twain and William Dean Howells were among the dignitaries expected for the occasion, but that cold, blustery day they never managed to get transportation, so crowded were the trains out of Cambridge. They missed hearing Emerson give a speech, James Russell Lowell recite an ode, the appearance of President Ulysses S. Grant and members of his cabinet, the military parade and the dinner in a tent for 4,000 people. They also missed a spectacular disaster, as the speaker's platform twice gave way under the weight of the distinguished guests, the dinner tent could not keep out the cold weather, and the town of Concord was trampled by 50,000 cold, hungry celebrators, a good many of whom were drunk by nightfall. The Boston *Daily News* said of the uproar, "There is no difficulty now in understanding the hurried retreat of the British from Concord and Lexington."

Ralph Waldo Emerson (1803–1882), present at the North Bridge in

1836 when his "Concord Hymn" was sung and at the debacle in 1876, knew greater renown than any other American writer of his time. He had lived in Concord since 1835, when he bought the house that stayed in his family until, after 1930, it became the museum that is open to the public today. Behind Emerson, when he moved in with his second wife Lydian, was his shocking resignation from Boston's Second Church, the Mather brothers' church; and before him were years of lecturing, essay writing, and increasing eminence. In July 1836, the group that would be named the Transcendental Club began to meet in Emerson's house. This included Margaret Fuller, with whom Emerson would edit *The Dial*; Thoreau; Elizabeth Palmer Peabody; Orestes Brownson; Theodore Parker; and Bronson Alcott. The following year he inherited $23,000 from his first wife's estate, giving him a measure of financial security, and gave "The American Scholar" as Harvard's Phi Beta Kappa oration. That day he was praised as "the spirit of Concord" who "makes us all one," and as the spirit of Concord he remained until his death in 1882. Today, the Emerson house's threadbare carpets and peeling paint give it the feeling of a lived-in house, as do the guides, who speak as if they enjoy their work. In Emerson's study, the books on the shelves belonged to him and there is a round desk that can be turned like a lazy Susan.

Emerson liked to fill up the desk's drawers—turning it to find a less full one—as he worked. This replica holds some of Emerson's working library, the bulk of which is at Harvard's Houghton Library. Walking through Emerson's house, it is clear that he was well off. It is a comfortable, middle-class home that then, more so than now, was crowded with the visitors who had come to see him. In the family dining room, twin tables are joined. These opened up to seat eighteen, a not uncommon number for lunch and dinner. In the first-floor study stands a placard listing some of Emerson's visitors. Walt Whitman came, and so did Eleanor Roosevelt and the bandleader Artie Shaw. My guide proudly told me she had shown Katharine Hepburn through the house. A signal feature of the place is the presence of Thomas Carlyle, the British historian and thinker. Emerson sought him out in England in 1833 and began a lifelong friendship that clearly had an element of hero worship on Emerson's part. A Guido Reni engraving, Carlyle's wedding present to the Emersons, hangs in their parlor and in the dining room there hangs a Julia Margaret

Cameron photograph of Carlyle in profile. He is white haired and looks like a prophet. Also in the dining room, and this is the most touching instance of Carlyle's importance to Emerson, is an engraving of Carlyle as a young man. Under it, Emerson affixed Carlyle's signature he had clipped from a letter. Emerson's fame spread, in part, because he gave at least 1,500 public lectures between 1833 and 1881. In 1865, he lectured seventy-seven times. He lectured in twenty-three states including California, but rarely in the South. In New England, he delivered more than 1,000 lectures in 143 cities and towns. Few American writers in any age have known their country on such first-hand terms.

Emerson lectured 100 times in the Concord Lyceum, and he gave his last lecture on Carlyle at the Boston Historical Society. Over the last five years of his life, Emerson descended into what the scholar Joel Porte has called "mental twilight." At Longfellow's funeral he is reported as saying, "That gentleman was a sweet, beautiful soul, but I have entirely forgotten his name." Despite this gradual enfeeblement, these years were serene. When he died on April 27, 1882, Thoreau had been dead for twenty years, Concord had become a backwater town, and only a few of the original Transcendentalists still lived.

Behind the Emerson house is his garden, much as it was during his lifetime. Across the street in the new brick Concord Museum is not only Emerson's study, but the third version of Thoreau's Walden cabin. This one displays a few Thoreau artifacts as if Ralph Lauren had arranged them. Every exhibit in the museum is so neatly laid out that the place is fussy and lacks spirit. It is the stuff of another time as no person then could have possibly lived with it. When I inquired about the books in Emerson's study I was given a dog-eared list and told not to go to far with it. Literary interest in this place is minimal.

Orchard House, the home of the Alcotts for nineteen years, is on Lexington Road not far from the museum. In 1857, **Bronson Alcott** (1799–1888) bought twelve acres of land on which stood two 18th-century houses. Although impractical in many ways, Alcott was a Mr. Fix-it, and he joined the houses together to make Orchard House. His daughter **Louisa May Alcott** (1832–1888) was twenty-six when the family moved in. She had already published stories and poems in *The Atlantic* and she would leave home during the Civil War to serve as a nurse, an experience she recounted in *Hospital Sketches* (1863). Her sisters Anna, an amateur actress who performed with the Concord Dramatic Union, and the artist May, who taught the sculptor Daniel Chester French when he was young, were also talented. There are examples of May's work throughout the house. Their mother, Abigail May, did her duty as homemaker, and was also the family's source of income. Active in many social causes, she worked as a social worker aiding, in particular, immigrant families. Bronson, philosopher, educator, writer, and indefatigable talker, worked at all four of his skills as he dreamed his great, and mostly unrealized, dreams. One that did come true is the Concord School of Philosophy, the home of which stands behind Orchard House and is still in use today. As with all the Concord houses, the Orchard House tour is first rate. Having been restored in 1912, the house looks substantially as it did during the Alcotts' time. In Louisa May's upstairs room there is a desk built into the wall, similar to the one Hawthorne used in the Old Manse. But hers allowed her to look out on the front yard and to watch the passing scene on Lexington Road. In the downstairs study there is a collage of authors' portraits in which you will find Hawthorne, Whittier, Emerson, and scientist and writer Louis Agassiz (1807–1873). Agassiz taught for many years at Harvard, where he was Henry Adams's favorite teacher. His presence in the collage testifies to the wide-ranging intellectual interests of the Transcendentalists. They lived before knowledge had been parceled out to experts, and they did not let their passionate minds be hemmed in by categories. Orchard House is open from April 1 until the last day in October. All Louisa May Alcott's titles are available in the book and souvenir store that adjoins the house.

As Bronson Alcott had cobbled together Orchard House, he did the same to Hillside, just down Lexington Road. Alcott, who is said to have moved once a year, brought his young family here in 1845 and stayed year-round, living pretty much hand to mouth until 1848, when they found the winters too harsh and moved into Boston. Hawthorne first saw Hillside in the winter of 1852 and found it a mess, but he bought it and, after some fixing up, moved in on the day his friend Franklin Pierce was nominated for the presidency. "It is no very splendid mansion," he wrote a friend, "but Mr. Alcott, the Orphic Sayer, of whom I bought it had wasted a good deal of money in fitting it up to suit his own taste—all which improvements I get for little or nothing. Having been much neglected, the place is the raggedest in the world but it will make, sooner or later, a comfortable and sufficiently pleasant home." It was to be the only home Hawthorne ever owned, but it was to be some years later before the Hawthornes, having rechristened it the Wayside, really lived there. That first summer, Hawthorne worked without pause to finish Pierce's campaign biography. When Pierce was elected, Hawthorne expected to get a job, and he was expected by several of his friends, including Melville, to help *them* get jobs. Despite his efforts, Hawthorne was unable to help Melville get a post, but Pierce did appoint Hawthorne American consul at Liverpool, England. Hawthorne served conscientiously throughout Pierce's four years in office, after which he resigned. He then took his family to France and Italy, where he began his last novel, *The Marble Faun* (1860), before returning to England and then to Concord and The Wayside. Upon his return, his first act was to add a new wing with a library on the ground floor, a bedroom above it, and above that, a tower room he expected to use as a study. This last proved all but useless, as it was too hot in the summer, stifling because of a stove in the winter, and comfortable only in the fall and spring. At this point, Hawthorne was writing little and, indeed, he was nearly finished as a writer. Shy as ever, he often avoided visitors who sought him out by retreating to a path on the ridge that is still behind the house. He also walked this path into Concord so as to avoid his garrulous neighbor Alcott who sat, like a kind of Ancient Mariner, before Orchard House, waylaying passersby and bending their ears for as long as he could keep them. The Civil War lowered Hawthorne's morale and he began to suffer from a nameless—though nonetheless debilitating—fatigue of the spirit. Physically, he began to deteriorate as well, and his once astonishing good looks aged quickly. In April 1864, he traveled south with his publisher William Ticknor, but this trip, undertaken to lift his spirits, ended in disaster when Ticknor died suddenly in Philadelphia. Returning to Concord, a shaken and agitated Hawthorne walked from the railroad station to his home, arriving pale, feverish, and confused. This foreshadowed the May trip to New Hampshire with Pierce, from which Hawthorne did not return. At his funeral, Emerson pointed to "the painful solitude of the man—which, I suppose, could no longer be endured, & he died of it." Hawthorne's wife and family kept the Wayside until 1870. In 1883 it became home to a third literary family when Daniel and **Harriet Lothrop** (1844–1924) bought it. Here Harriet, under the pseudonym Margaret Sidney, wrote the *Five Little Peppers* series of children's books, *Five Little Peppers and How They Grew* being the most famous. Her husband became a publisher of children's books, and their daughter Margaret both preserved the Wayside and wrote its history. The house is now open from mid-April through October.

All of Concord's major writers are buried on Author's Ridge in Sleepy Hollow Cemetery, which is on Route 62/Bedford Street just outside of town. Except for Hawthorne's, their graves are unremarkable. When Julian Hawthorne came to write his father's biography, he dedicated to his wife Minnie "these records of a happy marriage." By all accounts, and in the record of their constant loving attention to one another, Nathaniel and Sophia Hawthorne enjoyed an exceptionally happy and fulfilled marriage. Odd then that Hawthorne is alone on Author's Ridge. His grave is marked by stones at its head and foot, both of which say *Hawthorne* in raised letters. Nothing more. Small stones next to these announce that Sophia and their oldest daughter Una are buried in Kensal Green, London. Their other daughter, Rose, is buried in New York, and son Julian is buried in San Francisco. Hawthorne's solitary gravesite alone is one of the smaller of those "mysteries" that his friend Melville so cryptically brought up, but did not detail, in his interview with Julian.

During its literary heyday, there were also not-so-famous writers living in Concord. **William Ellery Channing** (1818–1900)—known as Ellery to distinguish him from his uncle, the clergyman William Ellery Channing—moved with his wife Ellen, Margaret Fuller's sister, to Concord, so as to be near Emerson, who had first noted his poems. The irascible, messy (Thoreau called his style "sublimoslipshod") Channing outlived his Concord friends by so many years that he wrote the first biography of Thoreau and became a source to those scholars and writers looking into the lives and works of the Transcendentalists. **Franklin B. Sanborn** (1831–1917) first came to Concord as a schoolteacher. His involvement with antislavery activities was so intense he joined the "Secret Seven" who raised money for John Brown's Harper's Ferry raid. The authorities came to Concord to seize Sanborn, implicated in the raid, but his friends and neighbors helped him remain free. In later life, he wrote biographies of Thoreau, the Alcotts and, with a collaborator, Emerson. **Margaret Fuller** (1810–1850), a prodigy who is said to have read Ovid at eight, belonged to Emerson's "Hedges Club," in which were held the discussions that led to Transcendentalism. She edited *The Dial* from 1840 to 1842 and published what has been called "the first mature consideration of feminism," *Women in the Nineteenth Century*, in 1845. She went to Europe in 1846 and soon found herself in Italy, where she became a follower of the revolutionary Giuseppe Mazzini and married one of his associates, the Marquis Angelo Ossoli. While there, she wrote a book on the Roman revolt which she planned to publish upon her return to New York. In a storm off New York's Fire Island, the ship bearing her and her family ran aground and, over a night and day, broke up. The bodies of Fuller and Ossoli were not found, but the body of their infant son washed up on shore. Emerson sent Thoreau to the site of the disaster in the hope that he might find some of Fuller's papers or other effects, but he returned only with vivid memories of the bodies washed ashore, and a button from Ossoli's coat.

Visitors entering Concord by car—and it requires a car to get around to all the sites—can stop at the Visitor Information Booth on Heywood Street to pick up an excellent map of all the places written about above. This map will also direct them to the Concord Free Public Library, where one of the pencils manufactured by the Thoreau family is on display, and to all the many historical sights in town. The booth is open weekends from mid-April through May, and daily from June through October. What visitors will *not* find there is an answer to why all this literary activity occurred in such a small town. Emerson's standing, and his sense of intellectual community, was such that he would have drawn like-minded souls to him most anyplace he lived. An accident of birth placed Thoreau in Concord. Channing and Fuller sought out Emerson; the Alcotts and Hawthorne came to the place, in large part, because Emerson and Thoreau had put it on the literary map. Perhaps the town itself, and the surrounding landscape, helped attract them. While Boston was water- and hill-bound, Concord's rich farm lands were watered by three rivers. There was less woodland than now, the wood being cleared for building, fuel, and to make fields. In the first half of the 19th century, Concord evolved into a modest mill town which still functioned as a market center. It was, in short, the country but not the boondocks, and it was convenient to Boston by train. "Hell, half the world wants to be like Thoreau at Walden," the painter Franz Kline said, "worrying about the noise of traffic on the way to Boston; the other half use up their lives being part of that noise." In Concord, writers could have their portion of both.

CUMMINGTON

William Cullen Bryant (1794–1878) was born and raised here, and today his home, the William Cullen Bryant Homestead, is open to the public during the summer months. In it he spent his boyhood there, and at age eighteen (although some say he was sixteen), he wrote one of his two or three most famous poems, "Thanatopsis." As he was determined to make a career in the law, he did not publish the poem until 1817. The poem made him famous, and he ended his legal career in 1825 to begin work as an editor in New York. Among his many books are translations of *The Iliad* and *The Odyssey*. Although he summered at his Cummington home, his decidedly New York orientation makes him something of a peripheral figure in New England. The Homestead, originally a one-and-a-half-story house, was expanded and elevated to two-and-a-half stories in 1856. Bryant's study was in the house's smaller wing. Today some of his personal effects and souvenirs from trips abroad are on display.

DEDHAM

In the summer of 1921, **Nicola Sacco** (1891–1927) and **Bartolomeo Vanzetti** (1888–1927), Italian anarchists who spoke no English at the time, were tried for murder and found guilty in the Dedham courthouse. Their crime was the April 1920 murder of a South Braintree shoe factory paymaster and his guard. On August 27, 1927, they were electrocuted in Charlestown. Fifty years later, Massachusetts Governor Michael Dukakis proclaimed the anniversary of their executions "Nicola Sacco and Bartolomeo Vanzetti

Memorial Day." No New England crime or trial has ever excited such passionate political and literary interest as the Sacco and Vanzetti case. But this was not true at the moment they were pronounced guilty. In fact, for several years as their lawyers filed appeal upon appeal, interest in the case was limited to radical political circles. In the spring of 1927, Harvard law professor Felix Frankfurter, who became a United States Supreme Court justice, published in *The Atlantic Monthly* "The Case of Sacco and Vanzetti." His accusations of "Red hysteria," outside and inside the Dedham courtroom, and of prejudice on the part of trial judge Webster Thayer, helped make the case an issue worldwide. Neither Frankfurter's eloquence nor the work of Sacco and Vanzetti's lawyers—nor a commission appointed by Governor Alvah T. Fuller and chaired by Harvard president Abbott Lawrence Lowell—overturned the guilty verdict. As their executions drew near, thousands picketed the Massachusetts State House. In her 1977 memoir *The Never-Ending Wrong,* novelist Katherine Anne Porter remembers John Dos Passos and Edna St. Vincent Millay among the picketeers. At their deaths, Sacco and Vanzetti became martyrs as foreigners and anarchists to America's post-World War I Red Scare, and their innocence became an article of faith for American political radicals and liberals. The trial transcripts, records of appeals, leads of all manner, and ballistic tests have been raked over in attempts to prove their innocence or to make the convictions stick. At this date, it is unlikely that their guilt or innocence will ever be conclusively proven. Many who know the case agree that the best presentation of the facts is available in the novel *Boston* (1928) by **Upton Sinclair** (1878–1968), who covered the trial. The case has a wealth of other literary associations. When it was discovered that the original 1937 edition of the WPA guide *Massachusetts: A Guide to its Places and People* gave more lines to the case than to the Boston Tea Party, an uproar ensued that led to the publisher, Houghton Mifflin, to delete all references to the case. Evidently, some copies of the guide were destroyed before Harry Hopkins of the WPA intervened to thwart the censors. Sacco and Vanzetti's letters—they both learned English in prison—have long been in print. Vanzetti especially had what Francis Russell, who began by doubting their guilt but has become convinced of at least Sacco's participation in the crime, calls "the gift of words." In a final interview Sacco declared, "Our words—our lives—nothing! The taking of our lives—lives of a good shoemaker and poor fish ped-dlar—all!" At the fiftieth anniversary conference held to discuss the case at the Boston Public Library (a book reprinting the papers given is for sale at the Library's Copley Square main branch), it was revealed that a portion of the ashes of Sacco and Vanzetti are held there, among papers relating to the case.

EASTHAM

Henry Beston (1888–1968) came to this Cape Cod town in 1927 and moved into a 16' × 24' shack on the beach. Intending to spend no more than a month, he fell in love with the sea, the isolation, and the area's flora and fauna and stayed for a year. He wrote of this experience in *The Outermost House*, a classic of its kind. Beston gave the shack to the Audubon Society, but a storm washed it away in 1964. In 1957, Sylvia Plath and her husband Ted Hughes spent the summer in Beston's cabin.

GLOUCESTER

In 1896, **T. S. Eliot**'s (1888–1965) father built the summer house Eastern Point. Eliot remembered his summers here, and his love of sailing, in the third of his *Four Quartets*, "The Dry Salvages." It takes its title from the rocky ledge and outcropping, visible sometimes at low tide, off the Northeast coast of Cape Ann. These rocks were originally named by French sailors "Les Trois Savages," but this was gradually corrupted, yielding the present name. A buoy marks the "salvages." As Eliot piloted his boat out of Gloucester har-bor and around Cape Ann, he used it as a marker. This is where Eliot, born and raised in St. Louis, Missouri, first heard the sea's "many gods and many voices."

Charles Olson (1910–1970), too, came to Gloucester as a boy. His mail-man father first brought the family here for summer holidays in 1915, and Olson was to return throughout his life until he settled here after closing Black Mountain College in the mid-1950s. Here Olson met his first mentor, the novelist **Edward Dahlberg** (1900–1977), who encouraged Olson's work on Melville and who was to be responsible for introducing Olson to Black Mountain, the experimental college dedicated to the arts which struggled to survive through Olson's tenure as rector in the late forties until he closed the college in the mid-fifties. It was at Black Mountain that Olson began to see Gloucester as his abiding subject—"my front yard," he called it—and to write his epic *The Maximus Poems* set there. He originally conceived of the poems as "letters" and in his first letter Maximus blesses "the roofs, the old ones, the gentle steep ones/on whose ridge-poles the gulls sit, from which they depart,/And the flake-racks/of my city!" At six feet, eight inches tall, Olson was himself a Maximus, and he came to think of Gloucester as his city, writing many letters to the editor of the Gloucester newspaper and filling his poem with the city's history and geography. A map of Gloucester, a chart of its harbor and surrounding waters, and a map of the area called "Dogtown," often painted by Marsden Hartley, will illuminate Olson's poem as much as any work of criticism yet written. In the kitchen of his apartment at 28 Fort Square, now a private home, Olson kept tacked to the wall a chart of Gloucester's inner harbor, on which he made notes for his Maximus letters. From this apartment Olson could look out at Babson's Ledge, Cresseys Beach, and Stage Head Point, all of which figure in his poem. Olson spent the last years of his life working in this apartment, between teaching semesters at the University of Connecticut in Storrs, which now has his papers. Olson's burial in Beechwood Cemetery has—as with much else about this outsized man—become mythologized. Olson's biographer Tom Clark has the poet Allen Ginsberg "accidentally triggering the coffin-release mechanism" to send Olson's coffin "plunging through the portals of the underworld." I was there, and this is not what happened. Ginsberg was present and sang Kaddish, but it was the officiating priest under whose nervous foot the mechanism jammed. The coffin shuddered, tipped, and got stuck. There was no "headlong rush akin to that of his poetry," but there were copious drinks afterwards at the Tavern, one of Olson's watering holes. The bartender knew him, as did many in the town in which he had rooted his poems, mindful of place as no other American poet save William Carlos Williams. Olson was, as he writes in his great poem "The Librarian," "caught/in Gloucester."

Gloucester has numerous other literary associations. Louisa May Alcott was a frequent summer visitor, as was William Rose Benét. It was here that Rudyard Kipling came to research *Captains Courageous* (1897). Norman's

Woe, a reef off West Gloucester, causes disaster in Longfellow's poem "The Wreck of the Hesperus" as "Like a sheeted ghost, the vessel swept/Tow'rds the reef of Norman's Woe."

GREENFIELD

Frederick Goddard Tuckerman (1821–1873), a Boston lawyer, retired here after the death of his wife and lived as a recluse. His one published book, *Poems* (1860), met praise from Emerson and from Tennyson, whom Tuckerman visited in England. While in Greenfield, he studied botany and astronomy and added occasionally to his sonnet series. His work was redis-covered by the poet Witter Bynner, who edited *Sonnets* (1931). A *Complete Poems* appeared in 1965. The critic Yvor Winters rated Tuckerman's poems above those of the British Romantics for their "description of natural detail."

HARVARD

Fruitlands represents the hippie streak in Transcendentalism. In a red farmhouse on a valley floor here, **Bronson Alcott** (1799–1888) and English Transcendentalist Charles Lane gathered a "Con-Sociate Family" determined to found a new Eden. Including Alcott, his wife, and four children, there were a dozen in the family. They planned to live on fruits and vegetables and to wear linen, so as to leave the sheep his wool. Cotton was banned, as it was a product of slave labor. Fruitlands began June 1, 1843. Among the members were Joseph Palmer, said to have the most famous beard in America; the Adamite (nudist) Samuel Bower; Samuel Larned, who had lived one year on crackers and the next on apples; and Wood Abram, who announced his Transcendentalism by reversing his name from Abram Wood. Beside the five Alcott women, the only other woman was Anne Page, who was soon sent packing for keeping—or so the rumor went—cheese in her trunk. Emerson visited the group in midsummer and reported, "I will not prejudge them suc-cessful. They look well in July; we will see them in December. " They were there in December, but by mid-January 1844 the family, not eight months old, had broken up. Alcott and Lane had been off talking up the virtues of Fruitlands when they should have been minding the crops, and Lane's increasing convictions against marriage had added to the disharmony. He decided to join a nearby Shaker community. Alcott took his family to the town of Still River and then to Concord. After the failure of Fruitlands, Alcott wrote to his brother: "Such a disproportion between my desires and deeds!" Today, Fruitlands is a museum open from April to the end of October. The farmhouse has been recently painted and contains not only "Family" memorabilia but a desk used by Thoreau and a collection of arrowheads found by him. The rooms are small, too small you might think for all the "Family" members, and their low ceilings and layout impart a sense of how intimate New England farmhouses of this period must have been. Fruitlands comprises several other buildings, including a museum of Indian artifacts. There is also a restaurant that overlooks the valley in which the farmhouse sits. On bright fall days after the leaves have turned, the view is splendid.

HAVERHILL

The handsome white farmhouse where **John Greenleaf Whittier** (1807–1892) was born still stands on Whittier Road, and is open from Patriots Day in April to Columbus Day in October. This is the setting for Whittier's poem "Snow-Bound," and the desk on which he wrote his early poems is on display. Before selling the house and moving down the Merrimack River to Amesbury, Whittier edited the *Essex Gazette,* one of a number of newspapers he worked on.

HOLYOKE

Born here, **John Clellon Holmes** (1926–1988) met Jack Kerouac, Allen Ginsberg, and Neal Cassady in New York City in 1948, and became a father of the "Beat Generation." Holmes's first novel *Go* (1952), dedicated to Kerouac "who talked it," begins the saga of the generation he—and, more famously, Kerouac—continued through the 1950s. Like Kerouac's *On the Road,* Holmes's *Go* can be described as a roman à clef. This is accurate but overly literary. In it, Cassady, Ginsberg, Herbert Huncke, and William Burroughs are all easily recognizable. Unlike Kerouac, who returned again and again to his hometown Lowell, Holmes wrote little about growing up in

Holyoke. In 1967, Holmes published *Nothing More to Declare*. Its autobiographical essays vividly recreate the Beat scene.

IPSWICH

Anne Bradstreet (c. 1612–1672), the daughter of one Governor of the Massachusetts Bay Colony, Thomas Dudley, married another, Simon Bradstreet, at age sixteen, and came to America in the "great Migration" of 1630. She found the country "a new world and new manners, at which my heart rose." Bradstreet spent nearly a decade here before moving—they were pioneers then—to North Andover, where she lived the rest of her life. She is the author of the first book of poems written by an English woman in America. In 1650, her brother-in-law took her poems to England, where they were published under the title *The Tenth Muse Lately sprung up in America: Or, Severall Poems, compiled with great variety of Wit and Learning, full of delight.* Critics have pointed out how derivative and stiff these poems are, but that does not make their sentiments any less heartfelt. "If ever two were one, then surely we./If ever man were loved by wife, then thee," Bradstreet wrote "To My Dear and Loving Husband." Her manuscripts are now at Harvard's Houghton Library. In 1956, John Berryman published his biographical poem *Homage to Mistress Bradstreet*.

LANCASTER

Mary Rowlandson (c.1635–c.1678) begins her account of her eleven-week captivity during King Philip's War like this: "On the tenth of February, 1675, came the Indians with great numbers upon Lancaster. Their first coming was about sun-rising. Hearing the noise of some guns, we looked out: several houses were burning, and the smoke ascending to heaven. There were five persons taken in one house. The father, the mother, and a sucking child they knockt on the head, the other two they took and carried away alive."

Mary, wife of the Reverend Joseph Rowlandson, was ultimately released for ransom. Her account of her weeks in captivity was published in Cambridge, Massachusetts, in 1862 as *The Soveraignty and Goodness of God: Together with the Faithfulness of His Promises Displayed; Being a Narrative of the*

Captivity and Restoration of Mrs. Mary Rowlandson. Her book became immediately popular, has been published in at least forty editions, and is in print today as *The Captive.* Indigenous to America, captivity narratives such as Rowlandson's were much written and read during the 17th century and into the 18th century. They are usually testaments to the captives' religious faith, but the horror stories described therein are grisly enough to hold any imagination.

LAWRENCE

At the age of ten, **Robert Frost** (1874–1963) came with his mother came to Lawrence. He stayed through high school, graduating as valedictorian. His co-valedictorian was Elinor Miriam White. Three years later, after at least one upheaval that caused Frost to consider suicide in Virginia's Great Dismal Swamp, Frost and White were married.

Born here, **Ernest Lawrence Thayer** (1863–1940) wrote, in 1888, one of America's few truly popular poems, "Casey at the Bat." Lines such as "There is no joy in Mudville" and "Mighty Casey has struck out" have entered the language.

LEOMINSTER

Look up **Johnny Appleseed** (c. 1775–1845) in the current American Heritage Dictionary and you will be directed to his real name, John Chapman, where the definition reads: "American pioneer and subject of many legends. He traveled widely in the Ohio River valley, planting apple seeds and pruning apple trees." The citizens of Leominster claim that Chapman was born there in a log cabin on the banks of the Nashua River, and they have a plaque saying so. In Springfield's Stebbins Park, there is another plaque claiming that Chapman spent his boyhood "in this pleasant valley or somewhere near by." Springfield rests its claim on what the farmers in Indiana and Ohio, on whose lands Chapman became Johnny Appleseed, remembered him as having told them. B. A. Botkin, who edited *A Treasury of New England Folklore,* judges Springfield to be correct. He also writes that Chapman's father drowned while fishing in South Hadley, leaving the boy on his own at the age of eighteen. In the 1930s, Leominster librarian Florence Wheeler was able to determine that Chapman, son of the Minuteman Nathaniel Chapman and his first wife, was indeed born in Leominster in 1774. At some unknown time, the Chapmans moved west to Springfield. It seems appropriate that a legend's early years be surrounded by such confusion. When Appleseed walked the Ohio River valley, he must have struck the farmers as having been born out of thin air, so wondrous was his behavior.

LOWELL

Lowell bears the name of Francis Cabot Lowell, "the Father of American Cotton Manufacturing," who first arrived around 1800. After studying British textile mills, he invented a workable power loom, and saw—in the waterpower of the Merrimack River and the transportation possibilities of the Pawtucket Canal—features that would make Lowell one of the state's foremost mill towns. It took men and women working fourteen-hour days, six days a week, to make it so. Throughout the 19th century and into the 20th century the mills hummed, but they were brought low by the Crash of 1929. The city suffered a slow deterioration as more and more mills went south in search of cheap labor. Today, Lowell's mills and canals are a sort of theme park. Refurbished by the federal government in the 1980s, Lowell's industrial center is perhaps the best place in New England to get some sense of the industrial energy that drove the region for more than 100 years. Those who come in search of **Edgar Allan Poe** (1809–1848) and **Jack Kerouac** (1922–1969) will find the brick bones and watery arteries of industry, and be able to imagine the giant that was.

Poe made three visits to Lowell, each one rife with romantic or financial complications. In July 1848, he came to lecture on "The Poets and Poetry of America," after which he read "The Raven." But he made that visit as much to pursue the poet Jane Locke, with whom he had been in correspondence. She greatly admired Poe's work, and Poe took her to be a widow and worthy of his attentions. On this visit he discovered that she was married, but he met another married woman, Nancy Richmond, and developed a crush on her. That fall he returned to Lowell, repeated his lecture, and while remaining friendly with Jane Locke he pursued Mrs. Richmond, whose first name—he decided—ought to be changed to Annie. His 1849 poem "For Annie" ("But my heart is brighter/Than all of the many/Stars in the sky,/For it sparkles with Annie") is dedicated to her. At the time, Poe was torn between her and Sarah Helen Whitman of Providence. The following spring he came for the third and last time to Lowell, still in pursuit of Nancy/Annie and also of subscribers for his magazine, *Stylus*. On this trip he bounced a check, had two daguerreotpyes taken for which Annie paid, picked up few *Stylus* subscribers, and seems to have been a delightful guest in the Richmond home. Today the Worthen House bar, which claims Poe drank there, has Poe tee-shirts for sale next to idealized portraits of native son Kerouac.

The mills that hummed during Kerouac's youth in Lowell still stand, but today they are quiet, part of a refurbished, if not a revitalized, Lowell. In the late 1970s and early 1980s, the downtown and adjacent mills were made into a sort of theme park administered by the National Park Service. The planners fit Kerouac, the town's most famous son, into this concept, and he has been honored by a public space of simple dignity but still greater in scale than any other memorial to a writer in New England. On Bridge Street, eight red granite columns by the sculptor Ben Woitena are inscribed with Kerouac quotations from *Mexico City Blues, Lonesome Traveller, Doctor Sax* (Kerouac's great Lowell novel), *On the Road,* and other of his books. There are benches where the visitor can sit and think Kerouac thoughts as he scans round at the mills, now made over into apartments, a tenement block housing Sully's Formal Wear and an old-fashioned dining car-type diner, Arthur's Paradise Diner. One column bears *On the Road*'s last paragraph:

> So in America when the sun goes down and I sit on the old broken-down river pier watching the long, long skies over New Jersey and sense all that raw land that rolls in one unbelievable huge bulge over to the West Coast, and all that road going, all the people dreaming in the immensity of it, and in Iowa I know by now the children must be crying in the land where they let children cry, and tonight the stars'll be out, and don't you know that God is Pooh Bear? the evening star must be drooping and shedding her sparkler dims on the prairie, which is

just before the coming of complete night that blesses the earth, darkens all rivers, cups the peaks and folds the final shore in, and nobody, nobody knows what's going to happen to anybody besides the forlorn rags of growing old, I think of Dean Moriarty, I even think of Old Dean Moriarty the father we never found, I think of Dean Moriarty.

At the National Park Center information center, where Market Street meets the Merrimack Canal, visitors can get a serviceable map that will help them find many sites associated with Kerouac. He and his family lived in eight houses in the city's Centralville, Little Canada, and Pawtucketville sections. Kerouac's Lupine Street birthplace, his Sarah Avenue, Moody Street, and University Avenue (number 118, on the fourth floor above Astro's Sub Shop) apartments still stand, and you can cross the Moody Street Bridge as the boys do in *Maggie Cassidy* (1959) and see "The Grotto" behind the Franco-American Orphanage which haunts the boy in *Doctor Sax.* It was Kerouac's star play as running back for Lowell High School—still there today—that earned him a scholarship to Columbia, where he played for Lou Little before taking up with the generation of writers, dreamers, misfits, and outlaws he named "the Beat Generation." Kerouac came back to Lowell rarely after 1940, but his imagination never left the place, and the city and his growing up in it became one pole of his work. In 1967 he did return, drunk and exhausted, a bloated shadow of his youthful self—"almost beyond injury," as one friend described him. He stayed a short time, then moved with his wife and mother to St. Petersburg, Florida, where he died of an abdominal hemorrhage moments after watching "The Galloping Gourmet" on television (shades of Charlie Parker's death by heart attack while watching the "Tommy Dorsey Show"). Kerouac was waked at the Archambault Funeral Home, and he was buried out of St. Jean Baptiste Church on Merrimack Street. He is buried in the Sampas—his third wife Stella's maiden name—family plot in Edson Cemetery, two miles from the center of Lowell. Maps are available at the National Parks information center. His footstone reads:

"Ti Jean"
John L. Kerouac

Mar. 12, 1922–Oct. 21, 1969
He Honored Life

Kerouac was called "Ti Jean" (Little Jean) as a boy at home. He published his first novel, *The Town and the City*, under the name John L. Kerouac. On my last visit, pilgrims had left a typed Gregory Corso poem, a color lithograph of the young Kerouac, and an empty jug of Gallo port. Annually, on the first weekend in October, "Lowell Celebrates Kerouac" with readings, lectures, tours, films—a mixed bag of activities.

MALDEN

There is a plaque identifying the hard-to-find house at 17 Dale Street in which **Erle Stanley Gardner** (1889–1970) was born. The inventor of Perry Mason, Gardner's "The Case of . . ." novels began to appear in 1933. Thirty years later, they had sold, in the United States, exactly 135,740,861 copies!

Elliot Paul (1891–1958), also born in Malden, is best known as a founding editor, with James Joyce's friend Eugene Jolas, of the Paris magazine *Transition*. He wrote the novel *The Last Time I Saw Paris* (1942) based on his years as an expatriate. It was made into a movie starring Van Johnson as the writer hero, and Elizabeth Taylor as his wife.

MARBLEHEAD

H. P. Lovecraft (1890–1937) based his fictional town, Kingsport, on Marblehead. Several of his stories, including "The Festival," are set here. For three years at the end of his life, a very ill **Eugene O'Neill** (1888–1953) lived here.

MARTHA'S VINEYARD

A great many writers have vacationed on this island, but only a few have done more than pass a few weeks or a summer. Henry Beetle Hough came to Edgartown in 1920 and edited the *Vineyard Gazette* for many years. He produced a number of books about his experiences as a country newspaper editor, as well as a biography of Thoreau. **Lillian Hellman** (1905–1984), playwright, screenwriter, and autobiographer, came here first in the summer of 1948 to work on a play based on Norman Mailer's novel *The Naked and the Dead*. She soon dropped the Mailer project, but she returned to the Vineyard as a renter before buying, in 1956, the first of two houses she was to own. The house stood on a bluff overlooking one of the island's many private beaches. Hellman liked the privacy—"if," as she wrote a friend, "you can discount the army of young who fornicate, I guess, during the nice summer evenings." **Dashiell Hammett** (1894–1961), the mystery writer who for more than thirty years was *the* man in Hellman's life, lived in a guest house on the property. A heart attack had slowed him and intensified his reclusive nature, and he often steered clear of Hellman's guests. By this time in their relationship he was totally dependent on Hellman, and he remained so until he died in New York City in 1961. After Hammett's death, Hellman moved to a smaller house she had designed for herself, with a view of Vineyard Haven harbor. Hellman enjoyed fishing in the ocean. In the first of the autobiographical works she wrote late in life, *An Unfinished Woman* (1969), she tells a gripping story about how, when fishing alone, she survived a fall from her boat into the sea. **Thornton Wilder** (1897–1975) had a house on the island toward the end of his life. Here he worked on *Theophilus North* (1973), the novel set in Newport that was to be his last book. In late August 1990, **A. Bartlett Giamatti** (1936–1991), the only commissioner of major league baseball to have been president of Yale University and to have written a book on Edmund Spenser's poetry, died here suddenly of a heart attack. A week before his death, Giamatti had banned Pete Rose, who has the most hits in major league history, from the game—making it impossible for Rose to be a candidate for the Hall of Fame. In addition to his scholarly work, Giamatti wrote a book about the glories he found in the game of baseball.

MEDFORD

The poet and translator of Dante John Ciardi graduated from Tufts University here; historian Francis Parkman lived on his uncle's Medford farm for five years as a boy, and while at Harvard, Thomas Wolfe visited the Medford home of his uncle. A thin thread of literary associations, except for the brief time the novelist **Nathanael West** (1904–1940) spent as a Tufts student, during which he went under his real name, Nathan Wallenstein Weinstein. Weinstein's first-semester (1921) grades were so abysmal that Tufts asked him to leave. He transferred to Brown and arrived there to find himself a second-semester sophomore. An error by the Tufts registrar had given Weinstein the credits of his namesake, Nathan Weinstein. Never one to take college seriously, West registered no complaint about his sudden change in status, and he graduated from Brown in 1924. During the 1970s, poet Denise Levertov taught at Tufts. Poet Marie Howe, MacArthur Award-winning novelist Jay Cantor, and novelist Jonathan Strong are among the writers who teach there today.

METHUEN

During the French and Indian wars, **Robert Rogers** (1731–1795) commanded a band of "Rangers" who used Indian-style guerrilla tactics against Indians menacing villages up and down the Connecticut River. Rogers led them in the famous Battle on Snowshoes. He later defended Detroit against Chief Pontiac, an action described by Francis Parkman in his *History of the Conspiracy of Pontiac*. Rogers was a writer as well as a warrior. He published his *Journals* and *A Concise Account of North America* in 1765, and the following year his play *Pontech* was the first American play to use Indians as its subject. Kenneth Roberts (1885–1957) wrote about Rogers in his historical novel *Northwest Passage* (1937), and Spencer Tracy played him in the popular movie made from the book.

NANTUCKET

Nantucket! Take out your map and look at it. See what a real corner of the world it occupies; how it stands there, away off shore, more lonely than the Eddystone lighthouse. Look at it—a mere hillock, and elbow of sand; all beach without a background. There is more sand there than you might use in twenty years as a substitute for blotting paper.

So wrote **Herman Melville** (1819–1891) in *Moby Dick*. The whaler *Pequod* in the novel, owned by the Quaker captains Peleg and Bildad, sails from Nantucket. Robert Lowell's "The Quaker Graveyard in Nantucket," his elegy for his cousin Warren Winslow, takes its name from an actual Nantucket graveyard. The poem's opening is lifted almost verbatim from Thoreau's description of the bodies washed ashore after the *St. John* wrecked on the Massachusetts coast. **Robert Benchley** (1889–1945), writer, humorist, Algonquin Round Table wit, and actor, is buried in the Benchley family plot in Prospect Hill Cemetery. Many remarks have been attributed to him, the most famous being, "Why don't you slip out of those wet clothes and into a dry martini?" His son **Nathaniel Benchley** (1915–1981), novelist, screenwriter, and biographer, lived here for his last decade, and *his* son **Peter Benchley** set the bestselling novel *Jaws* (1974) on another island, Martha's Vineyard. In the late 1940s the playwright **Tennessee Williams** (1911–1983) rented a cottage here and had his friend, the novelist **Carson McCullers** (1917–1967), as a houseguest. Through the summer, they worked at opposite ends of a long table; Williams wrote the play *Summer and Smoke* and McCullers wrote the successful Broadway adaptation of her novel *The Member of the Wedding* (1946). **John Cheever** (1912–1982) rented several cottages here over several summers and often used the island as a setting for short stories, "The Seaside Houses" notable among them.

NEW BEDFORD

On January 3, 1841, **Herman Melville** (1819–1891) shipped out of this whaling port on the maiden voyage of the *Acushnet*. He jumped ship in the Marquesa Islands, and his adventures there and on subsequent voyages and in Hawaii (he set pins in a Honolulu bowling alley) became the source for his first three books, *Typee, Omoo,* and *Mardi.* He did not return to America until 1844. New Bedford's "Seaman's Bethel"—it faces the Bourne Whaling Museum—is the model for the church in *Moby Dick* where Ishmael hears Father Mapple's sermon. Anyone interested in Melville and *Moby Dick* will want to visit the Whaling Museum. There, among much else, they will learn, as the

WPA guide has it, that "Whaling was filthy, dangerous and uncomfortable work, but it was exciting."

Albert Bigelow Paine, Mark Twain's biographer and literary executor, was born here in 1861, as was Martha's Vineyard newspaper editor Henry Beetle Hough in 1896. William Ellery Channing worked here briefly as a newspaper editor; Frederick Douglass (1817–1895) stopped in New Bedford for a time after fleeing from Maryland; and Louisa May Alcott had a summer place south of the city. Conrad Aiken came to New Bedford to stay with his aunt after the murder-suicide of his parents in Savannah, Georgia. Aiken wrote of this tragedy in his short story "Silent Snow, Secret Snow." New Bedford appears in both his novel *Blue Voyage* (1927) and his autobiography, *Ushant* (1952).

NEWBURYPORT

A statue of **William Lloyd Garrison** (1805–1879), who was born here December 10, 1805, stands in Brown Square. Before he moved to Boston and began his abolitionist paper *The Liberator,* he argued the cause in the Newburyport *Free Press,* where he was among the first editors to publish John Greenleaf Whittier's poems.

John P. Marquand spent some part of each year of his boyhood at the family home in Curzon's Mill, just outside of Newburyport. In 1925 he published a biography of **Timothy Dexter** (1747–1806)—Lord Timothy by his own decree—a prominent local eccentric. Dexter's house on High Street, where the stately homes of shipowners and captains from Newburyport's heyday still stand, was notorious because he crowded into his yard wooden statues of famous men. Among them reared a bust of Dexter himself. His neighbors came to think him crazy. In 1802, he published the pamphlet "A Pickle for the Knowing Ones." His spelling was original, and he had not bothered to punctuate. When he became aware of the latter he printed an edition that included a few pages of commas and periods. Readers were invited to use these as they saw fit; in Dexter's words, to "peper and solt it as they plese." No matter how off-putting Dexter was, he did very well in business, and he laughed all the way to the bank. Eventually, the weather destroyed his collection of statues.

NORTHAMPTON

George Washington Cable (1844–1925), Confederate army veteran, friend of Mark Twain, and author of stories and novels set in Louisiana, came here in 1886 and spent the rest of his life in his house, Tarryawhile. Cable's fiction made him a leader of the local-color movement. His most famous work was also his first, *Old Creole Days*, a collection of stories published in 1879. Twain once called him "the south's finest literary genius." Cable came north because his mother was a New Englander, but he continued to write novels about the South. He taught at Smith and is buried in Northampton's Bridge Street Cemetery. Among other writers who taught at Smith are Daniel Aaron, Newton Arvin, the biographer of Melville and Whitman, **W. H. Auden** (1907–1973), the novelist and essayist Mary Ellen Chase (1887–1973), and the critic Granville Hicks (1901–1982). Margaret Mitchell (1900–1949), whose one book was *Gone with the Wind* (1936), studied briefly at Smith. Anne Morrow Lindbergh graduated as, in 1955, did **Sylvia Plath** (1932–1963). Plath came to Smith on an **Olive Higgins Prouty** (1882–1974, Smith graduate and author of *Stella Dallas*, 1922) scholarship. A few days after her arrival at Smith, Plath exclaimed in a letter home, "I still can't believe I'm a SMITH GIRL!" Prouty was to become something of a patron, encouraging Plath through letters and with checks on birthdays and at Christmas. In 1956, the year after her Smith graduation, Plath and her husband the British poet Ted Hughes came to Smith, where Plath spent the year teaching. "The Disquieting Muses" and "Full Fathom Five" are two of the poems she wrote in a year that was to end unhappily as she became increasingly paranoid.

NORWELL

John Cheever (1912–1982) is buried in the cemetery across the street from the First Parish Unitarian Church. He lies next to his mother and father. His slate stone copies those of the 17th century and is engraved with a weeping willow and his dates. John Updike gave the eulogy at his funeral held in the church.

PROVINCETOWN

Known as P-Town, Greenwich Village by the sea, this became a watering hole for writers when Greenwich Village was still the Village of literary legend. In 1915, **George Cram Cook** (1873–1924) and his wife **Susan Glaspell** (1882–1948) began the Provincetown Players, a theater company that they moved the following year to the Village, where the Provincetown Playhouse is open today. The Players produced **Eugene O'Neill**'s (1888–1953) first play "Bound East for Cardiff" in Provincetown, and he became their major discovery. O'Neill spent a few summers on the Provincetown dunes at Race Point. The shack he lived in has long since washed out to sea. The journalist **John Reed** (1887–1920)—who covered the Russian Revolution in *Ten Days That Shook the World* and who is buried in the Kremlin—and his wife Louise Bryant were members of the Players. Their Provincetown summer resulted in O'Neill and Bryant having an affair. As successful as the theater was, it did not satisfy Cook, who left it and journeyed to Greece, where he became some sort of holy man whom peasants were said to venerate. Glaspell wrote Cook's biography, *The Road to the Temple* (1926), with the Greek experience uppermost in her mind. She went on to write a number of plays, winning the Pulitzer Prize in 1930 for *Alison's House*. John Dos Passos, Sinclair Lewis, Edmund Wilson, Tennessee Williams, and numerous other writers spent summers in Provincetown, or passed through. Since the beginning of the century, Provincetown has been unusually attractive to painters. Charles Hawthorne had a school here, as did Hans Hoffmann. Robert Motherwell, Franz Kline, Helen Frankenthaler and Jack Tworkov, Ford Madox Ford's brother-in-law—all had studios in town.

Norman Mailer's novel *Tough Guys Don't Dance* (he also directed the movie made from it) will give readers a taste of what P-Town bohemia became in the 1980s. During the winter there is a great deal of literary activity, readings and workshops, at the Provincetown Center for the Arts. In the summer the place can be crazy with day-trippers and tourists, but there is peace and quiet aroung the town's edges. P-town has not been the quiet retreat artists discovered in the teens since the beatniks brought bohemia into the mainstream in the 1950s. Like most seaside resorts, it is wonderful out of season. The wily summer visitor can avoid the carnival and find a patch of secluded beach, but this takes doing.

QUINCY

Peacefield, bought in 1787 by **John Adams** (1735–1826), then ambassador to the Court of St. James and soon to be the second president of the United States, has been maintained by the National Park Service since 1946. Adams wrote a great deal on social questions and government, and worked on the drafts of the Declaration of Independence. He was also a prolific letter writer, whose letters and papers had a decisive effect on Ezra Pound. Not only do Adams's political ideas play a key roll in Pound's *Cantos*, but Pound took his use of the ampersand and slash, as in spelling should *shl/d*, from Adams. **John Quincy Adams** (1767–1848), sixth president of the United States, followed his father at Peacefield. His memoirs—written, historian Allan Nevins quipped, "with malice toward all"—take up ten volumes. He also wrote poems and the famous *Report on Weights and Measures* (1821). His son, **Charles Francis Adams** (1807–1886), ambassador to the Court of St. James during the Civil War, married money and enlarged Peacefield to its present dimensions. He also built the Stone Library adjacent to the house. He wanted a separate building as a precaution against fire. This beautiful, serene, domed single room holds 14,000 volumes and the desk on which his grandfather wrote the Massachusetts Constitution. Charles Francis edited the *Works of John Adams* (1850–1856), the letters of John's wife Abigail, and the *Memoirs of John Quincy Adams* (1874–1877). He also fathered three sons: **Charles Francis, Jr.** (1835–1915), **Henry** (1838-1918), and **Brooks** (1848-1927). All three were writers, but Henry is the one remembered today because of the book many consider to be a masterpiece, *The Education of Henry Adams*, published in a limited edition in 1907 and made generally available in 1918. There is no American autobiography remotely like it, both for what it reveals and for what it doesn't. Adams's wife Clover, for example, is never mentioned, but the book goes into his theory of history at length. Perhaps in its detachment and insistence on his "failures," the book most resembles the Puritan practice of keeping a spiritual diary, an account of the progress of one's spiritual nature. Adams also wrote novels, a history of the Jefferson and Madison administrations (he worked on this during summers at Peacefield), a great many letters, and *Mont-Saint-Michel and Chartres* (1904), in which he argues that humankind attained a measure of perfection in the 13th century through service to the Virgin. He must have had this last book in mind when he wrote, "My idea of paradise is a perfect automobile going thirty miles an hour on a smooth road to a twelfth-century cathedral." Charles Francis, president of the Union Pacific Railroad and the Kansas City Stockyards, wrote on a great many subjects, despite the demands of his business life. He produced books on railroads, education, politics, and Massachusetts history, and by all accounts he saw his family with a clear eye. Reading James Russell Lowell's letters, he came across the observation, "the Adamses have a genius for saying even a gracious thing in an ungracious way." He was so taken with this that he spoke to the book's editor, Charles Eliot Norton, his feeling that the passage was "keen and true," and that he was glad Norton had left it in. Brother Brooks was the last Adams to live at Peacefield. His bedroom remains as it was then, and the guide will tell you about his dressing for dinner each night, black in winter and white in summer, and his penchant for long baths. He was a historian with a particularly dour view of the world, even for an Adams. The poet Charles Olson admired his book *The New Empire* so much that he wrote an introduction to the reprint that appeared in the late 1960s. Peacefield is in wonderful shape and can be visited from April to the end of October. There are roses in the garden planted by Abigail Adams and the grounds, though small, are a pleasure to stroll.

Quincy is also the birthplace of **Henry Beston** (1888–1968) and, on May 27, 1912, of **John Cheever** (1912–1982).

REVERE

Horatio Alger, Jr. (1832–1899) was born in this small working-class city north of Boston out of which few Ragged Dicks or Tattered Toms have come.

A graduate of the Harvard Divinity School, he served briefly as a Unitarian minister before he was, according to *The Oxford Companion of American Literature*, "ousted for questionable relations with his choirboys." It is hard not to want to believe this. One must have, to borrow from Oscar Wilde, a heart of stone not to chortle over Reverend Alger's history. His Ragged Dick, Luck and Pluck, and Tattered Tom novels, which sold more than 20,000,000 copies, turn Emerson's self-reliance on its ear, and add a dash of Benjamin Franklin, whom D. H. Lawrence called "a mechanical man", to create an American dream world of remarkable appeal. Alger's heroes always stiff-arm temptation and they never fail to triumph over poverty on their way to wealth and fame! It is a story Americans wanted to believe through Alger's 130 books—he always wrote the same story—and one that, in their heart of hearts, they would like to believe today. Nathanael West's cold-blooded and ferociously funny novel *A Cool Million* (1934) takes Alger's novels to the woodshed. A gift for satire is uncommon among American writers; West had it in spades. Alger died at his sister's house in Natick, Massachusetts.

ROCKPORT

While staying at the Yankee Clipper Inn, **Katherine Anne Porter** (1890–1980) finished her first and only novel, *Ship of Fools* (1962). Her reputation as a writer had been based on her short stories, particularly "Noon Wine" and "Pale Horse, Pale Rider," but it was assumed—an assumption that still obscures American literary judgment—that real fiction writers write novels. When, the question was asked so often it became impossible to ignore, will Porter write a novel? It took her years and, so the story goes, the handholding of Boston publisher Seymour Lawrence, to coax out the novel everyone knew she had in her. Upon publication *Ship of Fools* caused a stir, but Porter's best work, then as now, are her stories, for which she received both a Pulitzer Prize and the National Book Award in 1966.

SALEM

Nathaniel Hawthorne (1804–1864) was born on the Fourth of July in a Union Street house that was moved in 1958 to the grounds of the House of the Seven Gables, where it can be visited today. This site, with its ample parking lot, is a major tourist attraction/shrine for visitors to Salem. Hawthorne spent only his first four years in the house of his birth. His family was forced to leave that house when his father, Nathaniel Hathorne (Hawthorne added the *w* while at Bowdoin College), a sea captain, died of a fever in Surinam. Hawthorne's mother, Elizabeth Clarke Manning, went to live in her family's Herbert Street house. This was Hawthorne's home until he left to work at the Boston Custom House in 1839. The house still stands, but it was carved up into apartments years ago. It was to this house that Hawthorne returned upon graduating from Bowdoin to serve one of the strangest apprenticeships in American writing. For a decade he worked in his "chamber under the eaves" in the house he called Castle Dismal. In 1836, his stories making their way into print and his vocation as a writer firmly set, he wrote, "In this dismal and squalid chamber FAME was won." As Hawthorne remembered these years of solitude and painstaking work at his craft, he tended to exaggerate his melancholy and reclusiveness. He did leave Salem, usually alone, to wander, by stagecoach and on foot, through New England. He also liked not only to walk through Salem at night, but to be anonymous in the crowds at celebratory bonfires and musters on the Salem Common. If he was less the recluse than he later claimed, it is understandable why Hawthorne created a mythic glow around those years. He knew that no other American writer had spent the first ten years of his majority working alone, without the comfort or encouragement of friends and colleagues, to meet his destiny. In fact, Hawthorne made it sound as if in that chamber his destiny had found him: "And year after year I kept on considering what I was fit for, and time and my destiny decided that I was to be the writer I am." During these years Hawthorne had "slender means" to support him, but by 1839, as he desired to marry Sophia Peabody, he needed a job, and this, with the help of his soon-to-be sister-in-law Elizabeth Palmer Peabody brought him to Boston. The historian George Bancroft appointed him weigher and gauger at the Boston Custom House, and Hawthorne did not return to Salem until 1845. In 1846 his second child, son Julian, was born and Hawthorne needed a steady income. His Bowdoin friends Horatio Bridge and Franklin Pierce used their influence, and Hawthorne got a political appointment as surveyor in the

Salem Custom House. This stands not far from the House of the Seven Gables on Derby Street and is free and open to visitors, who can see Hawthorne's office as it was during his tenure. After Zachary Taylor's election as president, the Whigs came in and Hawthorne was ousted, not without controversy and some bitterness on Hawthorne's part. He bid "farewell forever to this abominable city" and moved his family to Lenox in the Berkshires where he wrote, in 1850, *The Scarlet Letter*, which established his name and fortune as a writer. Hawthorne's introduction to the novel, "The Custom-House," gives a picture of his work routine and satirizes some of his Salem colleagues. Today, Hawthorne is clearly Salem's favorite son. A statue of him stands on Hawthorne Boulevard, and there are portraits of him in the Essex Institute, which also displays his wallet, a red leather case for calling cards with his monogram, and the lamp he used on Herbert Street. On my last visit, the lamp was in Japan where, the curator assured me, "Hawthorne is very big." The portraits are fascinating. William Inman's depicts Hawthorne at the age of thirty-one, the last year under the eaves, with a mustache and modified Van Dyke beard. He looks scruffy, and is not at all the stunningly handsome man who was said to cause people to gasp when they passed him in the street. The Charles Osgood portrait, painted in 1840, is the handsome Hawthorne and the image by which most of his readers will recognize him.

Few writers are as inextricably linked to their birthplace as Hawthorne. His family arrived in Salem in 1636 and, as Hawthorne well knew, one of his ancestors, John Hathorne, was active in the Salem witchcraft trials. Hathorne, a magistrate, was one of two who examined the first three women to be charged with witchcraft. He and his colleague sent the three women— Sarah Good, Sarah Osborne, and the slave Tituba—to Boston for trial. Critics and readers have traced Hawthorne's preoccupation with sin, guilt, and the Puritan past to these events in Salem and his family's role in them. At times the line drawn is too straight, but Hawthorne's greatest novel, *The Scarlet Letter*, gains in power when you encounter remnants of witchcraft's past in Salem. Nineteen people were hung as witches on Gallows Hill, and several more died in jail. Their deaths have left a permanent mark on the American literary imagination, and you will see it in the work of Stephen King's precursor H. P. Lovecraft, who modeled his fictional Arkham on

Salem, and Arthur Miller, whose play attacking McCarthyism, *The Crucible,* is set—irresistibly, it seems—in Salem at the witchcraft trials.

Two other writers of note were born in Salem. The mystic poet and essayist **Jones Very** (1813–1880), who for a time believed himself to be the second coming of Christ, was born here in 1813, and lived in Salem much of his life. Emerson, Very's champion, said of him, "Such a mind cannot be lost." Very's religious poems aimed at a "will-less existence." The complete opposite of Very is **Nathaniel Bowditch** (1773–1838), who was also born in Salem. Bowditch was the answer to the English Whig and man of letters Sidney Smith, who asked contemptuously, "But *are* there American writers?" It was pointed out to Smith that Bowditch's *The New American Practical Navigator* (1802) was indispensable. Finding 8,000 errors in Moore's *Practical Navigator,* Bowditch corrected them. As a sea captain, he used his experience to revise and expand the navigators then in use. Finally he created his own, which was trustworthy for a century. Bowditch is often held up as one of the triumphs of Yankee ingenuity.

SPRINGFIELD

Theodor Seuss Geisel (1904–1991)—Dr. Seuss—was born here at 162 Sumner Avenue, a house that still stands but is privately owned. It will doubtless be on the Seuss walking tour Springfield is currently planning. The city fathers have gone so far as to ask the owner who tore down 51 Mulberry Street to rebuild it. In that house, Dr. Seuss was born when Geisel wrote his first book, *And to Think That I Saw It on Mulberry Street.* The year 1957 was one of Seuss's most productive, introducing both *The Cat in the Hat* and *How the Grinch Stole Christmas.*

SUDBURY

The Wayside Inn on the Old Boston Post Road at Wayside Road is the original for **Henry Wadsworth Longfellow**'s (1807–1882) poem "Tales of a Wayside Inn," but it was not an inn when Longfellow wrote the poem. On one of his rambles, Longfellow discovered the place, which had been a working inn, the Red Horse Tavern, run by the Howe family for more than 175 years. He set this poem here:

> As ancient is this hostelry
> As any in the land may be,
> Built in the old colonial day,
> When men lived in a grander way.

In the late 1920s Henry Ford bought the three-story gambrel-roofed house, restored it, and opened it as an inn, taking Longfellow's name for it so as to capitalize on the poem's fame. Since then Wayside has survived two fires, and is open today as an inn and restaurant that serves "Yankee fare." It is furnished with period antiques and offers rooms advertised at reasonable rates.

TRURO

The generation of writers who came of age during World War I were the first to visit this town south of Provincetown on Cape Cod. **John Dos Passos** had a house here; Edna St. Vincent Millay spent the summer of 1920, and Edmund Wilson bicycled from P-Town to visit her; **Waldo Frank** owned a house here and is buried south Truro (at Frank's funeral in 1967 Edmund Wilson thought that "the Wellfleet undertaker looked at some of us with lecherous eyes") and, in 1919, **Eugene O'Neill** (1888–1953) and his wife lived here in a converted Coast Guard station at Peaked Hill Bar. The station, the first house O'Neill ever owned, was practically in the ocean during the 1920s when he summered here. In 1930 a storm swept it away. Mary McCarthy gives this picture of some of the writers who gathered in Truro in the "Hiroshima summer" of 1945:

> Dwight [MacDonald] was living in what was called "the fish house" in North Truro. Jim Agee came, Philip Rahv, many others. [Nicolo] Tucci came to Truro too, to stay with Nicola Chiaromonte in a cottage above Dyer's Hollow beach. I remember Chiaromonte in a blue ruffled apron tied around his waist sweeping out the cottage he shared with Miriam, his wife, and I remember our beach picnics at night around a fire and our discussions of Tolstoy and Dostoyevsky. Thinking back

on Nika, I remember how he delighted in the group of New York psychoanalysts who came to swim a dune or so down the beach, wearing Noxzema, sunglasses, boldly striped beach towels—he understood them when they spoke German; they reciprocated with a frank, professional interest in *him*. Another source of amusement was a heavy-drinking rich woman from Chicago who believed that George Orwell had stolen *Animal Farm* from a book she had written; when in her cups she would utter, and reiterate, a single word—"Communication!"

Each summer *The Boston Globe* seems to run a feature on the writers who make Truro their home. The psychoanalysts continue to come to the Cape as well, but they tend to gather around the ponds of nearby Wellfleet.

WALTHAM

Isaac Asimov (1920–1992) lived here between 1951 and 1956. During this time he published his science fiction *Foundation* trilogy. These were among the first of his more than 200 published books—a prodigious output in any case, but all the more so because Asimov did not publish his first book until age thirty. He wrote on a bewildering array of subjects, many of them scientific and technological, and he wrote for children as well as adults. Asimov's next Massachusetts address was West Newton, where he lived until 1970. Here he wrote the novel *Fantastic Voyage* (1966), in which a team of doctors in a submarine are miniaturized and shot into the bloodstream of a man whose life they must save.

From 1957 until his death, the critic **Philip Rahv** (1908–1973) taught in Waltham at Brandeis University. He has a place in American literary history as a cofounding editor of *Partisan Review*, the most significant highbrow journal of politics and literature from the 1930s to the early 1950s. But he is better known for one essay, "Paleface and Redskin," which delineated two kinds of American writers: the palefaces of imagination and the redskins of experience. Melville and Twain are redskins; Henry James is the quintessential paleface. Irving Howe, Saul Bellow, the British poet F. T. Prince, J. V. Cunningham, Milton Hindus, and Allen Grossman have all taught at Brandeis.

WAYLAND

Lydia Maria Child (1802–1880), a prominent abolitionist whose *Appeal in Favor of that Class of Americans Called Africans* (1833) had a significant impact on many court cases, lived here for the last twenty-eight years of her life. In 1857 she wrote the poem "Thanksgiving Day." Most who know the words—and they are part of America's collective poetic consciousness—will not know who wrote them.

> Over the river and through the wood,
> To grandfather's house we go;
> The horse knows the way
> To carry the sleigh
> Through the white and drifted snow.

Edmund Sears (1810–1876), pastor of the Unitarian church, introduced another memorable American poem here at Christmas in 1849, when he read his "It Came upon a Midnight Clear." After publication the poem was put to music, and "that glorious song of old" is heard at Christmas today.

WELLESLEY

Marcia Davenport, the novelist, biographer of Mozart, and passionate partisan of Czechoslovakia, attended Wellesley College, and the poet May Sarton taught here in the early 1960s. Recently arrived in America, **Vladimir Nabokov** (1899–1977) rented a house at 19 Appleby Road and did his first American teaching at Wellesley. He lectured here, with time out for a Guggenheim, until 1948, but moved to Cambridge before that so as to be near his part-time job at Harvard's Museum of Contemporary Zoology. At Wellesley, Nabokov made friends with the exiled Spanish poet Jorge Guillen, who also taught there. Guillen thought enough of Nabokov to dedicate a poem to him. Nabokov never really fit in at Wellesley. His incessant smoking, for one thing, often caused consternation on a campus where it was taboo. He had many "Pnin"-like adventures with cigarettes before he left Wellesley to teach at Cornell. The poets Frank Bidart and David Ferry teach at Wellesley today.

Two years after her father's death, **Sylvia Plath** (1932–1963) moved here with her mother and brother Warren in 1942. The Plaths lived at 32 Elmwood Road, and Sylvia attended Bradford Senior High School. Perhaps because she did not want to go to college in her hometown, Plath spurned a full scholarship to Wellesley College and chose Smith instead.

WELLFLEET

In October 1849, **Henry David Thoreau** (1817–1862) made his first trip to Cape Cod. His friend William Ellery Channing accompanied him, and they made their way from Cohasset to Provincetown before returning to Boston by steamer. As was Thoreau's habit he took notes, made entries in his journal, and later wrote up these impressions. He did the same on subsequent trips to the Cape and began to work this material into shape, the first section of which appeared in the summer of 1855 in *Putnam's Monthly Magazine*. But nothing more appeared until after Thoreau's death. His biographer Franklin B. Sanborn claims that the material "became the subject of controversy first as to price, and then as to its tone towards the people of that region." This "tone" can be glimpsed in the "The Wellfleet Oysterman" chapter that appeared when Ticknor and Fields published the book *Cape Cod* in 1865. Thoreau encounters a man of eighty-four who claims he heard the guns at the Battle of Bunker Hill. Thoreau seems to believe that the sound could have carried across the bay, but he describes the old man and his family as hicks. Thoreau appears to be drawing them out so they will make fools of themselves, but perhaps they are pulling his leg. In any case, it is a most entertaining chapter.

Many writers have summered here and still do, but beginning in the 1940s, **Edmund Wilson** (1895–1972)—that American rarity, a man of letters—made the town his home. He was known mostly as a critic, but he published poems, novels, journalism, and books that attest to his wide-ranging curiosity. He wrote about the Iroquois Indians, the Dead Sea Scrolls, Canada, Russian literature, the literature of the American Civil War, and several works of autobiography. The critic Alfred Kazin remembers Wilson appearing on Wellfleet's Newcomb's Hollow beach after a day of work, dressed in a white dress shirt worn over Bermuda shorts and a large Panama hat, holding forth on whatever currently interested him. He did not suffer fools and could be tigerish in argument. Wilson's third wife, the novelist **Mary McCarthy** (1912–1989) gives an unflattering picture of him in her novel *A Charmed Life* (1955), in which New Leeds is Wellfleet. She makes Miles Murphy, a character based on Wilson, a pedant who takes a taxi to New York to look up a word. Wilson, some years later, did several times take cabs to his summer home at Talcottville in upstate New York. He never learned to drive a car and was, by his own description, more a man of the 19th than the 20th century. His posthumously published journals reveal a writer who seems to have needed to turn his every experience into words before they could be real to him. His plain, lucid prose has an attractive directness. He is buried in Wellfleet's Congregational Cemetery on Gross Hill Road, under a stone inscribed with the Hebrew prayer, "Be strong, be strong, and we shall strengthen one another."

WESTON

Born in Weston and schooled in Wellesley, **Anne Sexton** (1928–1974) returned here to live with her husband and daughters, and here she took her life in 1974. She had not been shy about wishing for death, and like the poet she considered her soulmate, Sylvia Plath, she attempted suicide more than once before succeeding. In several biographical notes she was described as a "housewife," a term unlikely to be used in a poet's biography today, and at least part of her fame derived from the fact that she *was* a housewife (housewives were not supposed to write serious poetry!), writing poems in the suburbs, where serious poetry was not supposed to be written. Robert Lowell was her mentor, and he wrote mostly confessional poetry that drew on her troubled and tumultous life. For a brief time she sang her poems to the accompaniment of her own rock and roll band. Sexton won the 1966 Pulitzer Prize for *Live or Die*. Since her death she has been the subject of several biographies, the most recent of which (by Diane Middlebrook, 1991) caused a sensation by quoting tapes of her therapy sessions with one of her psychiatrists. The resulting furor seemed in keeping with Sexton's flamboyant personality.

WINTHROP

Sylvia Plath (1932–1963) spent her childhood at 92 Johnson Avenue, in a house that looked out on Boston Harbor. It was here that Plath's father, Dr. Otto Emil Plath, a Harvard-trained entomologist who wrote the book *Bumblebees and Their Ways*, developed diabetes. In October 1940, Dr. Plath was operated on and one of his legs was amputated. He appeared to be recovering when, in early November, an embolism reached his heart and he died. His daughter Sylvia had just turned eight years old. Her father's early and unexpected death haunts several of her famous poems, "Daddy" most especially.

WORCESTER

This industrial city is a cradle of 20th-century American poetry. **Stanley Kunitz** (1905), **Charles Olson** (1910), and **Elizabeth Bishop** (1911) were all born here. **Frank O'Hara** (1926–1966) was raised in nearby Grafton but went to high school and took piano lessons here. That said, it must be added that Worcester plays no important role in their poetry. **S. N. Behrman** (1893–1973), the playwright, biographer of the art dealer Duveen, and writer of short stories set in Worcester, was also born here, as was **Esther Forbes** (1891–1967), author of *Johnny Tremain,* and Yippie founder and author of *Steal This Book*, **Abbie Hoffman**. In the 19th century, the town was a major stop on the lecture circuit. Dickens, Matthew Arnold, Lincoln, Frederick Douglass, Emerson, and Thoreau lectured here. Thoreau also had contact with a group interested in literature who gathered at Theo Brown's tailor shop. Thomas Wentworth Higginson, Edward Everett Hale, and Thoreau's friend Harry Blake were of this company who, inspired by the Transcendentalists, gathered to talk. New England has never had a cafe or bar intellectual life, but in the mid-19th century—inspired by the news from Boston and Concord and the slavery question—groups of writers did come together, as they have rarely since. In 1909, Worcester's Clark University gave honorary degrees to Sigmund Freud and Carl Jung. Invited by the university's president, psychologist G. Stanley Hall, Freud and Jung took part in a scientific conference at which Freud delivered his "Five Lectures on Psychoanalysis." Freud never visited America again.

New Hampshire

———◆———

"LIVE FREE OR Die," the motto on New Hampshire's license plates, shakes its fist under every nose: its citizens are free of state income tax, free of liberal politicians, and free to do what they please with their enterprising Yankee selves. The state's many shopping malls celebrate this freewheeling business ethic. When motorcyclists cross the state line into New Hampshire, they are free to remove their helmets and let their hair flow in the breeze, and residents of neighboring states are free to steal across New Hampshire's borders and take advantage of its low sales tax.

New Hampshire, the Granite State, has New England's highest mountains. In 1672, the English naturalist John Josselyn looked toward these White Mountains and recoiled: "Beyond these hills Northward is daunting terrible, being full of rocky hills, as thick as Molehills in a Meadow, and cloathed with infinite woods"—hard going for settlers from Connecticut and Massachusetts who came north to farm. The demands of this rugged country endure in the poems of **Robert Frost** (1874–1963), as much poet laureate of New Hampshire as Vermont. Frost knew firsthand what it meant to farm such rocky ground.

Terrain that daunted for centuries is now appealing. The White Mountains and New Hampshire's large, irregularly shaped Lake Winnipesaukee are two of New England's prime year-round "vacationlands." Skiing brings in visitors throughout the once fierce and isolating winters, and the state is a summer playground, with some of the region's most difficult hiking trails and rock climbs.

As the character of the state changes, so has its literary life. Twenty-five years from now, a guide like this will list dozens of writers who have arrived in the state within the past three decades, drawn by summer and year-round residence. Vermont is similar, and like its neighbor along the Connecticut River, New Hampshire has no native son or daughter who is a major American writer. Both might claim Frost, but he was—improbably—born in San Francisco.

New Hampshire does have a unique literary distinction. For six to eight weeks every four years, no state comes close to producing the volume of words produced in New Hampshire. These are the winter weeks of the first presidential primaries, which are held here. In what is now a year-long triathlon/roadshow, computers softly clock the candidates' every thought and deed. While little of this is memorable, Edmund Muskie's tearful response to an alleged slur against French Canadians and Ronald Reagan seizing the debate microphone from George Bush are the sort of thing Frost meant when he wrote in "New Hampshire":

> Just specimens is all New Hampshire has,
> One each of everything as in a show-case.

BOW

Born on a small farm and raised there, **Mary Baker Eddy** (1821– 1910) —founder of the Church of Christ, Scientist—lived in Bow until she was fifteen. A biographer describes her as "delicate, dainty and rather fragile in appearance and subject to hysterical seizures" during those years. Convinced that her brain was too large for her body, her father kept her out of school, and she learned by reading on her own, which left her deficient in grammar and with a weak grasp of syntax. This handicapped her when she came to write *Science and Health*, the first edition of which appeared in 1875 when she was fifty-four. By then she had been married three times and spent many impoverished years in ill health. Her Christian Science church established but her health again precarious, Eddy returned to New Hampshire, to Concord, where she lived the last nineteen years of her life.

The other prophet/founder of a large indigenous American religion, **Joseph Smith** (1805–1844), was also born in New England—south of Randolph, Vermont. In 1830 Smith translated and published *The Book of Mormon*, the bible of the Church of Latter-Day Saints. The following year, in upstate New York where he had been raised and where the angel Moroni first appeared to him, Smith founded his church. Murdered by a mob in Nauvoo, Illinois, Smith never saw Utah, where the church flourishes today. Near his birthplace, the Mormons maintain a museum open to the public.

BRISTOL

Above Newfound Lake, **John Cheever** (1912–1982) often summered at his wife Mary's family compound, Treetops. Cheever's daughter Susan, herself a novelist, wrote *Treetops; A Family Memoir* about the place and its role in her own life and the lives of her mother and father. In it she remembers Cheever "in baggy shorts and a frayed Brooks shirt, squinting down toward the lake to see if the water was too rough for canoeing." Cheever was also an enthusiastic hiker, and he wrote up his mountain hikes for *Holiday* magazine. He befriended the compound's caretaker, a Czech Communist, and as they worked together around the place, Cheever picked up from him a few stories that found their way into three of his own short stories: "The Summer Farmer," "Vega," and "How Dr. Wareham Kept His Servants." Today the compound remains in the hands of Mary Cheever's family.

CHOCORUA

William James (1842–1910) bought a farm here on the shores of Lake Chocorua in the Ossipee Mountains in the fall of 1886. In a letter to his brother **Henry James** (1843–1916), he descibed its "75 acres of land, mountain 3500 feet high, exquisite lake a mile long, fine oak and pine woods, valuable mineral spring, two houses and a barn, all for 900 dollars or possibly less. Two thousand five hundred dollars will give us the place in fine order." James and his family summered here, working the place as a farm and actively hiking in the mountains for the rest of his life. It still stands but is now privately owned. In late August of 1910, he and his younger brother Henry returned to this house from Europe, where William had traveled for his health. But it worsened steadily, and on August 26 he died. That day, Henry wrote to their friend Grace Norton, "My own fears are of the blackest, I confess to you and at the prospect of losing my wonderful beloved brother out of the world in which, from as far back as dimmest childhood, I have so yearningly always counted on him, I feel nothing but the abject weakness of grief and even ter-ror." Before he could send this letter, he had to reopen it and "add that William passed unconsciously away an hour ago—without apparent pain or struggle. Think of us, dear Grace—think of us!"

After the funeral at Harvard, Henry returned to Chocorua, where he wrote of the "unutterable, unforgettable hour" when his brother's ashes were interred beside his parents' in Cambridge. Over the next weeks, Henry poured out his grief in letters to Edith Wharton and other friends. Returning to his brother's Irving Street house in Cambridge, Henry decided to stay in America for a time. At least part of the reason was that William's wife was determined to hold seances in an attempt to contact her dead husband. No messages came, and Henry returned to England where, upon hearing that his brother's voice had been heard in Cambridge, denounced the seance as "the hollowest, vulgarest and basest rubbish."

Leon Edel, Henry's biographer, believes that his brother's death had pro-found consequences for Henry's work. In the final volume of what is one of the great biographies of an American writer, Edel writes, "Henry James now wore the mantle of Family; he was the last heir, the final voice; his would be the last word. Out of this came, indeed, during the next three years, the mas-ter's autobiographies, *A Small Boy and Others* and *Notes of a Son and Brother*.

CORNISH

Winston Churchill (1871–1947) was acclaimed as America's most popu-lar novelist of the early 20th century, with his *Richard Carvel* selling more than one million copies. So popular was he that Winston Churchill, the young British journalist, signed himself Winston S. (for Spencer) Churchill in order to avoid confusion. Following his success with historical romances, Churchill turned to the problem novel. *Conniston*, among others, is set in New Hampshire, and deals with the sort of corrupt practices involving out-of-state lobbyists that Churchill saw as ruining the state. He followed these novels by running for the state legislature, to which he was elected, and running for governor in 1906 on a reform platform, a race he lost.

DERRY

"I have lived, somewhat brokenly to be sure," **Robert Frost** (1874–1963) wrote, "in Salem, Derry, Plymouth, and Franconia, New Hampshire, from my tenth to my forty-fifth year." Frost and his family lived on the Derry farm from 1900 to 1912, when they left for four years in England. They came to Derry because Frost feared he had tuberculosis. He was able to buy the small farm through a complicated loan arrangement, which Frost never quite admitted he had entered into, with his grandfather. The old man lent Frost the $1,850 the farm cost, with the proviso that the farm could not be his for ten years. This, it seems, was meant to settle Frost down and spur him on to a successful farming career. Frost later called the arrangement his "sentence," and once the ten years were up he quickly sold the place and used the money to head for England, where his literary career effectively began.

The Derry house is a standard New Hampshire farmhouse. You'll pass thousands of them throughout the state. During the Frosts' residence it had no running water and was heated by a wood stove. Frost intended to support the place by egg farming. For a time he had a hired man to help, but, as was to be everywhere the case, Frost was an indifferent farmer. His daughter Lesley kept a diary while living here, and the number of times the family cow cannot be found in her pasture testifies to Frost's neglect of the simplest task—closing the pasture gate. He soon turned to teaching at Derry's Pinkerton Academy, which he could reach in a two- or three-mile walk.

On display in the house is the Morris chair in which Frost sat and worked on a writing board. Frost shaped his style here, as he drew his subjects from the people and countryside around him. His next-door neighbor, Nicholas Guay, instructed him in "spring mending time," from which evolved Frost's

"Mending Wall." The French Canadian Guay appears as Baptiste in "The Ax-Helve" and gives Frost another lesson, pointedly about craft: "He showed me the lines of a good helve/Were native to the grain before the knife/Expressed them." From Hyla Brook, which runs behind the house, and after which he titled a poem, Frost learned "We love the things we love for what they are."

In England in 1912 these poems began to find, with the help of the English poet Edward Thomas and Frost's champion Ezra Pound, a publisher and an audience. His first two books, *A Boy's Will* and *North of Boston*, appeared there.

Of the Frost sites in New England, Derry is closest to a replica of what Frost knew in life. His daughter Lesley, who had a keen memory of Derry, assisted in restoring the house, and the State of New Hampshire, which maintains it, has kept things as plain as they must have been. On a day in the spring or early fall before the house is closed for the winter, you can feel the cold that must have crept in when the Frosts lived here. If the day is overcast, it is not hard to imagine "Home Burial" taking place just outside the parlor window. The furnishings and books, most of which were in the family, speak of the modest, and sometimes strapped, circumstances in which the Frosts lived. Not that life here was exactly grim—but this was a working farm, and a sense of its cares and demands lingers.

Before New Hampshire took over the house, it was home to a junkyard named Frosty Acres. Today the place is well run by intelligent, knowledgeable guides. Skirting the pasture behind it there is the Hyla Brook nature trail, a pleasant stroll through the woods. The house is noted on most road maps, and there are signs directing you when you get within a few miles of it. Like most of the writers' homes in this book, it is closed from mid-October to April.

DUNBARTON

Robert Lowell (1917–1977) is buried beside his parents in the Stark Family Cemetery. His mother, Charlotte, was a Winslow who traced her line in America to the Mayflower. Her great-grandfather married Sarah Stark of

Dunbarton, daughter of Revolutionary general John Stark, hero of Bunker Hill and the Battle of Bennington.

Today the Stark Cemetery is off a back road and hidden by trees. Directions can be obtained at the town clerk's office. The cemetery was moved to this site when the Army Corps of Engineers built a dam that flooded the original graveyard. Granite steps in a low granite wall mark the cemetery's entrance. These lead to a wide path running a little way into the woods before coming to the iron fence that encloses the plot. The twenty or so stones have their backs turned, facing a standing Christ. The dead could be in church pews, accepting the figure's blessing.

Lowell's father died first, and his pink granite stone—all three Lowell stones are alike—has the Navy crest, his dates, and the epitaph:

> Stand and live
> The dove has brought
> An olive branch to eat.
> R. Lowell, Jr.

Since an enraged Lowell once knocked his father to the floor, an episode he wrote about in *Life Studies* and elsewhere, the epitaph reads like a peace offering. The *Jr.* seems wrong, as Lowell was junior to no one.

Lowell's mother is next to her husband. Her death and the original cemetery are described in Lowell's poem "Sailing Home from Rapallo." Charlotte Winslow Lowell's stone reads:

> Reserved and bracing lady
> Be buoyant now where time is love.
> R. Lowell, Jr.

Among the Winslows and Starks, admirals, architects, and soldiers and their wives, Lowell's stone is the most Spartan: name, dates, and the epitaph:

> The immortal is scraped
> Unconsenting from the mortal

Scraped—a typically violent Lowell verb—has the harsh music and hard action of his poems. This epitaph also reads like something of an apology.

Lowell often "scraped" his poems from the lives and letters of his family. Few poets have been so fixed on immortality as Lowell. He seemed to take the heights of Parnassus for granted, and for all his tragic frailty of mind, Lowell had an iron will.

DURHAM

Thomas Williams (1926–1991) came to New Hampshire at the age of fourteen and, with time out for study in the Midwest and Paris, he spent the rest of his life there, teaching at the University of New Hampshire in Durham and writing. His novel *The Hair of Harold Roux* won a National Book Award. After his death, his short stories were collected and published as *Leah, New Hampshire*, the imaginary town in which they take place. Williams began publishing them in 1957, and by the end of his life he had written fifteen. In his author's note, he has this to say: "Leah is an imaginary town in the State of New Hampshire, a state that can be cruel, especially to its poor, or sick, or old. In its public, or collective, stance, it can act as a skinflint and a buffoon among its neighbors. Its people, however, like most Americans, can be decent and generous if, for a moment, they forget dogma, forget 'conservatism,' and sanctimony, and the myths of an imaginary history." The novelist John Irving, a New Hampshire native and student of Williams's at U.N.H., wrote an introduction to the stories. **Russell Banks**, also a native of New Hampshire and the author of many stories and novels set here, taught at U.N.H. in the 1970s. **Charles Simic**, Pulitzer Prize-winning poet and prolific translator from his native Serbian, teaches at U.N.H. today.

EXETER

Exeter is the home of Phillips Exeter Academy, one of the nation's prestigious prep schools, founded in 1783. Robert Benchley, Booth Tarkington, and Gore Vidal are among its literary graduates. **Bliss Perry**, *Atlantic* editor from 1899 to 1909, died here, and the critic **Granville Hicks** (1901–1982) was born here.

FRANCONIA

There are large signs on Route 93 directing you to Frost Place, the last of **Robert Frost**'s (1874–1963) New Hampshire homes. Upon returning from England the Frosts lived here from 1915 to 1920. Except for its mountain view ("five mountain ranges one behind the other," Frost wrote), the house is nearly a carbon copy of the Derry farmhouse. Frost liked to pull his favorite Morris chair onto the porch and take in the view as he worked leaning on his writing board. In this house he wrote perhaps his most quoted poem, "Stopping by Woods on a Snowy Evening," but he also created some of the darker poems that are too often overlooked by Frost devotees. Out one night on the South Road in nearby Bethlehem, Frost and his son Carol had the experience on which the ghost story "The Fear" is based. Responding to the accidental death of a neighbor's son, Frost wrote the elegy "Out, Out—," which ends on the bleak lines:

> No more to build on there. And they, since they
> Were not the dead, turned to their affairs.

This has been said before and since but rarely with such grim finality.

Visitors to the house begin at the barn, where the guide shows a video made by Frost's great-grandson. This is a cut above what one usually gets in this sort of thing, but the images are still Dick and Jane, the poem says brook and the image is of a brook. The house is threadbare. There are a few of Frost's poem-Christmas cards on display, and some first editions and letters. The worn floors and sparsely furnished rooms let one imagine the Frosts' impoverished circumstances. Like the house in Derry, no attempt has been made to brighten or soften what often must have been the hard life common to many in these rural places. Behind the house there is a short nature trail.

For two months during the summer, a recognized poet and his or her family lives in an apartment that has been made in the house, runs a two-week workshop, hosts poetry readings, and soaks up whatever inspiration Frost left in the house. William Matthews, Cleopatra Mathis, and Julis Agoos have been among the resident poets.

Frost often spoke and wrote of his affection for New Hampshire. Both his parents and four of Frost's children were born in the state where he lived in fits and starts from the age of eleven to forty-six. When he came to leave he wrote a valedictory poem, "New Hampshire," that closes:

> I choose to be a plain New Hampshire farmer
> With an income in cash of say a thousand
> (From say a publisher in New York City).
> It's restful to arrive at a decision,
> And restful just to think about New Hampshire.
> At present I am living in Vermont.

GILMANTON

Grace Metalious (1924–1964) was born in Manchester of working-class French Canadians. She married and moved to this town where, living in poverty in her house It'll Do and raising three children, she wrote short stories and novels. *Peyton Place*, published in 1956, became an instant bestseller, making her the subject of an article in *Life* magazine and an overnight sensation. "Indian summer," the novel begins, "is like a woman. Ripe, hotly passionate, but fickle . . . " It was the sort of book librarians did not display, parents hid from their children, and high school kids read under their blankets by flashlight. It sold 300,000 hardcover copies and 8,000,000 in paperback, and then became a movie and a long-running television series. Before dying of chronic liver disease in Boston, Metalious wrote three more novels, all bestsellers, earning her total sales of $15,000,000. Thirty years after her death, James Hart did not deem her fit to include in his edition of *The Oxford Companion to American Literature*. Nor is she worthy of inclusion in *Benét's Reader's Encyclopedia of American Literature*.

HANOVER

The legend is that Daniel Webster, who graduated from Dartmouth College in the class of 1801, tore up his diploma upon hearing that he had been passed over for class valedictorian. He recovered his enthusiasm for the school, and in arguing the famous Dartmouth College Case that kept the school private, he delivered the oft-quoted line, "It is, sir, as I have said, a small college, and yet there are those who love it." **Robert Frost** (1874–1963) began his freshman year here, but left before the end of the first term never to finish college; the journalist and *New Yorker* writer A. J. Liebling (1904–1963) got through three years here before being expelled for skipping chapel. The poets **Richard Eberhart** and **Alexander Laing** taught here for many years, and the poets Philip Booth, Robert Pack, and David Rattray are Dartmouth graduates. **Lewis Mumford** (1895–1990) taught at Dartmouth for eight years, Walt Whitman read "As a Strong Bird on Pinions Free" at the 1872 commencement; and F. Scott Fitzgerald made a memorable visit one winter. Fitzgerald was a Hollywood screenwriter when, in 1940, he came to the college for its Winter Carnival. He was supposed to be getting background for a film, but he fell off the wagon and got little besides drinking accomplished. His guide was Dartmouth undergraduate **Budd Schulberg**, who went on to write the novel *What Makes Sammy Run?* and to recall Fitzgerald's stay in Hanover in his 1950 novel *The Disenchanted.*

Frost had a long association with the college. He read here in 1915 after returning from England, and today the library has a large Frost collection. His friend Edward Connery Lathem, of whom Frost said, "Ed, you're the only friend I've had who has never been a trial to me," not only built the collection but edited the concordance to Frost's poems and a book of interviews with Frost.

The poets Tom Sleigh, Cleopatra Mathis, and the MacArthur Award-winning Jay Wright are among the writers currently teaching at Dartmouth.

The Dartmouth library has recently been in the news because until the fall of 1992 it held the only copy of Samuel Beckett's unpublished novel *Dream of Fair to Middling Women.* Although Beckett permitted scholars to read the book, his refusal of publication was absolute. Somehow, someone photocopied the manuscript, and it has now been published—angering John Calder, Beckett's British publisher, and other keepers of the Beckett flame. At least that was the story as originally reported. Now that the novel has appeared, its editor Eoin O'Brien writes that Beckett approved publication and Dartmouth assisted in the project.

ISLE OF SHOALS

These islands, six at high tide and eight at low, and nine miles off the New Hampshire coast, are half in York County, Maine, and half in New Hampshire. Appledore, the largest, has a cairn on its summit built—so legend has it—in 1614 by John Smith. On his tour of the islands in 1853, Nathaniel Hawthorne heard this story, and wrote in his notebook, "The tradition is just as good as truth." During his visit Hawthorne stayed in Laighton's Hotel on Appledore. Thoreau, Emerson, Whittier, William Morris Hunt, and the painter Childe Hassam were other visitors to this hotel, which was managed by the poet **Celia Thaxter**'s (1825–1894) father.

Thaxter, born in Portsmouth, was raised on White Island, and spent some years on Star before moving to the mainland in 1860. Thaxter and her husband spent six years there before returning to Appledore upon her father's death and taking up the management of Laighton's Hotel. Hawthorne met her on his island visit, but she was seventeen and left little impression on him. By 1866 she was a published poet whose work had appeared in *The Atlantic* and she been encouraged by Whittier.

On Appledore, Thaxter made a garden famed for its splendid poppies. This became the source for her book *An Island Garden* (1894), illustrated by Childe Hassam and still in print today. In her time, Thaxter was well enough known to attract many literary guests to Appledore. One of them remembered that she read Hesiod while peeling cucumbers for salad.

Today the Appledore Hotel is gone. It burned to the ground in 1914, but Celia Thaxter's cottage still stands, and so does the John Smith cairn.

JAFFREY CENTER

Beginning in 1917, **Willa Cather** (1873–1947) often took two rooms during the summer at the Shattuck Inn. It is down the hill from the village of Jaffrey Center and looks directly at Mount Monadnock. One of Cather's favorite places to write, it was here that she finished *My Antonia*, began and finished *Death Comes for the Archbishop* and wrote most of *Shadows on the Rock*. Cather wrote of Nebraska, where so much of her work is set, "There is no place to hide in Nebraska, you can't hide under a windmill." This attitude may help explain her decision to be buried in the small cemetery to the left and behind the Jaffrey Center meeting house. Her grave is at the bottom of the slope, where through the now-grown trees Mount Monadnock can be glimpsed. Her epitaph comes from *My Antonia*: " . . . That is happiness, to be dissolved into something complete and great." Edith Lewis, Cather's friend of nearly forty years, is buried beside Cather's grave under a plain, flat stone marked only by her name and dates. Lewis lived until 1972 in the New York apartment she had shared with Cather, vigilantly following the letter of Cather's will—destroying Cather's letters when and where she could, and keeping her novels away from the movies. Their relationship has been described as a marriage, but Cather's biographer James Woodress thinks this is "misleading." Lewis had a career of her own as a magazine editor and advertising writer. Theirs was, according to Woodress, "a close, loving friendship."

Before Cather came to the Shattuck Inn, William Dean Howells was a guest. It is Mount Monadnock—called by Ralph Nading Hill "perhaps the most literary mountain in America"—that has drawn writers to the place. In 1845, Emerson wrote his poem "Monadnoc" after visiting the mountain, and Thoreau made at least four visits to the area, camping on the mountain's summit during one of them.

Hill claims that *monadnock* is not an Indian name but a term in physical geography. My *American Heritage Dictionary* tells me that monadnock, "a mountain or rocky mass that has resisted erosion and stands isolated in an essentially level area" is taken from Mount Monadnock. It offers no Indian history. Thoreau saw the mountain as having a "masculine front." Seen from Dummerston in Vermont by Rudyard Kipling, "Monadnock came to mean everything that was helpful, healing and full of quiet . . . " Mark Twain, whose vantage point was the porch of a Dublin, New Hampshire, cottage, saw the mountain in "the richest dyes the autumn can furnish" and was inspired to write, "the sight affects the spectator physically, it stirs his blood like military music."

NEWPORT

Few know the name **Sarah Josepha (Buell) Hale** (1788–1879) and fewer know of the poem, "Mary's Lamb," which she published in 1830 in *Poems for Our Children*. But everyone knows "Mary had a little lamb/whose fleece was white as snow . . . " While living most of her long life in this town, Hale was famous in her time for her work on behalf of child welfare, women's education, and other humanitarian causes. Her novels, stories, editorial work, and her history of distinguished women, *Women's Record* (1854), are typical of their period and are forgotten today.

NORTH HAMPTON

From the 1930s to the 1960s, light verse in America meant **Ogden Nash.** Nash (1902–1971) is buried in the Little River Cemetery on North Hampton's Atlantic Avenue, and is best remembered for his poem "Reflections on Ice-Breaking":

> Candy
> Is dandy
> But liquor
> Is quicker.

And he is often remembered for a poem he did not write,

> "Fleas":

> Adam
> Had 'em.

Not only did Nash not write this poem, but "Fleas" is not its title. The title is "Lines on the Antiquity of Microbes" and its author is Strickland Gillilan (1869–1954). The poem has been proclaimed the shortest poem in English, but the *Guinness Book of World Records* has given that honor to a single-letter poem by Aram Saroyan.

ORFORD

Charles Jackson's (1903–1968) novel *The Lost Weekend* (1944)—about five days in an alcoholic's life—was a bestseller that became even better known as a movie starring Ray Milland. Jackson had a house for eight years in Orford, but this slender connection is not the reason to visit the town. Along a ridge, known as "the Ridge," stand seven mansions that are among the finest colonial houses in the state. Nowhere else in New Hampshire is there such a dramatic concentration. They are not open to visitors, but their size and setting, at the end of wide lawns that sweep and rise up to them, is stunning. Jackson owned the northernmost house in the group. It is now known as the Vanderbilt House, and it was built between 1825 and 1828.

A footnote: In 1793, Samuel Morey, an Orford man, built a steamboat and sailed it on the Connecticut River. This was some years before Robert Fulton did the same—and much more celebrated—thing on New York's Hudson River.

PETERBOROUGH

The composer **Edward MacDowell** and his wife Marian Nevins Mac-Dowell, the pianist, founded the MacDowell Colony in 1907 but it did not open until after MacDowell's death a year later. MacDowell had built a cabin on what was once a farm, and their idea was to build more such cabins for the use of writers, artists, and musicians. Today there are twenty-nine such cabins, called studios, on the more than 400-acre site. Artists apply to the colony, and once accepted there is no charge for their residency. They may sleep in their cabins or in the main residence hall. Anthony Tommasini, who was at MacDowell working on a biography of the composer/critic Virgil Thomson, himself a three-time colonist, has described colony life when the artists are not working: "MacDowell is a special social place. Breakfast and dinners are chatty and relaxing. There are evening trips to the market, to the video rental store (Colony Hall has a tiny TV room), talks over wine, evening walks in the snow and, of course, ping-pong." This is in addition to frequent after-dinner readings and lectures by fellow colonists.

Edwin Arlington Robinson spent twenty-five straight summers at the colony; Willa Cather worked on *Death Comes for the Archbishop* here; Stephen Vincent Benét stayed three weeks; the painter Milton Avery was a colonist, as were the composers Leonard Bernstein and Aaron Copland. DuBose Heyward worked on the lyrics to "Porgy and Bess" at MacDowell, and at one point in their careers Sara Teasdale, Louise Bogan, and James Baldwin were in residence.

Few writers worked to greater effect at MacDowell than Thornton Wilder, who wrote much of *The Bridge of San Luis Rey* (1927) here. Eleven years later he wrote *Our Town* while in residence. Peterborough served Wilder as the model for his play's southern New Hampshire town, Grover's Corners.

Peterborough also boasts America's oldest free public library sponsored by public funds. It opened its doors in 1833.

The Peterborough visitor information center has maps to guide visitors to MacDowell. The colony's public areas are open to visitors from 2 to 4:30 p.m. Mondays through Fridays.

PLYMOUTH

On May 12, 1864, **Nathaniel Hawthorne** (1804–1864) and his friend Franklin Pierce left Hawthorne's Concord, Massachusetts, home on a trip to New Hampshire's White Mountains. Hawthorne had been ill for some weeks, suffering—he told Dr. Oliver Wendell Holmes, who examined him—from "boring pain, distention, difficult digestion." Pierce hoped the journey might revive Hawthorne's health and spirits. On the eighteenth, they reached the Pemigewasset House in this town at the entrance to the White Mountains. That afternoon Hawthorne had remarked to Pierce, "What a boon it would be, if when life draws to a close, one could pass away without a struggle." Early on the morning of the nineteenth, Pierce—awakened by a barking dog—went to check on Hawthorne and found him dead.

In 1883 Hawthorne's son Julian, himself a writer, visited Herman Melville in his New York home. Julian hoped Melville might have some of his father's letters, but these had been destroyed. As an agitated Melville spoke, Julian was struck by several remarks "among which the most remarkable," he remembered, "was that he was convinced Hawthorne had all his life con-

cealed some great secret,which would, were it known, explain all the mysteries of his career." Melville did not elaborate, but many critics have attempted
to search out this "secret." No biographer has done better than James R. Mellow in his 1980 *Nathaniel Hawthorne in His Times.*

PORTSMOUTH

Thomas Bailey Aldrich (1836–1907), **James T. Fields** (1817–1881),
and **Celia Thaxter** (1825–1894) were all born in Portsmouth, and all three of
them made their literary fortunes elsewhere. Fields went to Boston, where he
founded the publishing firm of Ticknor and Fields and began *The Atlantic.*
Aldrich followed William Dean Howells as editor of *The Atlantic,* and Thaxter wrote at her childhood home on the Isle of Shoals.

Aldrich, who described Portsmouth in his time as "the interesting widow
of a once lively commerce," wrote a semiautobiographical bestseller, *The
Story of a Bad Boy* (1870), about his youth in the town. He called his Court
Street home Nutter House. It is now part of Strawberry Banke, a ten-acre
outdoor museum, and can be visited May through October.

SILVER LAKE

e.e. cummings (1894–1962) began coming to Joy Farm, his parents' summer home, as a child. Upon their deaths he inherited the farm and spent summers here until his death of a cerebral hemorrhage on September 3, 1962.
cummings is buried in Boston under a footstone that reads E. E. Cummings.

In his next-to-last year at Joy Farm, cummings wrote his friend Hildegarde
Watson about his attempt to make a home for some barn swallows. Totally
absorbed in the project, he writes pure cummingsese:

> last autmun,at Marion's suggestion,I asked a firstrate carpenter (whose
> nothingifnotNewEngland name is Hidden) to make me a real—with a
> North light—studio in the barn. And this summer, shortly before our
> treeswallows had departed, a pair of barnswallows arrived;establishing
> themselves after a few days in the old nest. Presently three buffoonlike
> headsabsurdly masked with enormous lightcolored bills,appeared over

the nest's rim—30 feet above the barnfloor—& all day long the parents of these diminutive clowns magnificently swooped through height,capturing insects for their offspring:unless Hidden or his helper Nickerson or I came anywhere near the nest,when we were fiercely belaboured with wings and cries.

The fledglings do not survive, and cummings ends the letter on this note: "now the father&motherbirds are gone,& our hearts feel as empty as our skies."

Rhode Island

You, you come from Rhode Island
and little Old Rhode Island
is famous for you.
                    Dietz and Schwartz
            As sung by Weslia Whitfield

First of the thirteen colonies to declare independence from England and last to ratify the United States Constitution, Rhode Island is the nation's smallest state. The WPA guide dramatizes this by pointing out that "it could be contained in Texas two hundred times." It is forty-eight miles long and thirty-seven miles wide, land enough to fit under its one-word motto, "Hope."

William Blackstone, Boston's first white settler, became Rhode Island's as well when, striking out south because of his distaste for Boston's Puritans, he stopped at Study Hill, which is now in Lonsdale, North Providence. Blackstone remained a hermit, but he clearly found the congenial company of **Roger Williams** (1603?–1683), also in flight from the Massachusetts Puritans. Blackstone stayed put after Williams founded Providence, which would become Rhode Island's capital in 1636.

Beginning in the mid-19th century, Americans began to romanticize the Puritans as staunch defenders of religious freedom who preached religious tolerance. While this was true of the framers of the American Constitution, the opposite was true of the Puritans. They sought religious freedom only for themselves and demanded conformity within the areas under their control. Blackstone, unwilling to conform, left Boston of his own accord, but Roger Williams was banished from the Bay Colony by Governor John Winthrop for his "newe and dangerous opinions against the authorities."

Williams refused to accept that civil magistrates had the right to punish those who broke religious laws, and he argued persistently that the King of England had no right to give away Indian lands. He founded the colony of "Rhode Island and Providence Plantations" on the principle that "no man should be molested for his conscience," and he hoped for a "lively experiment" in religious liberty. By and large, Williams lived according to his principles. In 1657, Quakers began to arrive in Rhode Island, fleeing persecution in Massachusetts and Connecticut. While Williams attempted to talk the Quakers out of their faith, he did not prohibit its practice. The following year, families of Sephardic Jews began to arrive in Newport. A century later their congregation had a rabbi, Issac Touro, who established America's second synagogue, which still stands on Newport's Touro Street.

Like Massachusetts governors Winthrop and Bradford and like so many other leaders of the early settlements, Williams wrote down both his impressions of the new world and his religious and political ideas. Rhode Island was thickly populated with Indians and it seems natural that the curious Williams paid them a good deal of attention. His book, *A Key into the Language of America*, is a guide to Indian culture as he encountered it on living with them "in their filthy smoky holes." But his most famous work had to do with who would rule, and how. During a trip to England, Williams became friendly with John Milton and Oliver Cromwell, who influenced *The Bloudy Tenent of Persecution* (1644), his plea for total religious and political liberty.

Few writers of renown have been born or have spent their careers in Rhode Island, and of these few it is difficult to say how many have been marked by the independent streak of the state's founders. A belief in the individual runs through New England writers. Emerson exalted it; Horatio Alger vulgarized it; and Providence's H. P. Lovecraft can be said to represent it by writing books for which the adjective *Lovecraftian* had to be coined.

BRISTOL

Mark De Wolfe Howe (1864–1960), born here and raised in Pennsylvania, went to Harvard and became a Boston Brahmin who lived on Brimmer Street. He was a director of the Boston Athenaeum, editor of the *Harvard Alumni Bulletin,* and editor and author of a host of books about Boston. He gave us the memoirs of Mrs. James T. Fields (wife of the Fields of Ticknor and Fields); the letters of John Jay Chapman, Charles Eliot Norton, and General William Tecumseh Sherman; and books on the Boston Symphony, *The Atlantic Monthly,* and the Saturday Club. He also wrote *Bristol, Rhode Island, A Town Biography* (1930). Howe was—as his daughter the novelist Helen Howe says in her book *The Gentle Americans*—a "minor" writer, but he was a representative one. He married a Boston Quincy with three Boston mayors and a Harvard president in her family tree, and he produced, besides daughter Helen, son Quincy, the World War I radio broadcaster who moderated the last of the Kennedy–Nixon presidential debates; and son Mark, who taught law at Harvard and is the father of the poet Susan Howe and the poet and novelist Fanny Howe, who are active today, though not in Boston.

LITTLE COMPTON

Elizabeth Alden Pabodie, daughter of John and Priscilla Alden, is buried here in the Common Burial Ground. Elizabeth was the first white woman born in New England, and her parents are characters in Longfellow's poems "The Courtship of Miles Standish" (1858). The countryside surrounding Little Compton is rural, wooded, and warmed enough by the ocean and bay that there are several producing vineyards. It is farming country on the bay's shore, and the small barns are shingled as they are in Maine or Cape Cod. There is no tourist scene at all, and Little Compton and nearby towns like Tiverton and Sakonnet feel as if they have been bypassed and gone unreported, though they are not forty-five minutes from Providence.

171

MIDDLETOWN

George Berkeley (1685–1753), a bishop of the Church of England and a philosopher, spent three years here, 1728–1731, attempting to establish a college in Bermuda. Either on the ship to America or while waiting in Middletown at his home Whitehall, Berkeley wrote the poem "On the Prospects of Planting Arts and Learning in America." It has one oft-quoted line that is nearly always described as "prophetic": "Westward the course of empire takes its way!" That course did not take Berkeley to Bermuda, as the funds he was waiting for failed to materialize. He did, however, have an impact on local intellectual life, as he helped to found Newport's Philosophical Society, from which Newport's Redwood Library, the nation's oldest library building in continuous use (at 50 Bellevue Avenue), got its start. In the last year of his American stay he wrote *Alciphron, or the Minute Philosopher* (1731), being dialogues debating the existence of God. Connecticut's Berkeley Divinity School in New Haven bears his name, as does—it is said—Berkeley, California, where the University of California began. Today Whitehall is owned by the National Society of the Colonial Dames and is open to the public from July 1 to Labor Day.

NEWPORT

Famous as the "playground" of American millionaires, and a tourist attraction because of its mansions—some might best be described as palaces and some are what the English call follies—where these millionaires play, Newport, beyond its many literary associations, represents the triumph of 19th-century American monopoly capitalism as nowhere else in the country does. These mansions were built by a newly emerged American class that could call upon unlimited money and an imagination fed on ideas of European grandeur—an imagination that was desperate to turn its wealth into European "culture." Henry James and Edith Wharton, both of whom lived in Newport, William Dean Howells, and Mark Twain wrote about this class, if not about Newport itself.

Visitors will want to walk down Bellevue Avenue and perhaps tour the Breakers or Belcourt Castle or the Astors' house, and see for themselves some first-class examples of homegrown American surrealism. **Henry James** (1843–1916) spent two periods of his youth in Newport when it was a quiet seaside town, and looked back fondly on those years all his life. In 1858, Henry James, Sr., brought the family back from Europe and settled in Newport where Henry, then fifteen, studied with the painter John La Farge learning how to draw, at which he was adept throughout his life. In 1859, the peripatetic James family was back in Europe, only to return to Newport the following year. This time they stayed put for two years, which were to be significant years in James's formation as a writer. He read Hawthorne for the first time, and it struck him that "an American could be an artist, one of the finest." He also suffered an "obscure hurt" when serving as a volunteer fireman putting out a Newport fire. This injury may or may not have kept James from serving in the Civil War. Since James was so vague about exactly what happened to him, critics have gone so far as to suggest castration and have heaped all manner of psychological interpretation on the event. Leon Edel, James's biographer, thinks he suffered a back injury. James's brother William, sixteen months his senior, studied with the painter William Morris Hunt during this time but gave up art to enter Harvard's Lawrence Scientific School. The Jameses lived at a house on Spring Street, which is now a funeral home.

Edith Wharton (1862–1937) came to Newport first as a girl spending summers beginning in 1872 at the family home, Pencraig. Her New York, winter home, Europe, extended travel, and Newport orbit during those years was the one shared by many of her Newport neighbors. In 1878, her mother paid the Chase and Chase Bookstore at 202 Thames Street to publish a book of Wharton's poetry, *Verses*. The following summer, a neighbor passed some of the poems on to Longfellow, who in turn passed them on to Howells, who published one in *The Atlantic*, around the time Wharton made her debut in society. In 1893 Wharton, now the wife of Edward Robbins "Teddy" Wharton, bought Land's End at Newport for $80,000. She hired the Boston architect Osgood Codman to decorate the house, thus beginning a collaboration with him that resulted in her writing *The Decoration of Houses*. It was published by Scribner's in 1897 and achieved unexpectedly good sales. Two years later Wharton began to look for a summer place away from Newport, and eventually she discovered Lenox in the Berkshires where, after disagreeing with Codman about his fee and replacing him with another architect, she built the Mount.

A host of writers have summered or paused in Newport: Bret Harte, Richard Henry Dana, Jr., Longfellow, Whittier, Robert Louis Stevenson, and Jean Stafford. **Clement C. Moore** (1779– 1863), author of "'Twas the Night Before Christmas," spent his last twelve years at his home, the Cedars. After the Civil War. **Thomas Wentworth Higginson** (1823–1911) retired to Newport, where he lived and wrote many books—*Army Life in a Black Regiment* (1870) and *Oldport Days* (1873) among them—until 1877, when he returned to Cambridge. Higginson was not so retired that he missed many meetings of Boston's Radical Club.

Henry Adams's close friend **Clarence King** (1842–1901), the geologist, was born and raised here before graduating from Yale. He was an adventurer who traveled on horseback over much of the west and wrote an exceptional book *Mountaineering in the Sierra Nevada* (1872). King and Adams, Adams's wife Clover, and John Hay (1838– 1905), President Abraham Lincoln's secretary and author, spent a great deal of time together in Washington, D.C., in the 1870s, when Rutherford B. Hayes was president. The novelist **Thornton Wilder** (1897–1975), who served in the artillery at Fort Adams here in World War I, set his last novel, *Theophilus North* (1973), in Newport.

The Redwood Library at 50 Bellevue Avenue, which traces its history back to George Berkeley's Philosophical Society, displays a portrait of the good bishop.

PAWTUCKET

Galway Kinnell, born in 1927 in Providence, grew up here on Oswald Street. He has translated from the French, written a novel set in Persia, published many books of poetry, and is the poet laureate of Vermont.

PORTSMOUTH

The poet Robert Graves said that he liked to write every day so as to be there when lightning struck. Lightning struck **Julia Ward Howe** (1819–1910) but once, and the result was "The Battle Hymn of the Republic." This gregarious, and intellectually vibrant woman spent many of her summers at 745 Union Square, where she died on October 17, 1910. During the rest of the year she lived in Boston with her husband, **Samuel Gridley Howe** (1801–1876), with whom she edited the anti-slavery paper the *Boston Commonwealth*. Dr. Howe founded the Massachusetts School for the Blind (Perkins Institute) and was one of those who attempted to rescue the fugitive slave Anthony Burns. The Howes had two daughters, Laura Richards and Maud Howe Elliott, who lived in Newport for many years. They collaborated on their mother's biography, *The Life and Letters of Julia Ward Howe*, which was awarded the Pulitzer Prize for 1916.

PROVIDENCE

H. P. Lovecraft (1890–1937), whose stone in the city's Swan Point Cemetery proclaims "I AM PROVIDENCE," had the good fortune to be born and raised and to spend most of his writing life in a city thrice visited by his spiritual grandfather, **Edgar Allan Poe** (1809–1849). Poe's Providence visits were bound up with his love for, and fevered pursuit of, the poet **Sarah Helen Whitman** (1803–1878). Their courtship, as with so much of Poe's life, makes an incredible story. After reading one of his short stories and experiencing, as she wrote later, "a sensation of such intense horror that I dared neither look at anything he had written nor even utter his name," she sent, in 1848, a poem to New York to be read at a Valentine's Day party in his honor. She had no way of knowing that Poe had already seen her on a visit to Providence in 1845. His friend Fanny Osgood had wanted Poe to meet Helen, the name he preferred, on that visit, but Poe thought she was married—she was actually a widow— and did not approach her. But he saw her on a hot, moonlit night when, unable to sleep, he walked on the hill near her home, and glimpsed a woman he recognized as Helen from Fanny Osgood's description: she was dressed in white, with a white shawl covering her head. Three years later, her Valentine's Day poem set in motion his next visit to Providence and their romance. Before he laid eyes on her again he sent, through a friend, the poem "To Helen" (he wrote two poems with this title—this one is the second and longer one) which remembers the night he first saw her:

I saw thee once—once only—years ago;
I must not say *how* many—but *not* many.
It was a July midnight;

On September 21, 1848, Poe arrived at her 88 Benefit Street home, which still stands today, and in three days—one of which they spent on an outing to Swan Point Cemetery—Poe wooed her. He returned in November, despairing enough over his prospects that he rushed by train to Boston, his birthplace, where he took laudanum in a possible suicide attempt. Back in Providence, he and Helen decided on a conditional engagement. To satisfy her terms, he had to "never again taste wine," and her mother had to bless their marriage. There was also the matter of Helen's inheritance from her aunt. Dead set against the marriage, Helen's mother managed to have this money turned over to her, but when Poe returned to Providence in December to deliver his lecture "The Poetic Principle" with an admiring Helen seated in the audience, they determined to wed. But it was not to be. Poe stayed through Christmas and left early in the New Year, their marriage plans canceled. He was dead within the year. For her part, Whitman went on to publish a few books of poems that bear Poe's influence, and she defended him against his many enemies in her book *Edgar Poe and His Critics* (1860). Today, a small wooden sign marks Whitman's Benefit Street house, and at the granite Providence Athenaeum at 251 Benefit Street (it looks like a mausoleum), which welcomes visitors, there is a portrait of Whitman and a daguerreotype of Poe.

Lovecraft—his initials stand for Howard Phillips—was born at 454 Angell Street, the home of his maternal grandparents Whipple and Robie Phillips. His parents soon moved to Massachusetts, but his father went insane and died, causing Lovecraft and his mother to move back to Providence. Lovecraft spent all but two years of the rest of his life on the city's East Side, College Hill. His grandparents had a library of 2,000 books, and Lovecraft is said to have received his education from them. When his grandparents died, he moved with his mother to 598 Angell Street. Illness prevented his finishing high school, but he began to publish his stories in local newspapers. From 1926 (when his marriage failed) to 1933, he lived with his aunt at 1012

Barnes Street, where he wrote "The Dunwich Horror" and many other of his "tales of fantasy and supernatural horror." They are always described this way, and Lovecraft is nearly always referred to as a cult writer. He certainly has a passionate following who conduct "Lovecraft Lurk-Ins," walking tours of his East Side haunts and houses where he set some of his stories. In Lovecraft's case, *cult* seems to mean that the writing is not quite deserving of a place at literature's high table, and that its popularity is based on extra-literary values. This sort of ranking means as little to his devotees as highbrow rejection does to those who buy millions of copies of novels by Maine's Stephen King—Lovecraft's spiritual grandson. At 135 Benefit Street stands what was once called the "Shunned House." Built on a graveyard in 1764, screams in French were said to rise from its cellar. Here Lovecraft set his story "The Shunned House," and here his fans stop on their prowl to read the story aloud. The house is now painted a bright yellow and bears two enamel plaques on its gate. The larger reads "Attention *Chien Bizarre*" and the smaller, "*Chien Lunatique*." Lovecraft's stories and his more than 100,000 letters give a rich picture of his native city, through which he loved to take long walks. His last Providence address was 66 College Street. The house that stood there has been moved and now stands at 65 Prospect Street, at the corner of Meeting Street. Much of Lovecraft's work, including his story *The Case of Charles Dexter Ward*, was published after his death. The Wisconsin novelist August Derleth wrote the first biography of him, and founded Arkham House publishers to get Lovecraft's work into print. One Providence bookshop owner told me it is easier to find Lovecraft titles in Arizona than in Providence, so thoroughly have they been scouted out. Lovecraft is buried in the Phillips family plot at Swan Point off Blackstone Boulevard, a garden cemetery in the manner of Cambridge's Mount Auburn Cemetery but not nearly so grand. The cemetery office will provide a map, and they will also tell you that the novelist and diarist Anaïs Nin is not buried there. Somehow word got around that she is, and a few visitors inquire every year. Lovecraft's grave, like that of Jack Kerouac's in Lowell, attracts the sort of visitor who leaves offerings. When I was last there a stack of pennies, decaying gourd, and blue hydrangea flower sat before his scroll-shaped stone.

On the way out Blackstone Boulevard to the cemetery, there is a statue of

Constance Witherby, who died at the age of fifteen and whose book of poems was published posthumously. It is the only statue of a writer in Providence, and it quotes Ms. Witherby:

> The wind roars by I feel it blow
> And know that I am free to go.

George M. Cohan (1878–1942), who wrote the songs "Over There," "Give My Regards to Broadway," and "It's a Grand Old Flag," as well as some forty plays, and who starred in Eugene O'Neill's *Ah, Wilderness!*, was born at 536 Wickenden Street. Cohan had the good fortune to be played by James Cagney in the biographical film *Yankee Doodle Dandy*. Few American writers have been portrayed on screen, and none with the sass and vinegar Cagney brought to his portrayal of Cohan. When the film director Mike Nichols was a comedian, he suggested that Spencer Tracy could play Gertrude Stein as a baby. Had this come to pass, we might have had a performance worthy of Cagney's, who does an unforgettable stiff-legged dance and who is well worth looking up in the video store. George Pierce Baker, who taught playwriting at Harvard and Yale to O'Neill, John Dos Passos, Thomas Wolfe, and many others, was born here and is buried at Swan Point. The novelist **David Cornel De Jong** (1905–1967) set his 1942 novel *Benefit Street* in a Providence boardinghouse on the street of the same name. The journalist A. J. Liebling worked a few years in the 1920s for the *Providence Journal,* and Edwin O'Connor's stint at radio station WPRO gave him the background for his first novel, *The Oracle* (1951).

The poet **Ted Berrigan** (1934–1983) was born in Providence, and after a hitch in the army and college at Tulsa University, he went to New York, where his forceful, provocative presence stimulated two or three generations of poets. Officially a member of the second generation of the New York School, Berrigan was really a school unto himself. He taught at Iowa and in Chicago, but an apartment on New York's Lower East Side remained his home base. His books include *The Sonnets, Nothing for You,* and his selected poems, *So Going Around Cities.* A collected poems is overdue. Berrigan often returned to see his family in a working-class section of the city near Cranston. He wrote two wonderfully tender poems about these homecomings, "Things to Do in

Providence," and "Cranston Near the City Line," that cannot be reduced to quotation. Throughout his life he lived unconventionally, insisting on the honor and dignity due him as a poet. Following the memorial service after his death, a crowd of some 200 people carried aloft his portrait from New York's St. Mark's Church down Second Avenue, as if—in the words of the poet Michael Palmer—he were a minor Italian saint.

Brown University is the college on Providence's College Hill. **S. J. Perelman** (1904–1979), who grew up in Providence, where his father owned a dry good store, went to Brown, and there he met the novelist Nathanael West (1903–1940). They became friends, and Perelman married West's sister Laura. While at Brown, Perelman wrote and drew for the campus humor magazine, *Brown Jug,* which gave him a leg up when he went to New York and began to write for the comic magazines like *Judge* and the early *New Yorker.* West mostly loafed. An administrative error allowed him to transfer from Tufts a full year ahead of himself, but he kept mum about this and enjoyed himself.

Winfield Townley Scott (1910–1968), poet and longtime editor of *The Providence Journal,* also graduated from Brown. S. Foster Damon, the Blake scholar, poet, and biographer of Amy Lowell, taught at Brown from 1927 to 1963. Poet and translator from the Spanish Edwin Honig taught at Brown for many years. The poet John Berryman taught there for only one year in the early 1960s but is remembered for going to the blackboard on his first day and, suffering from a terrible hangover, scratching his name in chalk. Stepping back, realizing it was illegible, Berryman said, "Obviously, they didn't hire me for my penmanship." Poets Clark Coolidge, a Providence native, and Bill Berkson attended Brown at the end of the 1950s. The novelist John Hawkes taught there for many years and was partly responsible for establishing the school's currently flourishing creative writing program. Novelists Robert Coover and Edmund White teach in it today, as do poets Michael Harper, C. D. Wright, and Rosemarie and Keith Waldrop, who have operated the Burning Deck Press out of their Providence home for years. At 74 Waterman Street there is Brown's John Hay Library. Hay, secretary to Lincoln during the Civil War and friend of Henry Adams, graduated from Brown. The library holds the Harris Collection of Poetry and Plays, one of the dozen or so large poetry collections in the United States; a wealth of Lincoln material; a collection devoted to Walt Whitman; and some of H. P. Lovecraft's letters and manuscripts.

SAUNDERSTOWN

The brothers **Christopher** (1897–1956) and **Oliver** (1901–1963) **La Farge** summered here during their youth. Christopher wrote a number of novels, several in verse. *Hoxie Sells His Acres* (1934), a verse novel, is set in Rhode Island. Oliver, yet another Harvard graduate, spent much of his life in the American Southwest, where he wrote his Pulitzer Prize-winning (1929) novel of Navajo Indian life, *Laughing Boy*.

WOONSOCKET

Born and raised in this small industrial city, **Edwin O'Connor** (1918–1968) finished high school here before going to college at Notre Dame. After a tour in the Coast Guard during World War II, he went up to Boston, where he worked as a radio producer before making a name for himself as a novelist with *The Last Hurrah* in 1956. His novels, centering on Boston's Irish Catholics, gave that group a literary identity denied them by Boston's Brahmins, for whom they seem not to have existed in literary terms.

Vermont

VERMONT STANDS APART. When it joined the Union in 1791, it became the last New England state and the only one with a name of French origin. It is landlocked, more heavily wooded than it was a century ago, and so sparsely populated that it did not exceed half a million permanent residents until the 1990 census. It is New England's number one milk producer, and it is said that cows still outnumber people. By law there are no billboards, and it is more difficult to put up a shopping mall or housing development in Vermont than in any other New England state. In a region proud of its independence, Vermont goes its own way.

In 1606 Samuel Champlain explored the long, narrow lake that today bears his name. His descriptions of Vermont's green mountains were the first words written in the state. Since then the well-known writers associated with Vermont have come from elsewhere. "To top the roster," Charles Edward Cone wrote in 1937 in *Let Me Show You Vermont,* "of resident writers, if not natives, we have names such as those of Rudyard Kipling, Sinclair Lewis, Dorothy Canfield Fisher and Alexander Woollcott." Today Saul Bellow, Alexander Solzhenitsyn, David Mamet, Louise Gluck, and Grace Paley spend some part of their year in Vermont but not one of them was born there. Galway Kinnell, the state's poet laureate, is a native of Rhode Island.

Who can say why so few writers of renown have been born in Vermont? Population might provide some sort of answer, but Vermont kept pace with the other New England states until 1850. After that the state's population lagged. Indeed, this slow growth may have had more to do with why writers have come to live or, in most cases, to summer in Vermont. The state remains largely rural, and its only distractions are unsurpassed natural beauty. There is no "scene" in Vermont—nothing to compete with mountains, meadows, pasture, forest, lake, and river. Like the Native Americans who used Vermont as a hunting ground, writers tend to spend their summer months working undisturbed or relaxing in sweet repose; then they head home to avoid the hard winters natives are so proud to endure.

ARLINGTON

Dorothy Canfield Fisher (1877–1958) is one of those writers who produces bestsellers for one generation, only to be all but forgotten by the next. She spend childhood summers in Arlington, once the state's capital, returning to reside there after she married. As a writer, the 1920s was her decade. Her novels *The Brimming Cup, Her Son's Wife,* and *The Deepening Stream* sold in the hundreds of thousands. From 1926 to 1950 she held considerable influence as a member of the Book of the Month Club's selection board. Her book *Vermont Tradition* (1951), often found in Vermont's secondhand bookshops, sets down the values she lived by, formed as they were through her relationship with Vermont. She sees this relationship as having begun in 1763, when her ancestor first settled in Arlington. The book is part history, part meditation, and part—as her subtitle reads—"The Biography of an Outlook on Life." During her most productive years, Fisher traveled widely in Europe, where she became interested in Freud's ideas and worked with the educational theorist Maria Montessori. This led to Fisher's service on the Vermont Board of Education. It was Fisher who introduced Robert Frost to southern Vermont. She died in Arlington and is buried there.

During Fisher's lifetime, Arlington had the reputation of something of an artist's colony. Norman Rockwell lived and worked in West Arlington from 1939 to 1952. He painted portraits of Fisher and her husband and recruited many local friends and neighbors to pose for his *Saturday Evening Post* covers. The maverick composer Carl Ruggles (1876–1971) lived a great deal of his long life in Arlington, much of it in a converted schoolhouse that still stands. For a time, he shared a house in nearby Sunderland with the artist Rockwell Kent, who was then illustrating Melville's *Moby Dick*. Ruggles posed for Captain Ahab. He wrote little music—it takes up but two long-playing records—but it remains original and fresh. In Fisher's home he composed his set of three songs *Vox Clamens in Deserto* (A Voice Crying in the Wilderness). Her description of the middle movement of his chamber symphony *Men and Mountains* catches the texture of his music: "'Lilacs' tells . . . of dust on deserted hearthstones, of 'brush in the pastures'—that perfect New England phrase which to any Yankee brings up the whole picture."

BARNARD

After a whirlwind courtship, **Sinclair Lewis** (1885–1951) married the journalist **Dorothy Thompson** (1894–1961) in 1928 and that year bought Twin Farms, two houses on a large piece of land, the first he ever owned. Here he wrote *Dodsworth* and *It Can't Happen Here,* whose protagonist is a Vermont editor and whose title became a household phrase. In 1930, Lewis became the first American writer and the first Vermonter to receive the Nobel Prize. His best work was behind him. Until 1942 Lewis spent some time each year at Twin Farms, but he was restless and he rarely stayed anywhere for long. After their divorce Thompson, now at least as celebrated as Lewis, took over the property. Her celebrity began when Hitler ordered her expulsion from Germany in 1936. She became known as "the first lady of American journalism" and once caused a sensation by derisively laughing out loud over the air while covering a German–American Bund meeting from New York City. She has been the subject of a recent biography, *American Cassandra,* by Vermont-based writer Peter Kurth. The forlorn, agitated Lewis died in Rome, and is buried in his birthplace, Sauk Center, Minnesota. Thompson is buried in Barnard.

As this book goes to press, Twin Farms is being transformed into a sixteen-room inn. When it opens, there will be some Lewis memorabilia—first editions at least—on display. His "Library Room," a converted barn, will serve as the inn's living room. Visitors will be welcome, but only guests will be able to dine at the inn.

BENNINGTON

Robert Frost (1874–1963) and his family are buried in the graveyard behind the graceful Old First Church that fronts on the green in Old Bennington. Frost knew the town during the years he lived in South Shaftsbury, but his decision to bury his family there came after he was frustrated in honoring his wife Elinor's request to scatter her ashes near their first home in Derry, New Hampshire. For reasons that remain unclear, Frost was put off by the owner of the house when he came with his wife's ashes. Frost kept the ashes in an urn (she had died in 1938) until he bought the Bennington plot in 1941. He had helped dedicate the restored church in 1937, and he must have been impressed by the graveyard that goes down the steep hill toward the town. It dates to the Revolutionary War and holds the tomb of the Hessian troops killed at the Battle of Bennington. Frost deposited the ashes of his wife, his eldest son Carol—dead by his own hand in 1940—and those of the Frosts' first child Elliott, whose death at three from cholera so tested their young marriage. The ashes of Elinor Bettina Frost, who lived but a single day, were also buried without ceremony by Frost and Carol's family— his son William Prescott and wife Lillian. Frost joined his family, again without ceremony, after his death in 1963. Under his dates, his epitaph reads, "I had a lover's quarrel with the world." Next to this grave is a second slab where Frost's daughter Lesley, the only Frost child to survive into old age, and her family are buried. Green signs point the way to the graves behind the church.

William Ellery Channing (1780–1842), Unitarian minister of Boston's Federal Street Church for nearly forty years, is also buried here. He preached that "It were better to have no literature, than form ourselves on a foreign one. . . . A country, like an individual, has dignity and power only in proportion as it is self-formed." His emphasis on the great potential of human nature influenced Emerson, Longfellow, Bryant, Lowell, and Holmes, and his statue stands at the Arlington and Boylston Street entrance to Boston's Public Garden. His stone reads:

> In This Quiet Village
> Among the Hills
> William Ellery Channing
> Apostle of Faith and Freedom
> Died at Sunset
> October 2, 1842

Time of day is rarely recorded on gravestones. Perhaps sunset is meant to salute Channing's love of nature, intensified by his deep reading in and admiration for Wordsworth and the other English Romantic poets. The church is open to visitors. It has the bareness, severe and chaste, common to New England churches. The wooden fence that runs up to it has beautiful proportions and a stately rhythm.

BENNINGTON COLLEGE

Before Bret Easton Ellis and Donna Tartt, Bennington College in North Bennington had a literary heyday in the late 1940s and through the 1950s, when poet Howard Nemerov, novelist Bernard Malamud, and critic Stanley Edgar Hyman taught there. Poet Theodore Roethke also taught there for a spell, and there wrote his "Elegy for Jane, My Student Thrown by a Horse":

> Over this damp grave I speak the words of my love:
> I, with no rights in the matter,
> Neither father nor lover.

Yet during those years the most famous writer associated with Bennington did not teach there. **Shirley Jackson** (1919–1965), married to Hyman, came to the college in 1945. While she raised several children, the trials and pleasures of which she wrote about in *Life Among the Savages* and *Raising Demons*, she also wrote short stories for *The New Yorker*, among other magazines. On a spring day in 1948, she came home loaded with groceries, mail, and kids to write—in one two-hour sitting—her classic story "The Lottery." In this case, *classic* means once read not to be forgotten. She published the story in *The*

New Yorker to enormous response of the "I will never buy *The New Yorker* again!" sort. Outraged readers seemed to accept the story as a true account of New England village life—true enough, in spirit at least, to make its telling scandalous. "The Lottery" could have been set on any of a thousand New England village greens, and it does pack a wallop. While Jackson's other work has faded from sight, "The Lottery" has recently been republished as the title of a book of her short stories and is continuously anthologized.

For the past several years, Bennington College has sponsored writers' conferences in the summer. It boasts bigger names than most such conferences, and offers the usual fare of readings, workshops, panels, and lectures.

BOMOSEEN

Alexander Woollcott (1887–1943), born and raised in the Charles Fourierite Phalanx community in Red Bank, New Jersey, established a retreat in 1924, with a half-dozen friends, on Lake Bomoseen's Neshobe Island. During the summers he spent at the Neshobe Island Club, Woollcott was among America's most celebrated literary personalities as a playwright, critic, and radio broadcaster. Today, he is remembered as one of the Algonquin Round Table wits and as the inspiration for Sheridan Whiteside, *The Man Who Came to Dinner*. George S. Kaufman and Moss Hart, who wrote the play, often visited the island, as did the Marx Brothers, Dorothy Parker, Charles MacArthur, Ben Hecht, and countless other writers, movie people, and celebrities. Woollcott, who could not bear to stay alone on the island, ran the club with an iron hand, earning him the nickname *Der Führer*. Besides drink and talk, high-stakes croquet was the island's chief amusement. Woollcott, it is said, got along well with the natives. But like many summer people or flatlanders, he was accepted only up to a point. When he ran for trustee of the nearby Castletown Public Library, he was defeated.

BURLINGTON

Born in Litchfield, Connecticut, **Ethan Allen** (1738–1789) organized the Green Mountain Boys in Bennington, and helped in the capture of the British garrison at Fort Ticonderoga in 1775. He became Vermont's great Revolutionary hero, celebrated in song and story, but before this he was a writer as well as a rebel. He wrote *A Narrative of Ethan Allen's Captivity* after he had been captured by the British in a reckless attempt to claim Montreal. Proud of his deistic opinions, Allen wrote "Reason the Only Oracle of Man," which earned him a reputation for "godlessness," so much so that President Ezra Stiles of Yale noted Allen's death in Burlington, where he had spent his last years, in his diary: "Feb.13—Gen'l. Ethan Allen died & went to hell this day." By the mid-19th century, Allen's fame was nationwide. The Montpelier lawyer and writer **Daniel Pierce Thompson**'s (1795–1868) historical romance *The Green Mountain Boys* (1839) had a great deal to do with this.

John Dewey (1859–1952) was born here and graduated from the University of Vermont, which is in Burlington. He went on to teach at a number of universities before taking a position at Columbia in 1904. An educator and philosopher, Dewey wrote a number of books.

CALAIS (pronounced *callous*)

In this hamlet northeast of Montpelier, the state capital, are buried **Louise Andrews Kent** (1886–1969), author of the cookbook/memoir *Mrs. Appleyard and I*, and **John Latouche** (1915–1956), playwright and librettist. Robinson Cemetery will best be found by asking directions at the Maple Corners Store. Both graves are to the left as you enter the cemetery. Mrs. Kent is in a thicket of Kents, hers being a large local family. Latouche's is the tall obelisk behind her grave. Almost lost in the grass at the corners of his plot are four squat stone posts, carved with a ballerina, a doe, a cabin, and an apple. These commemorate the Latouche compositions: "Ballet Ballads," "The Ballad of Baby Doe," "Cabin in the Sky," and "The Golden Apple." Frank O'Hara remembers Latouche in his poem "A Step Away from Them":

> First
> Bunny died then John Latouche
> then Jackson Pollock. But is the
> earth as full as life was full, of them?

The poet **James Schuyler** (1923–1991) visited Calais on several occasions, usually in the fall, and was inspired there to write a number of poems. November was his Vermont month, and Schuyler responded with his accustomed clarity:

> Evenings
> in Vermont, the fire dies in the sky,
> the pond goes altogether black,
> and indoors all is coziness. I study
> the pattern in a red rug, arabesques
> and squares, and one red streak
> lies in the west, over the ridge.

CAVENDISH

Alexander Solzhenitsyn has lived in isolation here since his arrival from Switzerland in 1976. As this book goes to press his wife Natalya has announced that he and at least some of the family will return to Russia some time in 1994. Solzhenitsyn was expelled from Russia in 1974 after being arrested and stripped of his citizenship within the space of two days. In Cavendish, Solzhenitsyn isolated himself in a fortress-like compound where everything is rumored to have been set up so that he could write without distractions. His mother, who accompanied him from Russia, baked bread and his wife typed his manuscripts. However he actually lived, Solzhenitsyn was extremely productive here, as he worked to complete his epical cycle of books, *The Red Wheel.* He rarely bestirred himself from his home, but he did give a Harvard commencement address. There are stories that his Cavendish neighbors protected his privacy by giving nosy visitors either wrong directions to his house or no directions at all.

DANBY

Pearl Buck (1892–1973), Pulitzer Prize winner in 1931 for *The Good Earth* and Nobel Prize winner in 1938, lived here during much of the last three years of her life. Active in restoring houses and shops along Main Street, Buck bought some of them and formed a company to do the remodeling.

DUMMERSTON

After marrying Caroline Balestier, a local girl, British writer **Rudyard Kipling** (1865–1936) came to build a house, Naulakha ("Great Treasury"), in this town north of Brattleboro. Caroline was the sister of Wolcott Balestier, Kipling's sometime agent and collaborator on the novel *The Naulahka* (the misspelling is a mystery), who died of typhoid in 1891. The Kiplings married shortly thereafter and arrived in New York in 1892. They found the city, in Kipling's words, "grotesquely bad," and fled almost as once to the Balestier family home near Brattleboro. At first they lived in the Bliss Cottage. "My workroom," Kipling wrote, "was seven feet by eight, and from December to April the snow lay level with its windowsill." The Kiplings liked the long winters and isolation enough to build Naulakha on a hillside above the Connecticut River. They moved into the house in the spring of 1893 and lived there until 1896. "The night cometh when no man works," Kipling's father's motto was carved above the house's main fireplace. Kipling worked well there, producing *The Jungle Book, The Second Jungle Book*, numerous stories and poems, and the research in Gloucester, Massachusetts, that evolved some years later into *Captains Courageous*. Kingsley Amis, one of Kipling's biographers, notes that the one story Kipling set in Vermont, "A Walking Delegate," has for its characters horses. Amis theorizes that loneliness had a great deal to do with Kipling leaving Naulakha and Vermont. But there was another, more direct cause. A family quarrel erupted between Caroline and her older brother, Beatty Balestier, over the rights to property adjoining Naulakha. Balestier, bankrupt and drinking heavily, at some point may have threatened to blow Kipling's brains out. Whatever the exact threat, Kipling took his unstable brother-in-law seriously and had Balestier arrested. Kipling, who disliked being photographed, loathed the publicity provoked by this event. Before the case came to trial, he sold Naulakha and most of its furnishings and took his wife and two daughters, who had been born in Brattleboro, to England—never to return.

Although opened rarely, Naulakha stayed in the same family until 1992, when the British trust Landmark bought the house and the twenty-nine acres on which it sits. Since the Kiplings took with them only their books and Indian carpets, Kipling's writing desk, billiard table, and even his golf clubs remained in the house, which is now undergoing renovation. When work is completed, Naulakha will be open to tourists and might possibly be available for week-long rentals as well.

At the same time Landmark began work on the house, a safety deposit box belonging to Kipling was discovered in a Brattleboro bank. *The Boston Globe* listed its contents as "Kipling's wedding certificate, his will and the draft manuscripts of eight poems, including one apparently never published. Also among other papers, two pages of a letter that may shed light on Kipling's alleged homosexual affair with one of his wife's brothers, Woolcott Balestier." Martin Seymour-Smith, an Englishman, is the Kipling biographer who alleges the possibility of an affair, but the two pages have shed no light on anything but America's obsession with the sex lives of the famous. The "relationship" made the gossip columns and publicized Landmark's plans for his long-closed home.

Naulakha, open or not, is worth a visit. It is a long house, a single room deep and three stories high, situated to take advantage of a long, spectacular view down to the Connecticut River and east across New Hampshire to Mount Monadnock. Even with the trees now grown up and the new houses along the dirt road to Naulakha, the setting is as grand as any in New England.

Vermont has a green historic interest standard and plaque where Route 5 meets the road leading up to Naulakha. Soon Landmark will have made the house even easier to find, but until they do, a stop at the Brattleboro information booth will result in clear directions to the home.

GRAFTON

Famous for its cheddar cheese, Grafton has been so prettified that it resembles a 1930s movie set. Walking through the town, you expect to hear Bing Crosby croon "White Christmas." This is the work of the Windham Foundation, which restored houses and businesses and buried power, cable, and phone lines. The Grafton Inn dominates the center of town. According to old registers stored in the Grafton Historical Society, Hawthorne, Emerson, Holmes, U. S. Grant, Daniel Webster, Thoreau, Kipling, and the American Episcopal Bishop Phillips Brooks, who wrote the hymn "O Little Town of Bethlehem," have been among the inn's guests. There is a Kipling room on the first floor decorated with a few photographs of the great man but containing no other memorabilia.

GREENSBORO

This village on Caspian Lake, in the area known as the Northeast Kingdom, is as out of the way as a place in New England can be. At the beginning of this century, clergymen and academics began to summer here. Among them were Christian Gauss (1878–1967), who is buried here, Princeton teacher of Edmund Wilson; John Peale Bishop and F. Scott Fitzgerald; Bliss Perry (1860–1954), Harvard professor and anthologist; Lucy Sprague Mitchell (1878–1967), founder of New York's Bank Street School and author of the *Here and Now* storybooks; and her husband, Wesley Clair Mitchell, (1878–1948), chairman of the Economics Department at Columbia and author of a book on business cycles. Perry is buried in the small graveyard on the lake's west side. Also buried there is **John Gunther** (1901–1970), whose overviews *Inside Asia, Russia, Africa,* etc., made him as widely known as any of today's television anchors, from whom we now get a small measure of the information Gunther's books once supplied. His novel *Death Be Not Proud,* set in Deerfield, Massachusetts, at the Deerfield School and dealing with the death of the only son from his first marriage, continues to be read today. Not far from him, **Alfred Barr** (1902–1981) of the Museum of Modern Art, whose books on Picasso and Matisse introduced these artists to America, and his wife **Margaret Scolari Barr** (1901–1987), who wrote a book on the Italian sculptor Medardo Rosso, are buried under gravestones designed by the architect Philip Johnson. They are the only works by Johnson in the state.

Wallace Stegner (1909–1993) summered here for nearly fifty years, but this went unremarked upon in the obituaries published by both the *New York Times* and *Boston Globe.* Stegner was associated with the American West to such a degree that his relationship with New England must have been easy to overlook. He won a Pulitzer Prize in 1972 for his novel *Angle of Repose* and a

National Book Award in 1977 for his novel *The Spectator Bird.* He wrote two novels set in Greensboro, *Second Growth* (1947) and *Crossing to Safety* (1987).

GUILFORD

Born in Guilford, **Royall Tyler** (1757–1826) achieved fame as a writer before becoming chief justice of Vermont's Supreme Court. His play *The Contrast* is considered the first American play to focus on contemporary social life and the first American comedy. Tyler wrote it after seeing a 1787 New York production of Sheridan's *School for Scandal.* In 1797 Tyler published his novel, *The Algerine Captive*, which was the first American novel to be republished in England.

JAMAICA

Following the enormous success of *The Naked and the Dead,* **Norman Mailer** experienced difficulty in finding a second act. In Detroit he researched a novel on unions, but came away uninspired. With the germ of *Barbary Shore* in his mind, he spent January to May of 1949 at work in Jamaica. Mailer's five months residence stands here for all the many still living writers of the past fifty years who have sought refuge to work, rented a summer place or dug in for the winter, in Vermont.

MANCHESTER

Walter Hard (1882–1966), a sixth-generation Vermonter and poet, ran the Johnny Appleseed Bookstore for many years. Today the store occupies the brick building next to the Equinox House, and Hard's photograph hangs on the wall. He wrote mostly character sketches in the manner of Edwin Arlington Robinson, but in free verse and with a sentimental tinge. *Salt of Vermont* is regarded as his best book, and can be found in most Vermont secondhand bookstores. His wife Margaret also wrote poetry, and their son Walter Hard, Jr., edited *Vermont Life* for many years.

Here is what the 1937 WPA guide to Vermont says about **Sarah Cleghorn** (1876–1959): "Sarah Cleghorn is Vermont's most famous liberal spirit of recent decades, a combination of lavender and old lace and dynamite. Her lines

> The golf links lie so near the mill
> That almost every day
> The laboring child can look out
> And see the men at play

are the most widely quoted ever written by a Vermonter."

Socialist, pacifist, and antivivisectionist Cleghorn was to Robert Frost one of Vermont's "three verities" (Dorothy Canfield Fisher and Zephine Humphrey were the others), and he described her as "saintly and a poet." Today the mills are gone, and in their place stand outlet stores that clog Manchester streets with traffic, summer and fall.

MIDDLEBURY

Ralph Waldo Emerson (1803–1882) lectured eight times in Vermont, three of these at Middlebury College. We know he gave more than 1,470 lectures in all, and that Vermont was his least-visited New England state. The other confirmed figures for lectures in other states are: New Hampshire, 27; Maine, 35; Connecticut, 18; Rhode Island, 46; and his native Massachusetts, 899. Vermont's sparse population and few colleges may explain Emerson's rare appearances in the state. On August 11, 1868, Emerson lectured on "Greatness" at Middlebury. It was his last Vermont lecture, for which he was paid $50.

MONTPELIER

Montpelier's Historical Society is located in the Pavilion building on State Street, near the state capital. The Society library asks for a $2 donation, which entitles the visitor to the use of its open stacks and a seat at one of its tables. Most who come here do genealogical research, but the library has substantial holdings in even the more obscure Vermont writers. Historical societies are everywhere in New England, and are worth contacting if your interest in a particular writer or locale requires detailed attention.

ORLEANS

James Hayford (1913–1993) lived here for most of his adult life. Born in Montpelier, Hayford went to Amherst College where, upon graduating, he received the Robert Frost Fellowship from the hand of Frost himself. As he wrote his short, tightly rhymed poems, Hayford taught school and supported himself at a number of other jobs including goat farming. At the time of his death, his work had begun to reach a wider audience. Many of his books were self-published. This is how he introduced his 1976 volume *The Furniture of Earth*:

> You can use a poem the next time your life threatens to become too crowded or too empty, or too anything, to give you some feeling of order or companionship. A spell against "chaos and old night." A comfort in these uncomfortable times.

PLYMOUTH

Born here, **Calvin Coolidge** (1872–1933), like most American presidents of the 20th century, published little of note, but he earns a place here on the strength of two sentences he spoke, and two sharp lines delivered about him. In a 1925 speech Coolidge declared, "The chief business of the American people is business." This sentence has often been quoted—or misquoted, as it consistently appears as "The business of America is business"—as *the* home truth about American aspirations. To questions about whether or not he might seek a second term as president, Coolidge's "I do not choose to run" has stood as a model of Yankee taciturnity.

Coolidge was memorably, if tartly, served by the wit of others. Legendary wit Alice Longworth Roosevelt thought the dour Coolidge "had been weaned on a pickle." At his death, Dorothy Parker was at the theater seated in the middle of a row. When the whispered message "Calvin Coolidge is dead, pass it on" reached her, Parker turned and whispered back, "How did they know?"

RIPTON

At age sixty-five, **Robert Frost** (1874–1963), one year a widower and, as his friend Hervey Allen described him, "a great and powerful engine without the control of its flywheel," came to the Homer Noble farm in 1939. He already owned a house in South Shaftsbury, and his son Carol and family lived there. Frost also owned two houses in Concord Corners outside St. Johnsbury, but these proved inadequate. When he bought the Noble farm he gave the use of it to Theodore Morrison, a friend who ran Bread Loaf, and moved into a simple log cabin behind and above the Nobel house. Until his death in 1963, this was Frost's summer home. Today you are permitted to look at the cabin, but visitors are not allowed inside. First you must find the road that leads to the Noble farm. It is made of dirt and is unmarked, to discourage those who have only a casual interest in Frost. You will find it just past the Robert Frost Wayside Area going uphill toward Bread Loaf. There is a plaque at the Area that proclaims Frost Vermont's poet laureate and reads, in part, "A distinguished American poet by recognition and a Vermonter by preference." Frost's cabin looks south over the Green Mountains, a view similar to the one he enjoyed of the White Mountains from the front porch of his Franconia, New Hampshire, home.

Down the hill on state Route 125 is the Robert Frost Interpretive Trail. It is a half-hour woodland walk, broken by poems on weatherproof placards beginning with "The Pasture":

> I'm going out to clean the pasture spring,
> I'll only stop to rake the leaves away
> (And wait to watch the water clear, I may):
> I shan't be gone long.—You come too.

Today Middlebury College owns the Noble farm, Frost's cabin, and Bread Loaf, home of the Bread Loaf Writers' Conference co-founded by Frost. For two weeks in August, writers and students of writing from throughout America meet here for a workshop, where all writing workshops began. The Bread Loaf grounds are spacious, and its large yellow buildings give it the air of a resort.

There are many stories of Frost's participation at Bread Loaf, and few are entirely flattering. He was—as many who knew him attested—tirelessly, bitingly competitive and, in his later years, a curmudgeon. At Bread Loaf he was the star, and determined to be treated as such. The poet Donald Hall, who went to Bread Loaf as a teenager, remembers Frost—some forty years his senior—taking pleasure in one-upping him.

By the time Frost came to Ripton his family had died or grown, and he was as celebrated as any American poet has ever been. For the remaining twenty-four years of his life, more attention was lavished on Frost than on any American writer of this century save Hemingway, whose competitiveness Frost equaled. Ornery as he could be, Frost gloried in every minute of his fame.

This entire area has a simple dignity. Frost, a most complicated man, has been remembered without fuss. Visitors will not be distracted by mugs, tee-shirts, or even books, until they drive into nearby Middlebury itself.

RUTLAND

Charles Tuttle (1915–1993) opened a book publishing company here in 1938 that bore his name and published books about Japan. He did so because at the time, as he said later, "There were no Japanese books on publishers' lists. It was taboo." In 1946, after the war, he started up a Japanese branch of his firm in Tokyo to import American books. By the early 1960s both ends of the business were thriving. In 1983 Emperor Hirohito of Japan awarded Tuttle the "Third Order of the Sacred Treasure" for his contribution to improving Japanese-American relations.

ST. ALBANS

This town near the Canadian border was the family home of **Frances Frost** (1905–1959; no relation to Robert), Yale Younger Series Poet and mother of the New York poet and translator **Paul Blackburn** (1926–1971), who was born here. After she separated from her husband, Frost left Blackburn and his younger sister in St. Albans under the care of her parents. There they endured—so Blackburn later wrote—a miserably pinched and cruel childhood before rejoining their mother in New York City.

ST. JOHNSBURY

The St. Johnsbury Athenaeum at 30 Main Street is both library and picture gallery. It was built in 1871 by Horace Fairbanks, nephew of the inventor of the platform scale still manufactured in St. Johnsbury, and was presented to the town. The brick building (to quote the Athenaeum handout) "is characterized by high cathedral ceilings, tall windows, elaborate woodwork, floors with alternating strips of oak and walnut, and spiral staircases." It is like being inside a hive of books. An art galley was added in 1873. Among the copies of Italian Renaissance paintings and numerous 19th-century genre scenes by now-forgotten painters, there hangs a Durand, a Cropsey, and the gallery's one knockout, Albert Bierstadt's "Domes of the Yosemite." It takes up the entire far wall of the gallery, and as you walk toward it, it is easy to imagine continuing into the painting and taking your place beside the grass-nibbling deer beneath the dramatic mountains under the even more dramatic weather.

SOUTH SHAFTSBURY

In 1920 Dorothy Fisher introduced **Robert Frost** (1874–1963) to this town, and he moved here from New Hampshire. He bought and remodeled the half-stone, half-timber Peleg Cole house, named it the Stone House, and expected to farm, with the help of his son Carol, an apple crop. Frost counted on the relatively low maintenance required by apples to give him time to write. As with Frost's other farming ventures, this was not a success, and he spent a good deal of time away from South Shaftsbury. Carol stayed on with his family to tend the orchard, and it was here that he took his life. At some point Frost bought another house, the Gulley, not far from the Stone House. This house, now in private hands, was so completely gutted for renovation more than a decade ago that Frost partisans reacted with consternation. Frost spent some part of every year in South Shaftsbury until 1939, when he moved north to Ripton.

STRATTON

Robert Penn Warren (1905–1989), a longtime summer resident, died here. In 1985 he was appointed the first poet laureate of the United States. The position is, it seems, totally ceremonial, as Warren produced no poems in praise of Reagan and Bush or their achievements. It is meant to honor and promote poetry, but the truth is that most Americans, even those interested in poetry, could not list those who have held the position, nor tell you who the present poet laureate is. Warren, a Southerner, is buried in the Union Cemetery.

Eleanor Clark, Warren's wife, is the author of several novels but is best known for her nonfiction: *Rome and a Villa* (1952), *The Oysters of Locmariaquer* (1964) and *Eyes, Etc.* (1977). The Warrens' daughter, Rosanna, is a poet who teaches at Boston University.

WINDSOR

Maxwell Perkins (1884–1947), the legendary Scribner's editor of Hemingway, F. Scott Fitzgerald, and, most particularly, of Thomas Wolfe, whose gargantuan manuscripts (one filled a steamer trunk) Perkins helped shape, spent childhood summers here. After marrying, Perkins and his family continued to vacation in and around the town.

While Perkins has an entry, more or less the above, in *The Oxford Illustrated Literary Guide to the United States* and is listed in *Benét's Reader's Encyclopedia,* he is omitted from *The Oxford Companion to American Literature.* Editors in general go unacknowledged in reference works on American literature. The *Companion* does not list Katherine White, Saxe Cummins, or Harold Ross of *The New Yorker.* Benét does much better by editors and so a fuller picture of what makes American literature emerges from its pages. But the point is that editors, along with agents and publishers, are not as well represented as they should be. Nor are bestselling authors.

A Partial Bibliography

———◆———

ORE THAN THIRTY years ago, Edmund Wilson lamented that there existed no standard edition of America's classic writers. Today the Library of America means to remedy this, at least in part. While they publish definitive texts in a handsome and sturdy format, the Library has no plans to publish any writer's complete works. You will find, for example, a volume of Hawthorne's *Tales and Sketches* and another of his *Novels*, but the Library will probably not republish his wonderfully detailed *Notebooks*. Still, it is best to go first to this series for work by the following authors: Henry Adams, Willa Cather, W. E. B. Du Bois, Ralph Waldo Emerson, Nathaniel Hawthorne, William Dean Howells, Henry James, William James, Flannery O'Connor, Eugene O'Neill, Francis Parkman, Edgar Allan Poe, Harriet Beecher Stowe, Henry David Thoreau, Herman Melville, Mark Twain, and Edith Wharton.

The books of Van Wyck Brooks, so often cited in this book, are out of print. Dutton was his publisher, and they published *The Flowering of New England* and *New England: Indian Summer* in hardcover and paperback. Dutton also published Brooks's picture book *Our Literary Heritage*. All three of these titles show up regularly on the shelves of most New England second-hand bookstores. Brooks also gathered an anthology of New England writing, *A New England Reader: William Bradford to Robert Lowell*, published by Alfred A. Knopf.

There are three other anthologies worth looking up. Nancy Hale's *New England Discovery* (Coward McCann) includes a great deal more than the Brooks, but is also out of print and will have to be rooted out in secondhand shops or the library. Currently in print are Richard Nunley's *The Berkshire Reader* (Berkshire House) and Charles and Samuella Shain's *The Maine Reader* (Houghton Mifflin).

Three picture books are worth the time it will take to find them. *The Oxford Illustrated Literary Guide to the United States* is in print but not often in bookstores. I found my copy at the bookstore run by the National Park Service at Longfellow's Cambridge home. *The Writers' America* (American Heritage) is especially strong on 19th-century drawings and engravings. It is out of print and hard to find. Out of print but easier to find is *Who Lived Where* (Bramhall House) with text by Mark De Wolfe Howe and photographs by Samuel Chamberlin. The book takes a look at thirteen New England homes—Emily Dickinson's, Longfellow's, the Old Manse, and James Russell Lowell's among them.

John Harris has written two extremely thorough walker's guides to Boston and Cambridge. Both contain a wealth of literary detail. They are: *The Boston Globe's Historic Walks in Cambridge* and *The Boston Globe's Historic Walks in Old Boston.*

Two books that I encountered in researching this guide gave me great pleasure, and I want to recommend them. Richard O'Connor of the Thoreau Lyceum put me onto Robert A. Richardson's *Henry Thoreau: A Life of the Mind* (University of California Press). It is the best book I have read on Thoreau. I had read James R. Mellow's *Nathaniel Hawthorne in His Time* (Houghton Mifflin), but it was even better the second time around.

Index
